IMAGES
of America

SANDY

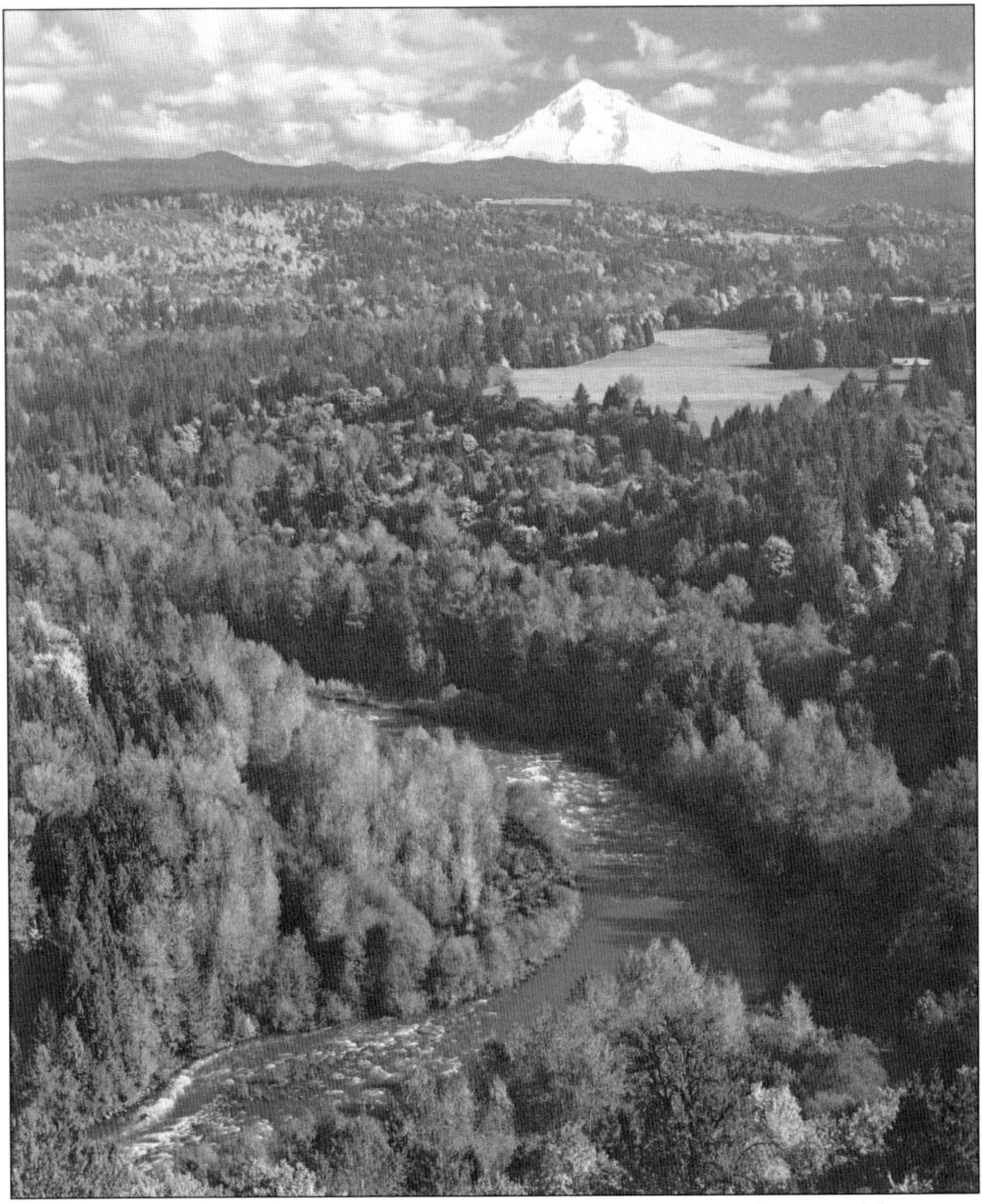

This view of the Sandy River and Mount Hood shows the most imposing character of the region. To the first inhabitants, Mount Hood was Wy'east, a thunderous god. To Samuel K. Barlow, it was a challenge, almost religious in nature. To the settlers, it was a constant reminder of unpredictability. But to many today, Mount Hood is an ever-present remembrance of those who have gone before. (Courtesy of the Sandy Historical Society Museum.)

On the Cover: Taken in the 1950s, when Highway 26 was still a two-way street through town, this aerial photograph offers a sweeping vista of Sandy, with a view looking east toward Mount Hood. The line of trees leading down to the left at the far end of town, where the two main streets join, marks the route of the Barlow Road, used by pioneers to go around Mount Hood. (Courtesy of the Sandy Historical Society Museum.)

IMAGES
of America

SANDY

Dan Bosserman

ARCADIA
PUBLISHING

ISBN 978-1-4671-3433-0

Published by Arcadia Publishing
Charleston, South Carolina

Printed in the United States of America

Library of Congress Control Number: 2015936989

For all general information, please contact Arcadia Publishing:
Telephone 843-853-2070
Fax 843-853-0044
E-mail sales@arcadiapublishing.com
For customer service and orders:
Toll-Free 1-888-313-2665

Visit us on the Internet at www.arcadiapublishing.com

To Connie Revenue Selzler, whose forebears,
Francis and Lydia Revenue, started it all.

Contents

Acknowledgments

No publication about Sandy history would be complete without paying homage to Philip Jonsrud, Miles Aubin, and Morton Spence. From the time a small museum was started in the late 1970s in the Community Center Building and later moved into a vacant portion of Sandy City Hall, people have donated museum items to what is now the Sandy Historical Society. The society struggled with storage challenges, often relying on garages and barns. Bryon Tolle, in particular, has been tireless in locating the sites of buildings and enterprises long destroyed and nearly forgotten.

Finally, after struggling for funds, and with the aid of a grant from the Clackamas County Tourism Commission, and some very generous donations by members of the society, a modern museum was built and dedicated in 2007, across the street from city hall, at the top of the hill on the Old Barlow Road. From this museum's treasure trove of artifacts, books, family records, and a vast collection of digitized photographs, I have gleaned most of the contents of this book.

Everyone at the museum was exceptionally helpful as I worked my way through the maze of images and reports, but special thanks must go to Ann Marie Amstad, Kenneth Funk, Nancy Spencer, Albert Gagnon, and Sandra Jordan, who volunteer tirelessly at the museum and were always there to help me, even when I called them at home in the evening. Connie Revenue Selzler and Jean Bacon Rolli provided immense support by inviting me into their homes and sending me back to my house with stacks of research material.

I wish to thank Arcadia Publishing for affording me the opportunity to embark on this amazing journey, especially my persistent title manager, Matt Todd, for keeping me on track in this sometimes perplexing process. Before his passing in 2012, Dennis Gray volunteered countless hours at the Sandy Historical Society, restoring and archiving photographs dating back to the pioneers. The digitized photographic archive center in the museum is appropriately named in his honor.

Finally, to my wife, Kathleen, thank you for your patience and encouragement, not only on this enterprise, but in everything we have shared, particularly our three children.

Unless otherwise noted, all images appear courtesy of the Sandy Historical Society Museum (SHS).

Introduction

They came in the thousands and tens of thousands, crossing the Great Plains in ox-drawn and horse-drawn covered wagons that contained everything they owned, seeking a promised land they knew little about. The Oregon Trail from Illinois and Missouri to Oregon City, Oregon, had gradually become established as a road, although, in many places, it was still more trail than road. The Oregon Trail followed Indian trails that had been there for centuries.

Still, by 1840, a few covered wagons were getting through as far as The Dalles. There, pioneers had to break down the wagons and load them, along with their supplies, onto rafts for the rest of the journey through the Columbia Gorge to Portland. There, they reassembled their wagons for the last leg of the trip to Oregon City. Cattle were driven separately on trails on the north side of the Columbia River, or on Indian trails over the Lolo Pass to Oregon City.

About 70 wagons left Independence, Missouri, in 1841. A year later, there were 100. On May 22, 1843, a single train of 1,000 wagons left Elm Grove, Missouri, and started the Great Migration of 1843. In 1845, Samuel Kimbrough Barlow led one of many smaller wagon trains as far as The Dalles and decided there must be a better way to reach the Willamette Valley than rafting down the perilous waters of the Columbia River.

But the hardy and adventurous pioneers were not the first inhabitants of the Oregon Territory. Lewis and Clark had made an exploratory trip in 1803 and had spent the winter of 1805–1806 in Fort Clatsop. The British had built and dedicated Fort Vancouver in 1825 to protect the fur-trading post nearby, overseen by Chief Factor Dr. John McLoughlin. Beginning in the 1830s, missionaries were coming to the Oregon Country with the idea of converting the Indians to Christianity. The best known of these were Marcus and Narcissa Whitman.

But, for at least 10,000 years, the land had been occupied by Native Americans of many small tribes. They lived within sight of three mighty volcanic mountains, and their legends reflect the volcanic activity. The Multnomah name for Mount Hood was Wy'east. In one version of the legend, the two sons of the Great Spirit Sahale fell in love with the beautiful maiden Loowit, who could not decide which man to choose. The two braves, Wy'east and Klickitat, burned forests and villages in their battle over her. Sahale became enraged and struck down the three lovers. In another version, Wy'east (Mount Hood) battles Pahto (Mount Adams) for the fair La-wa-la-clough (Mount St. Helens). Yet another version has Wy'east, the chief of the Multnomah tribe, competing with the chief of the Klickitat tribe, and their great anger leads to their transformation into volcanoes. In each version of the legend, their battle is said to have destroyed the Bridge of the Gods and thus created the great Cascades Rapids of the Columbia River. The ancient legends were given new credibility in 1980, when Mount St. Helens erupted: first on May 18 and again on May 25, ejecting more than a cubic mile of material nine miles into the atmosphere.

Regretting his rash action, the Great Spirit Sahale erected three mountain peaks to mark where each fell. He made beautiful Mount St. Helens to represent Loowit; the somber Mount Adams symbolizes Klickitat, mourning for the lost Loowit; and proud, erect Mount Hood stood for Wy'east.

Mount Hood was an obstacle for the wagon trains when they came to The Dalles. The pioneers sought an alternative to rafting down the Columbia River to reach the Willamette Valley.

One

THE FIRST SETTLERS

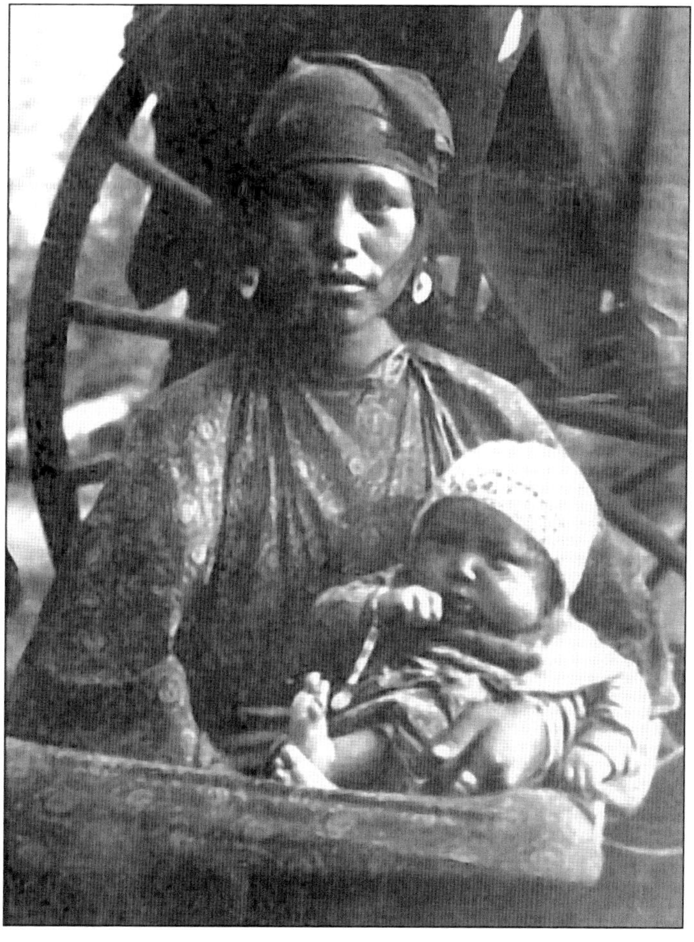

Before white men came, no permanent settlements were in the area now called Sandy, but it was well traveled by the native population as they moved with the seasons to trade and harvest huckleberries, salmon, and other goods between permanent settlements. This unidentified Indian mother cares for her baby as she camps near Brightwood, a few miles upriver from Sandy.

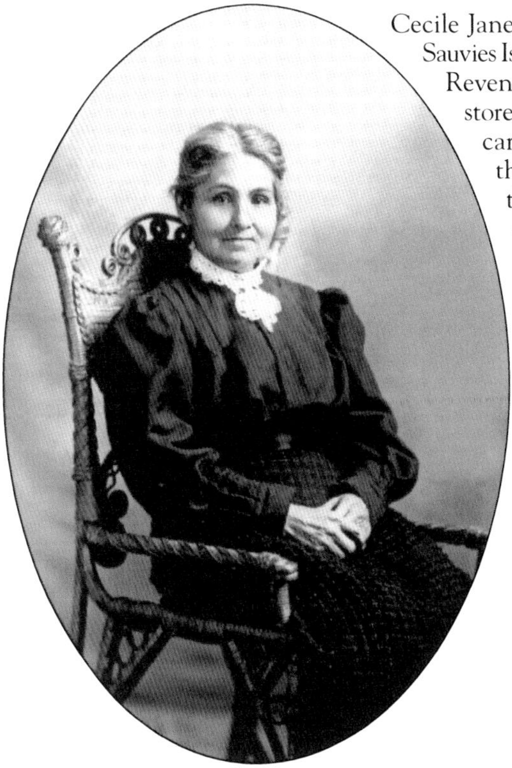

Cecile Jane Haguet was kidnapped from her home near Sauvies Island before she was 10 and was rescued by Francis Revenue when the kidnapper stopped at Revenue's store. The Revenues took her into their home and cared for her as their own for several years, until they could locate her parents. She was grateful to the Revenues and visited them often. (Courtesy of SHS and Connie Revenue Selzler.)

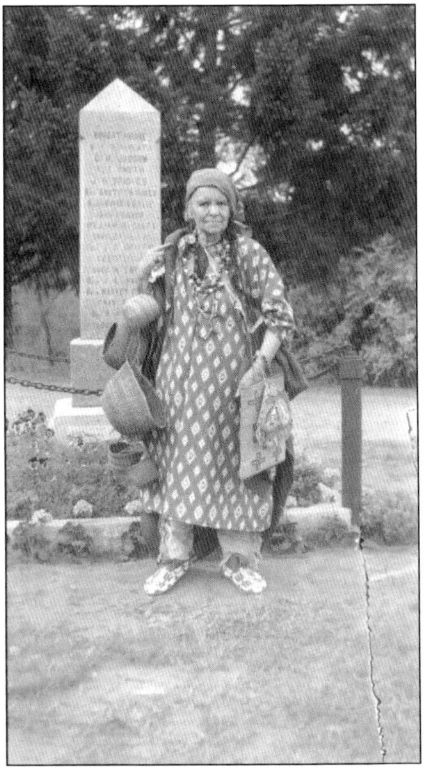

Each year at Champoeg, Oregon, the Friends of Champoeg Park present a pageant celebrating Oregon's history. One feature that is not celebrated is the white man's treatment of the native population and the latter's relegation to the Grand Ronde Reservation. Alice Reveue Webster is shown here representing the Clackamas tribe, which hunted and fished along the Clackamas and Sandy Rivers. (Courtesy of Connie Revenue Selzler.)

Since there were no permanent settlements of Native Americans in the Sandy area, very few large implements are to be found. Some camps were semipermanent, however, as migrating travelers would return to familiar campgrounds. At such camps, a large mortar and pestle like this one, weighing nearly 50 pounds, would be left for the next group of travelers to grind meal.

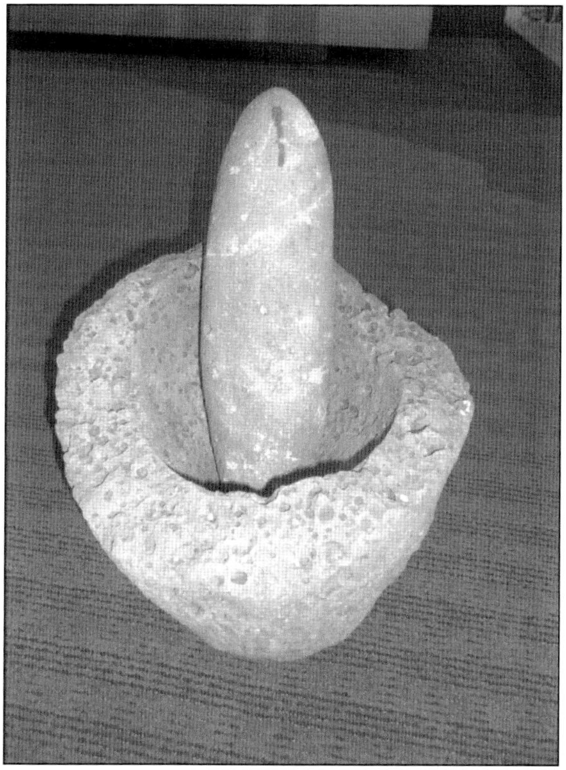

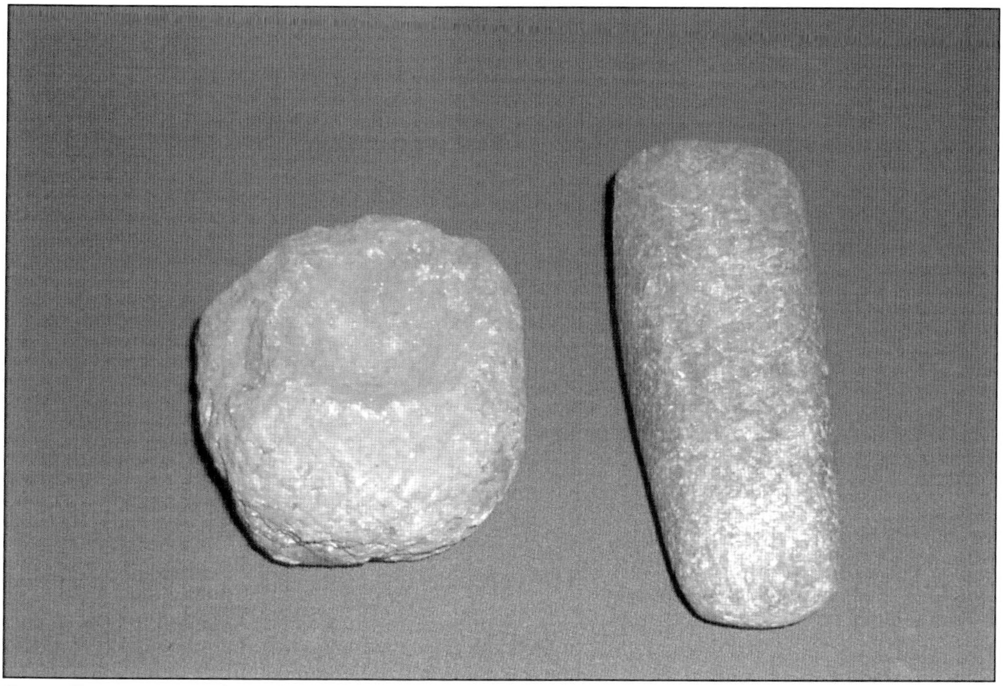

A smaller mortar and pestle, like this one, could be carried in a sling or pouch and was used to grind enough for a family's evening meal. This pestle, only seven inches long, was found near the rapids of a stream where salmon swam in abundance on their way to spawn.

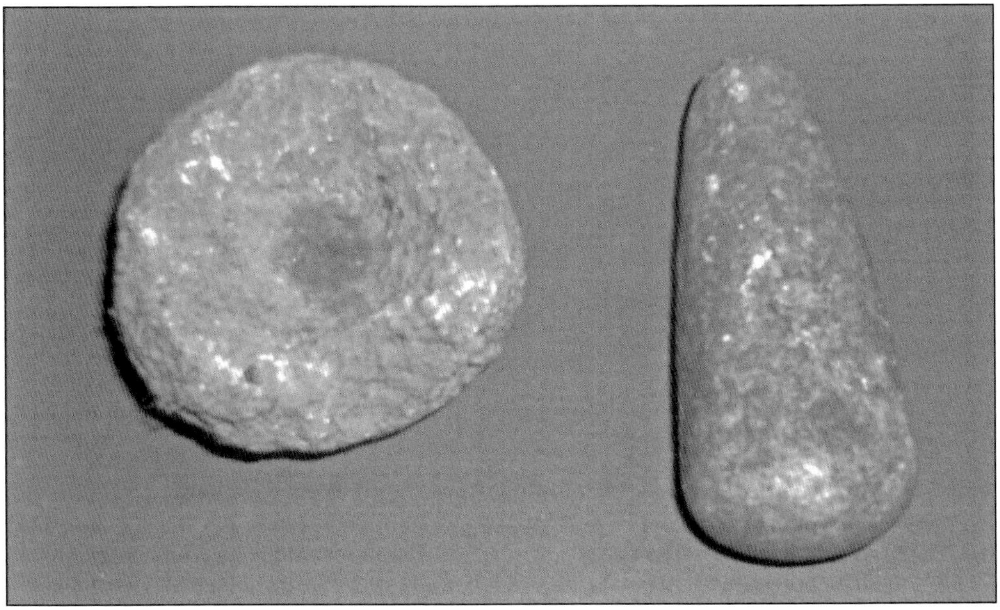

Smaller yet, this mortar and pestle might have been carried by a single individual traveling light—perhaps a messenger or a scout, or even a fugitive. It is not generally acknowledged, but some natives of the Northwest practiced slavery, a phenomenon borrowed from the northernmost tribes of the Pacific Northwest.

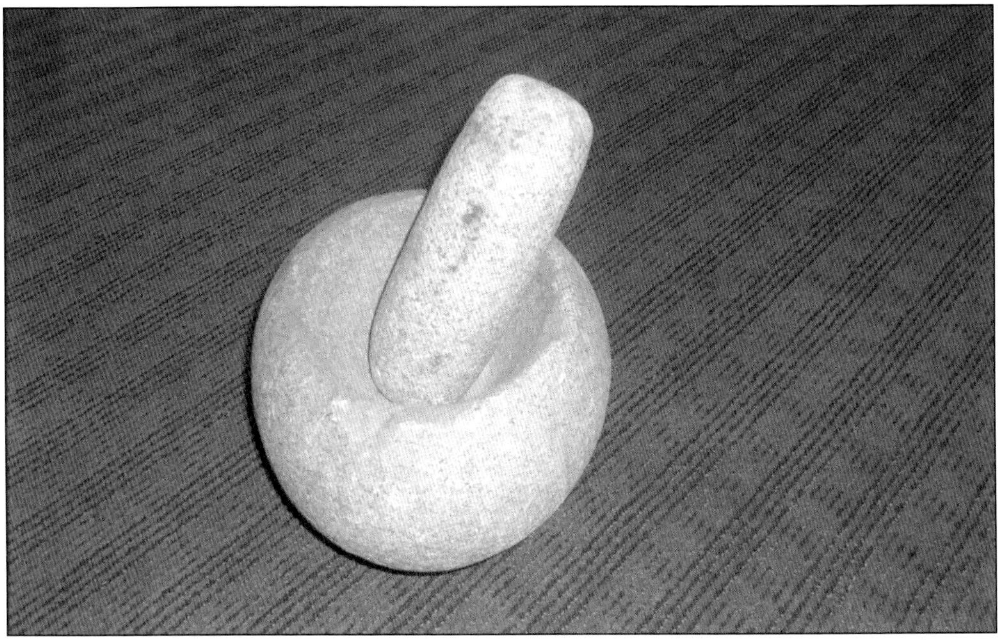

This midsized mortar and pestle, with its fine, regular features, might have been used by a shaman, not just for acorns or grain, but for herbs and spices to cure diseases or even mental maladies. These maladies were often thought to be influenced by, according to F.A. Shaver's 1905 *An Illustrated History of Central Oregon, Embracing Wasco, Sherman, Gilliam, Wheeler, Crook, Lake and Klamath Counties, State of Oregon*, "a dancer jumping, and invoking his 'tam-an-was' or familiar spirit; until, exhausted, he falls as one dead, by the overpowering influence of his familiar."

This carefully formed stone would have been used for the head of a war club by wrapping thongs around the smooth grooves and attaching it to a stout limb. The handles of the stone ball clubs were made with hardwood or different types of bone, including whale bone.

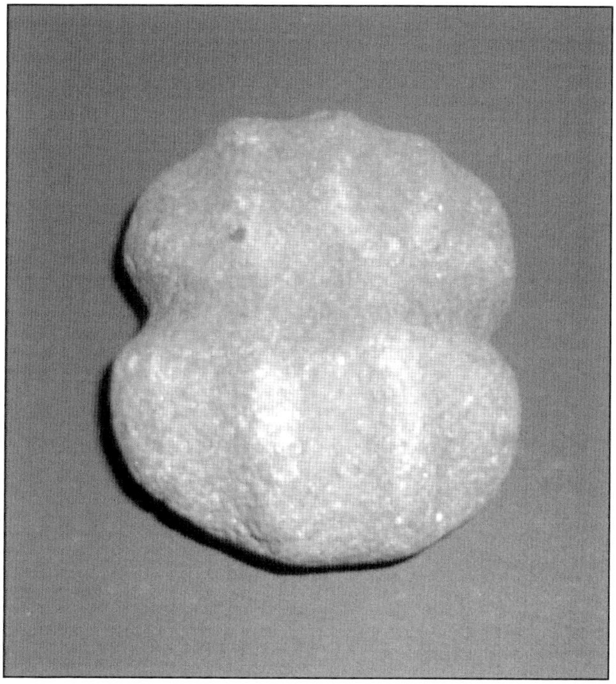

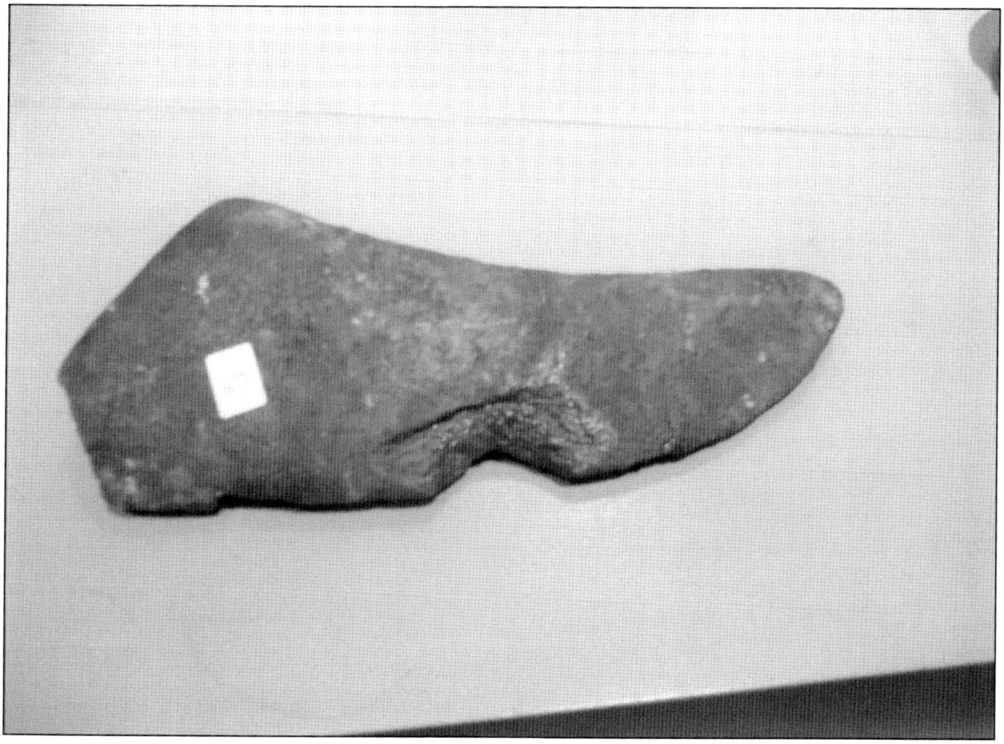

The hatchet was used as a weapon by Native Americans and consisted of a fighting axe, specifically known as a tomahawk. The hatchet axe had a wooden handle. When first developed by Native Americans, the axe had a head made of stone. It was further developed using European technology, when the stone head was replaced by iron, steel, copper, or brass.

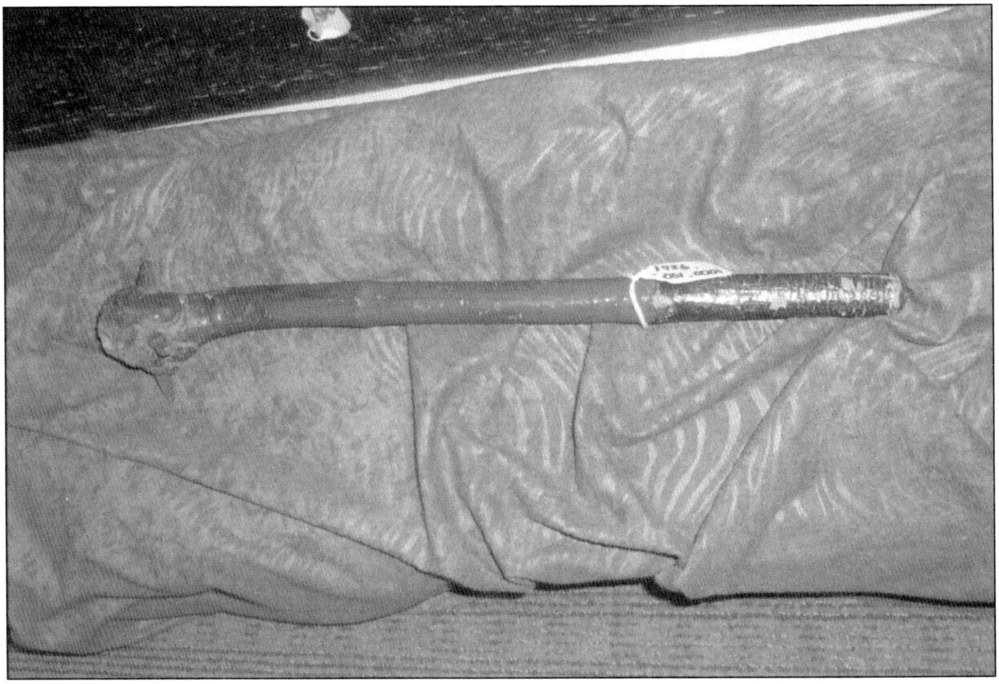

When not used in full-scale warfare, a small war club with spikes attached would have been sufficient for self-defense, if one was traveling light but still needed protection. In such times, a short, light club like this would have been carried by a traveler.

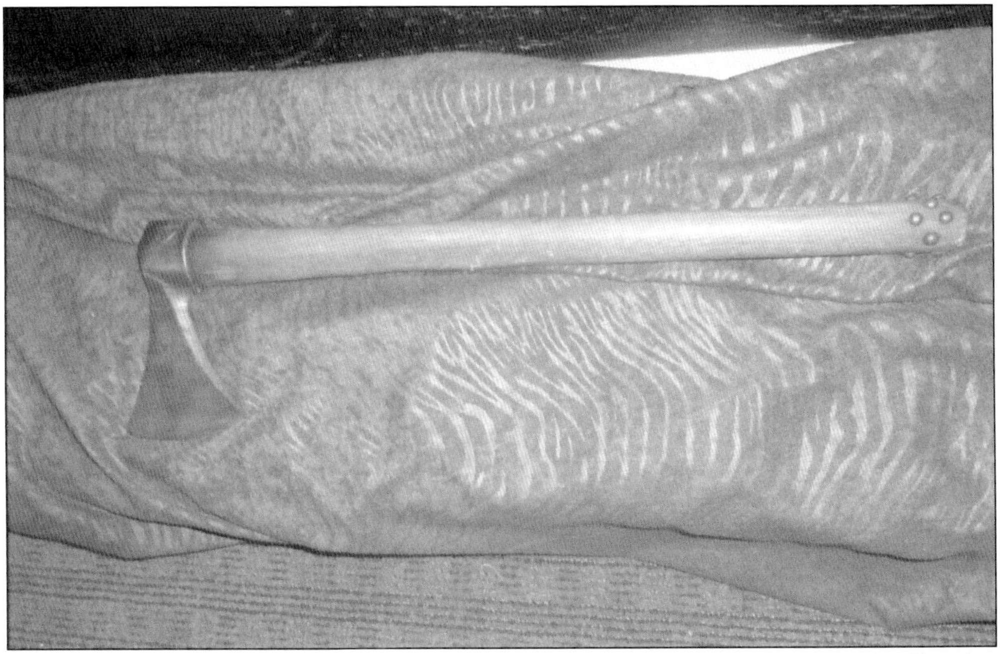

The coming of the white man brought an arms race, of sorts. This new, lightweight style of hatchet axe had a metal edge on a solid wooden handle. It was used in deadly hand-to-hand combat, or as a throwing weapon. The hatchet axe was developed into a variety of different shapes and designs. It was sometimes traded for furs or other supplies.

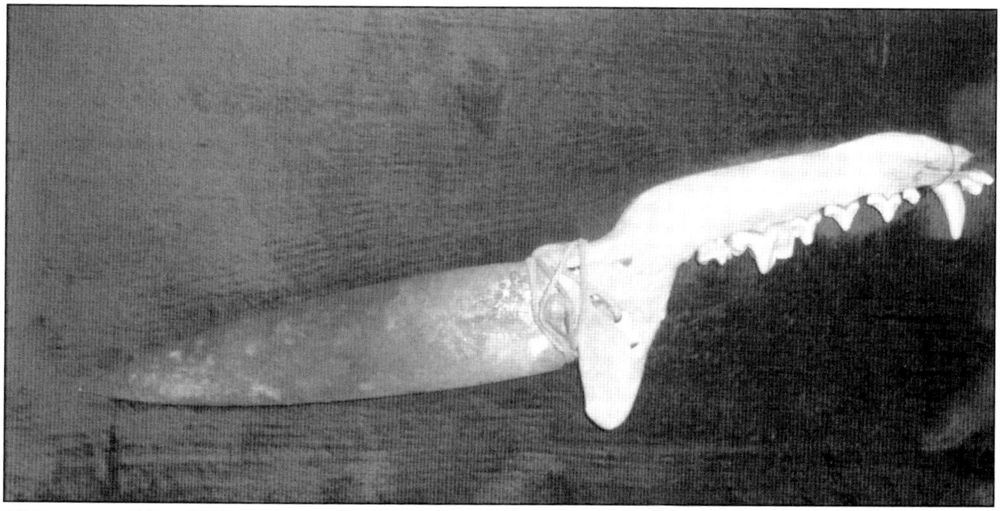

This unusual knife, found not far from the Barlow Road, has for its handle the jawbone of a mountain creature, probably a mountain lion. Cutting weapons were used by Native Americans for combat as well as hunting. They preferred shorter blades over long cutting weapons, like the swords that the Europeans used at the time.

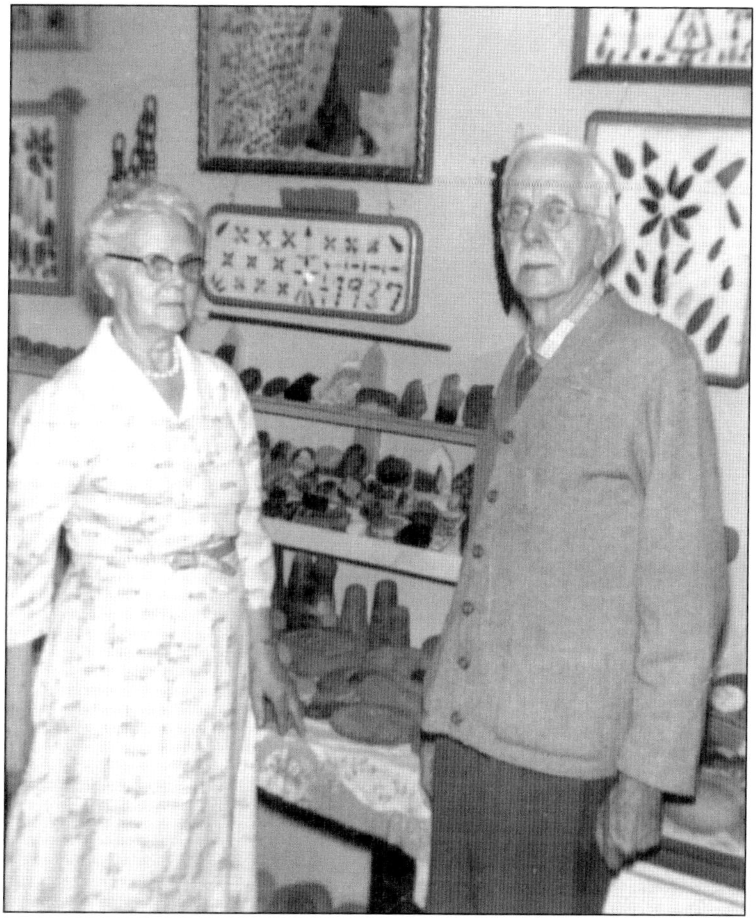

Anthony Schedeen lives on Tickle Creek, near Sandy, and has inherited a lifelong collection of Native American artifacts from his grandparents, Ernest and Annie Schedeen, shown here in 1937 with part of that collection. Ernest provided wood for Columbia Brick Works, founded in 1906. The company dug 100 tons of clay a day, perhaps accounting for the discovery of many of the artifacts.

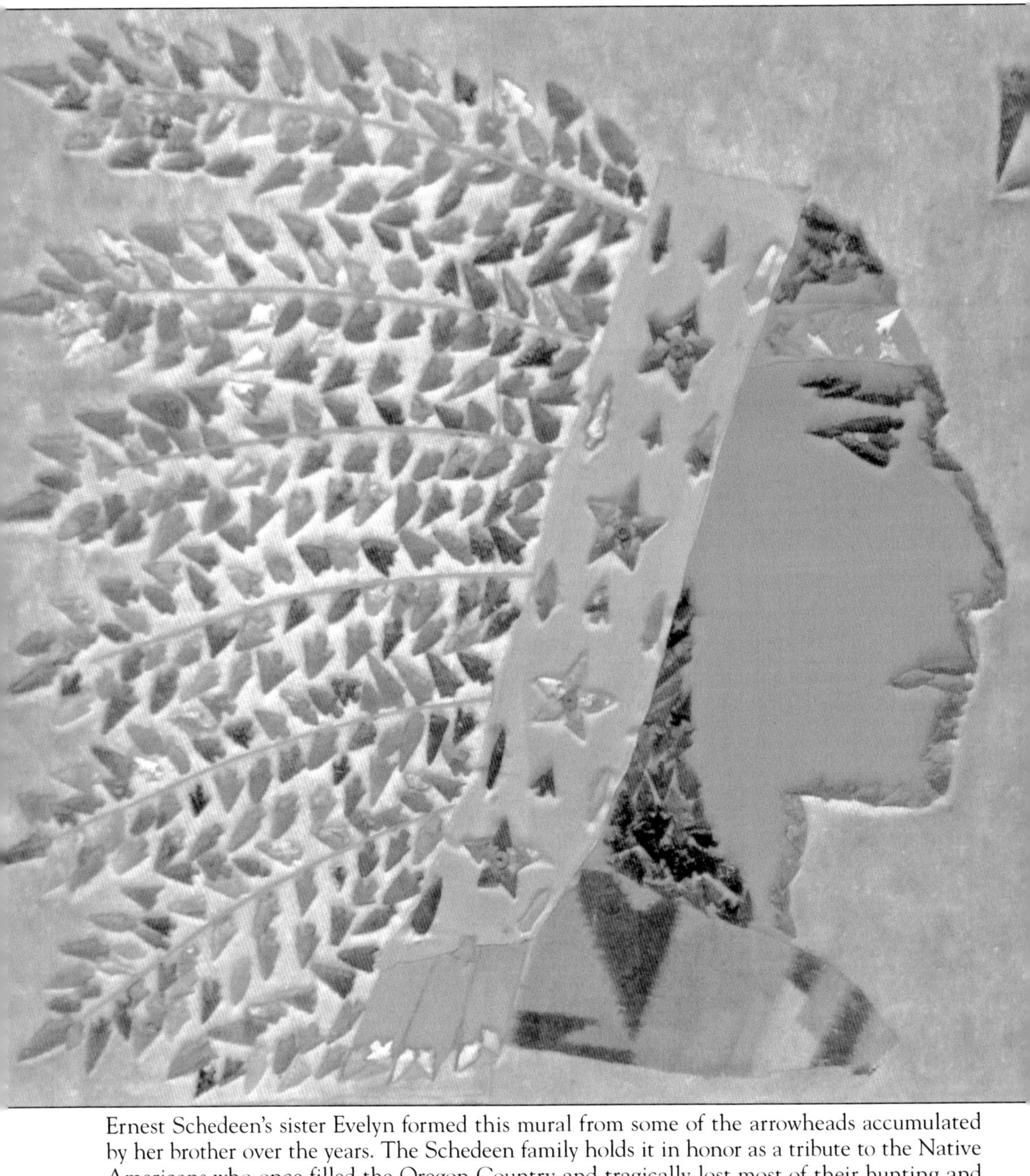

Ernest Schedeen's sister Evelyn formed this mural from some of the arrowheads accumulated by her brother over the years. The Schedeen family holds it in honor as a tribute to the Native Americans who once filled the Oregon Country and tragically lost most of their hunting and fishing grounds.

Two

A WAY AROUND THE MOUNTAIN

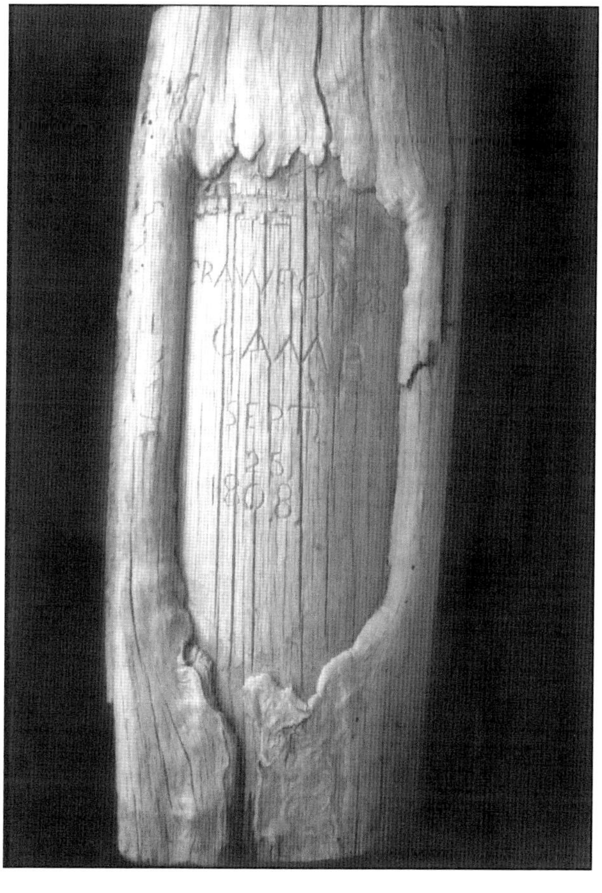

This carving, believed to have been made by a trapper in 1808, was found on a tree near a lake south of Mount Hood. The late Duane Knapp, owner of Skyline Logging Co., saved it for the Sandy Historical Society Museum. (Courtesy of SHS and Duane Knapp.)

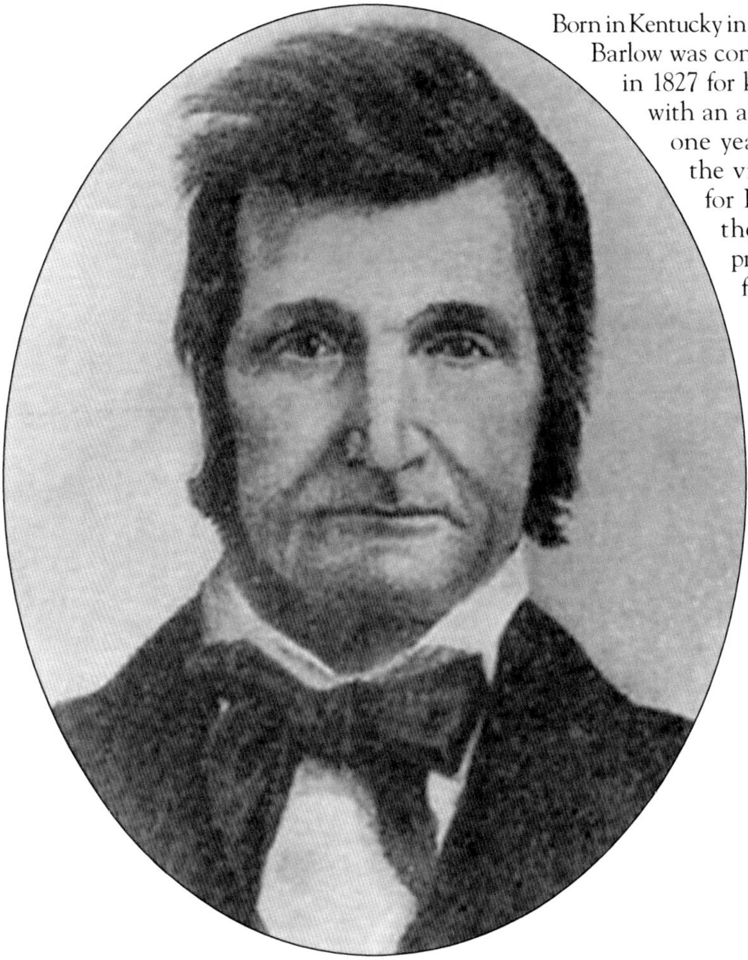

Born in Kentucky in 1795, Samuel Kimbrough Barlow was convicted of manslaughter in 1827 for killing George Matlock with an ax. He was sentenced to one year of hard labor. Even the victim's brother pleaded for Barlow's pardon, since the killing was done to prevent harm to Matlock's family. The governor of Indiana pardoned him, and in 1845, Barlow led a wagon party to Oregon.

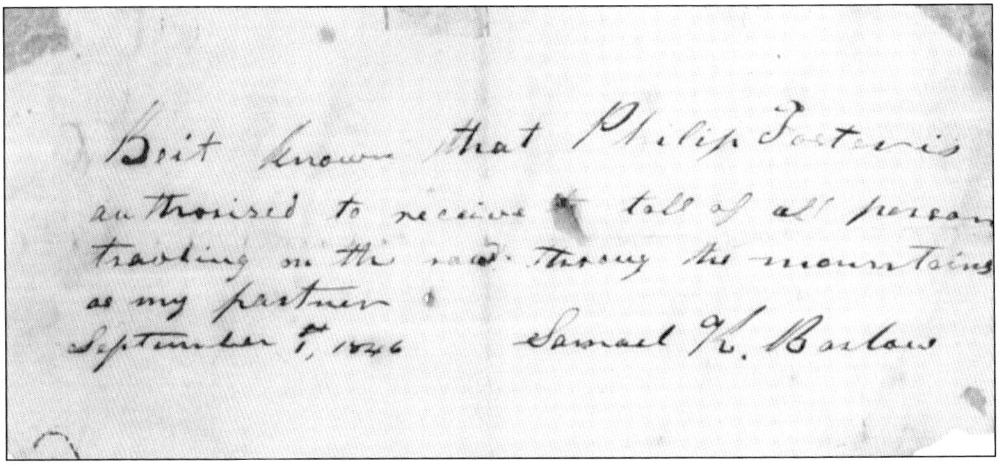

Be it known that Philip Foster is authorised to receive the toll of all person traveling on the road through the mountains as my partner.
September 7, 1846 Samuel K. Barlow

This scrap of paper has handwriting by Samuel Barlow from 1846, authorizing Philip Foster "to receive the toll of all persons traveling on the road through the mountains as my partner." The Barlow Road (originally the Mount Hood Road) was built in 1846 by Sam Barlow and Philip Foster, with authorization of the Provisional Legislature of Oregon.

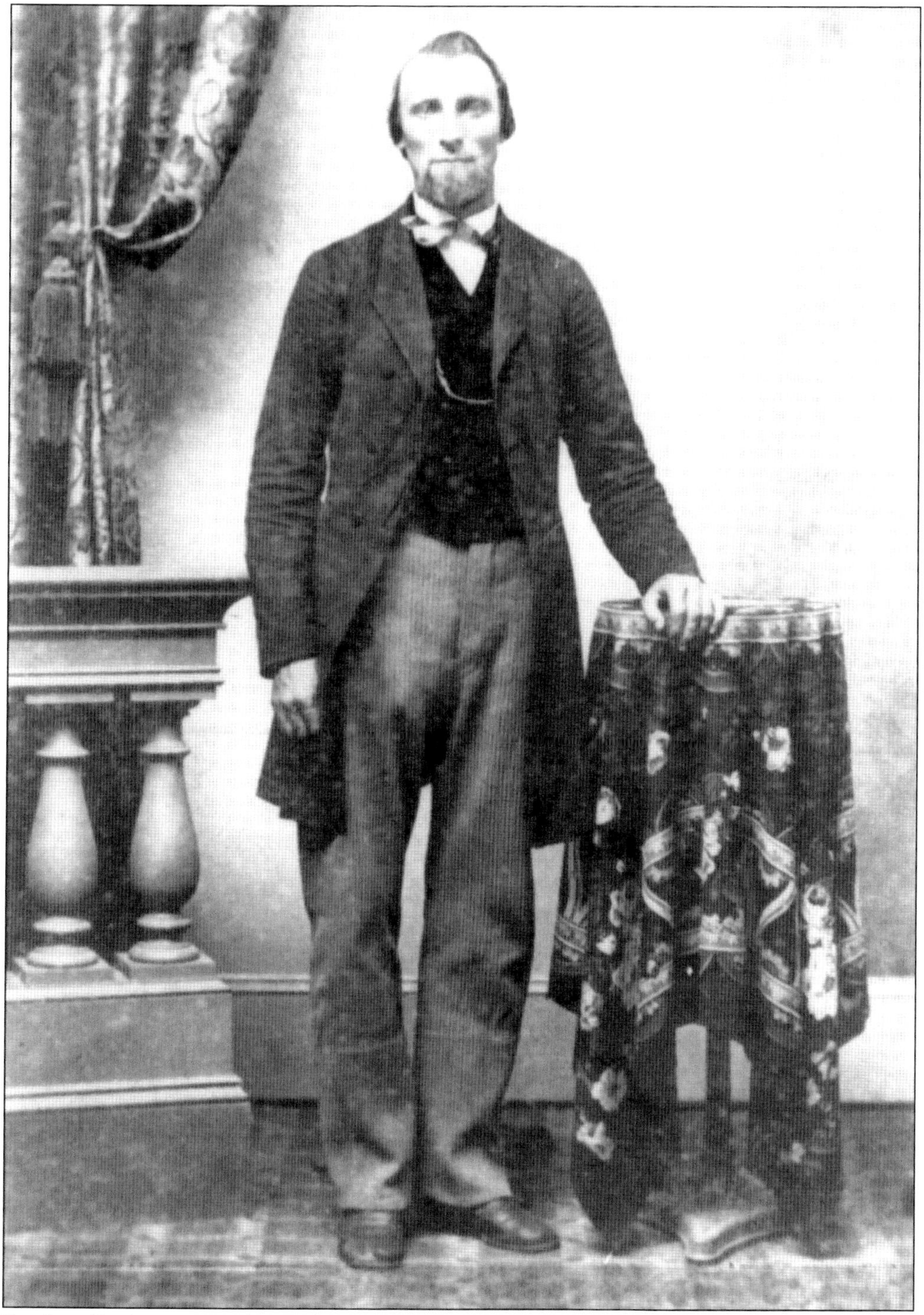

Stephen Coalman came from Ohio to Oregon in 1852 when he was 18. He settled on 160 acres near Sandy and was instrumental in building and maintaining the Barlow Road. He and his wife, Elizabeth, were the parents of famed Mount Hood mountaineer Elijah "Lige" Coalman. (Courtesy of SHS and the Coalman family.)

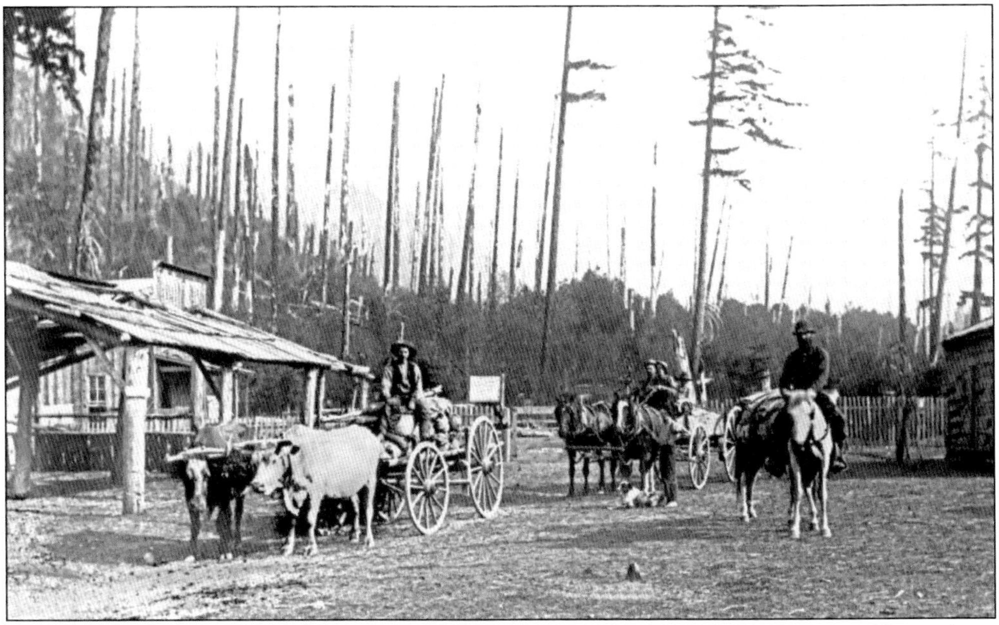

The Barlow Road tollgate, located a mile or two east of Rhododendron, is pictured here about 1885. Ernest Sievers sits atop the loaded wagon at left. Samuel Bacon drives the horse-drawn wagon. Adam Kotzman sits to the left of Bacon, and Mary Bacon (Samuel's mother) sits in the wagon to the right. The rider and the boy standing are unidentified. (Courtesy of SHS and Edward Green.)

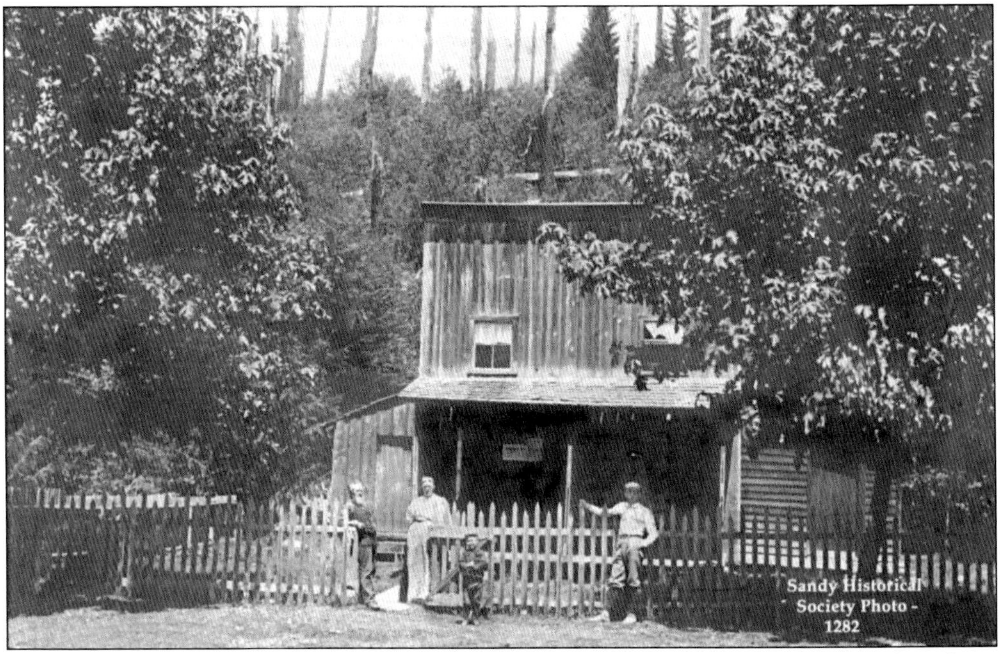

There were five different tollgates at different times in different places. The one that lasted was about a mile east of Rhododendron, and one of its earliest staffers was John Maronay Sr., shown here with his wife, Amanda, inside the fence. Theodore Collinger leans against the fence, and the little boy is George L. Lanphere.

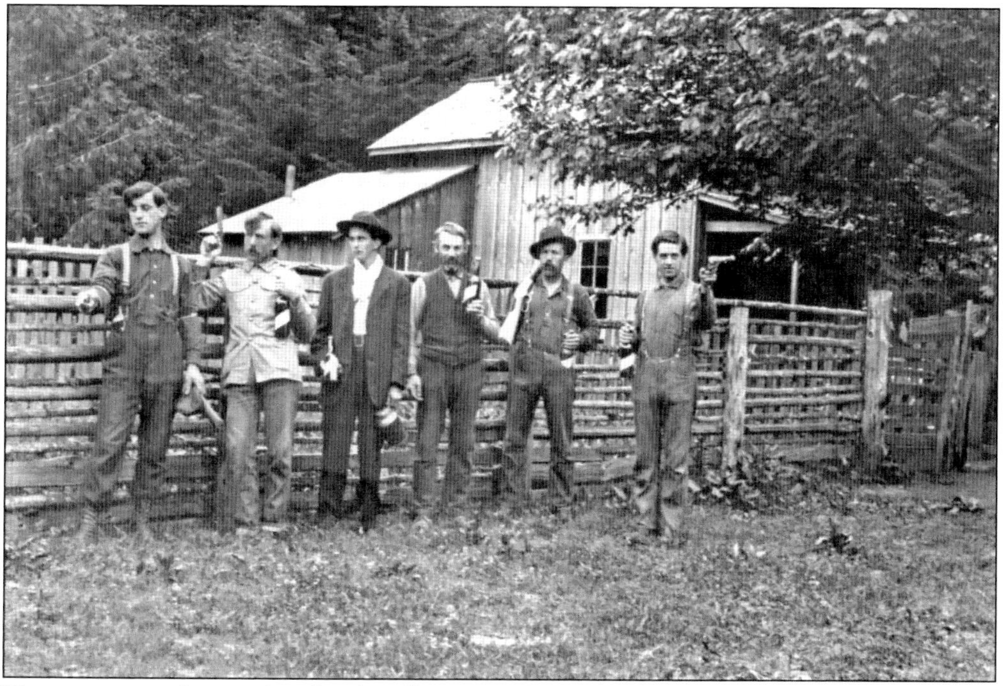

These young men have gathered at the tollgate to go shooting and, by the looks of the bottles, perhaps drinking. They are, from left to right, Gustave Stucki, Lloyd Baker, Harry Thornton, unidentified, John Maronay Sr., and Arleigh Mitchell. (Courtesy of SHS and the Mitchell family.)

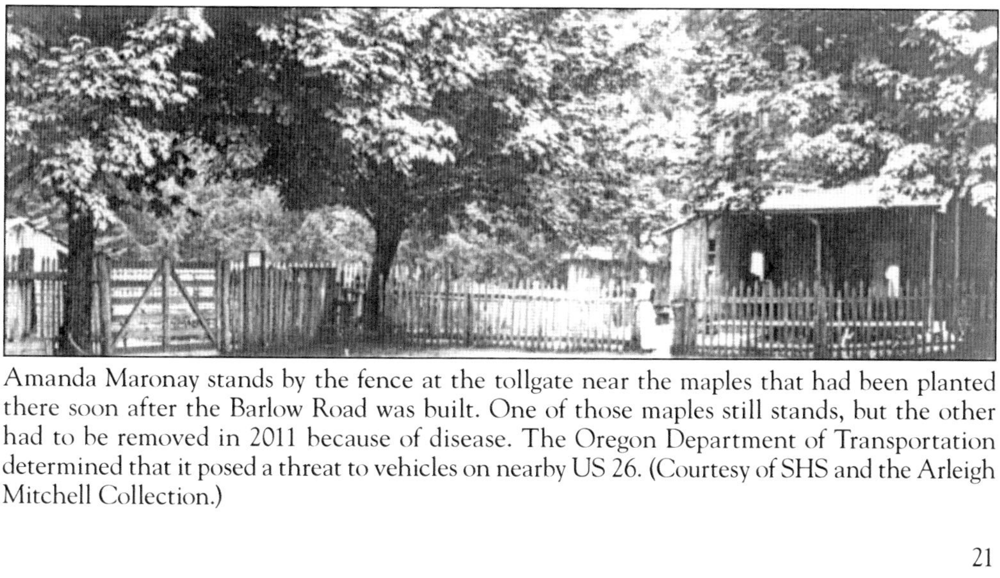

Amanda Maronay stands by the fence at the tollgate near the maples that had been planted there soon after the Barlow Road was built. One of those maples still stands, but the other had to be removed in 2011 because of disease. The Oregon Department of Transportation determined that it posed a threat to vehicles on nearby US 26. (Courtesy of SHS and the Arleigh Mitchell Collection.)

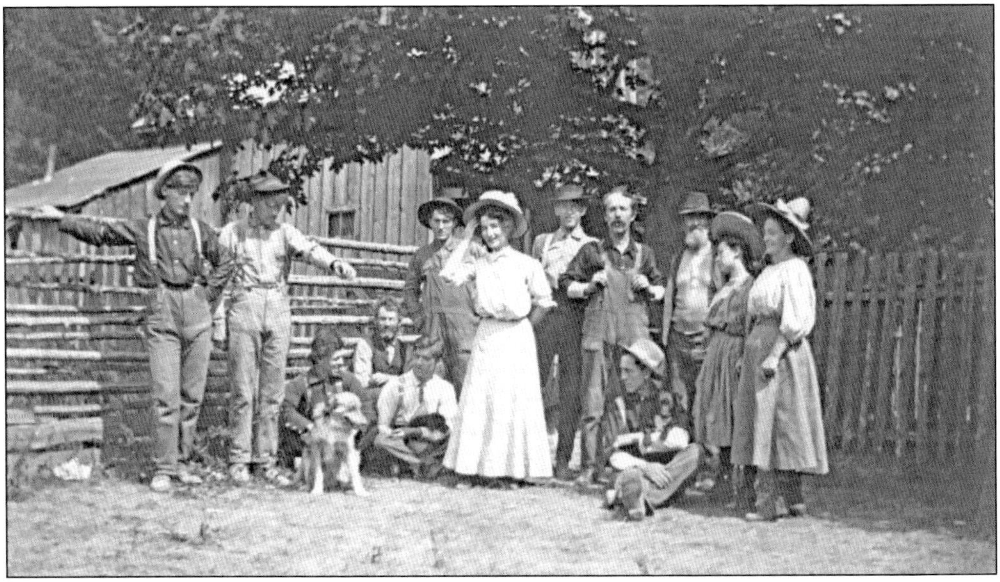

This gathering at the Barlow Road tollgate a mile above Rhododendron in 1907 includes, from left to right, Gustave Stucki, Peter Swan, Sam Miles and dog, Richard Ten Eyck, Arleigh Mitchell (holding puppy), Fred Waespe, Mary Waespe, John Roberts, John Maronay Jr., Steven Mitchell (Arleigh's father), Hazel Murray, Lena Murray, and Lloyd Baker (sitting with puppy).

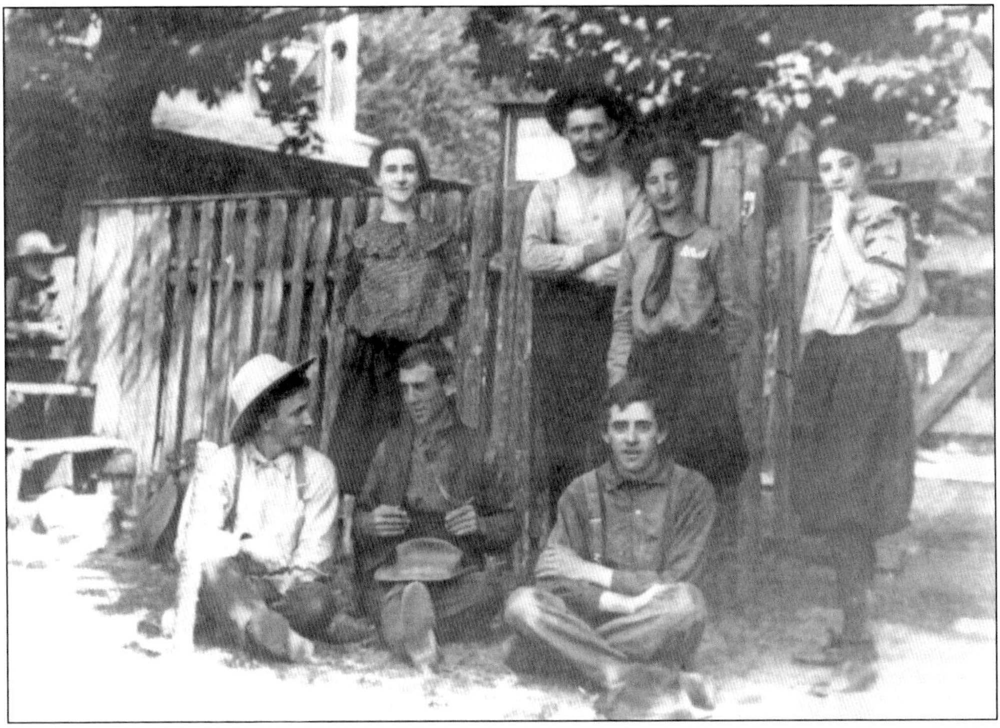

Arleigh Mitchell was the last tollgate keeper on the Barlow Road. The tollgate became a popular gathering place and jumping-off point for mountain excursions. Shown here are, from left to right, (seated) Otto Meinig, unidentified, and Arleigh; (standing) Mary Mitchell, Frederick Waespe, Mary Waespe, and Clara Mitchell.

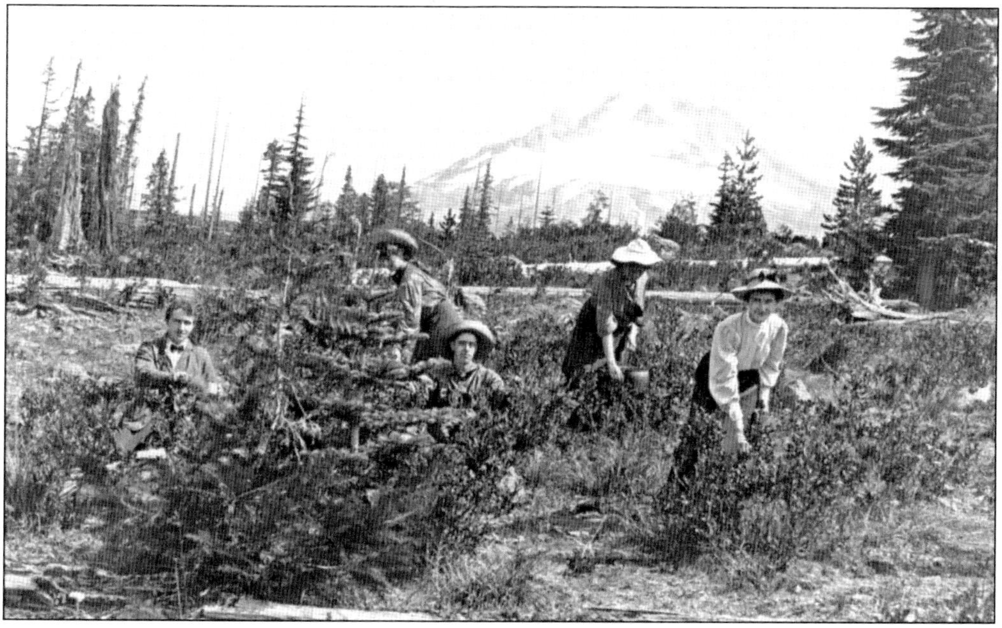

At the turn of the century, before movies, television, and digital devices, these young folks, friends since school days, had to be creative in their search for entertainment. Shown here picking huckleberries are, from left to right, Otto Meinig, unidentified, Arleigh Mitchell, unidentified, and Mary Waespe. Mount Hood looms in the background. (Courtesy of SHS and Richard Meinig.)

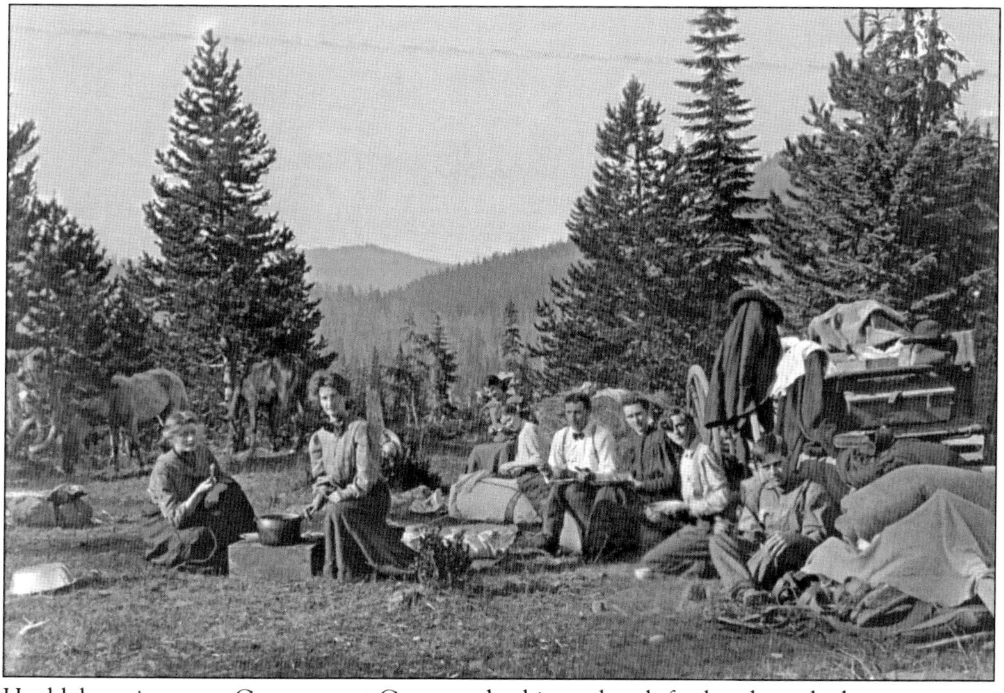

Huckleberrying near Government Camp and taking a break for lunch cooked over an open fire are, from left to right, Minna Hoffman, Mary Waespe, Nell Forrester, Clara Mitchell, Otto Meinig, Mary Mitchell, Harry Thornton, and Arleigh Mitchell. (Courtesy of SHS and John and Ruth Mitchell.)

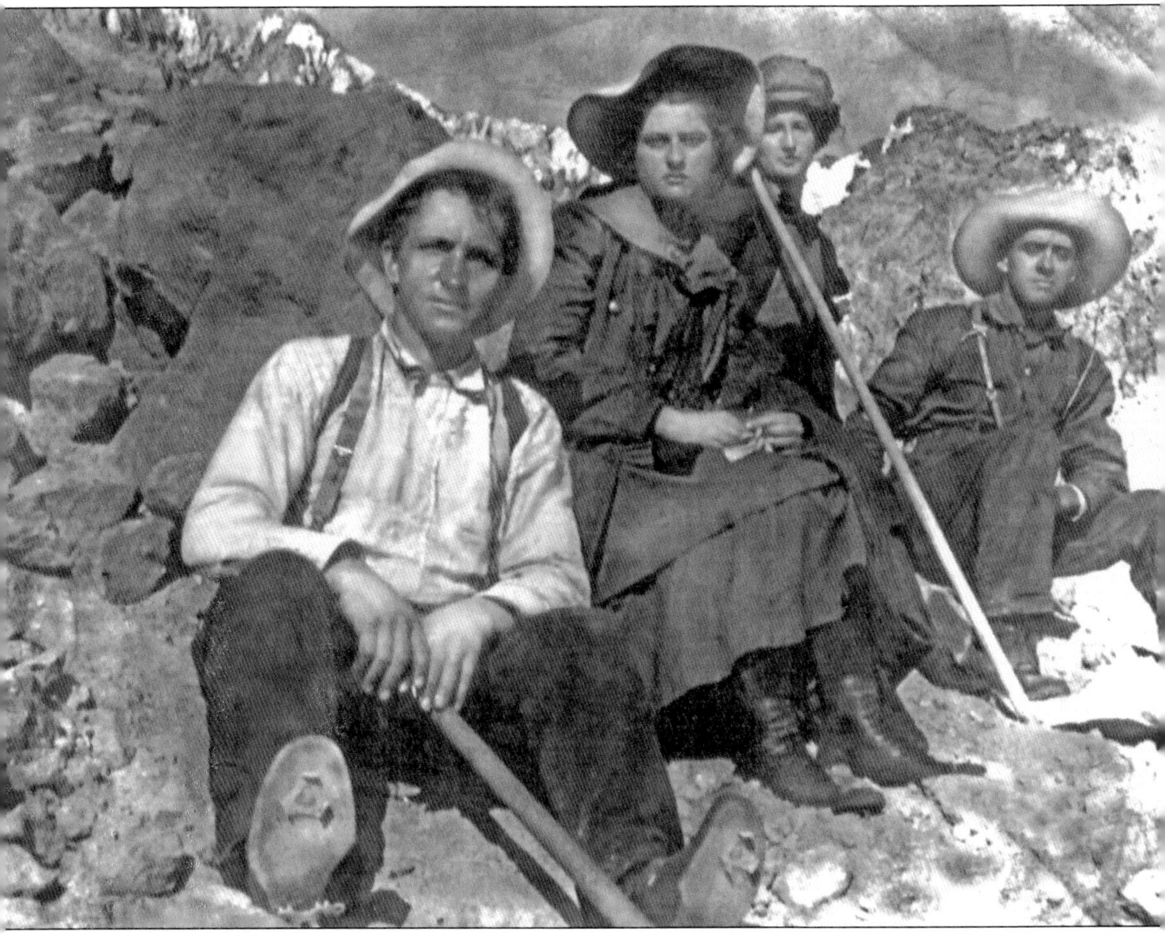

Another favorite activity of young "Sandyites" was taking an afternoon jaunt on the slopes of Mount Hood. Posing here are, from left to right, Otto Meinig, Minna Hoffman, Mary Waespe, and Arleigh Mitchell. They are at Crater Rock on Mount Hood in 1906. Otto's cleated boots seem prepared for any terrain. (Courtesy of SHS and the Mitchell family.)

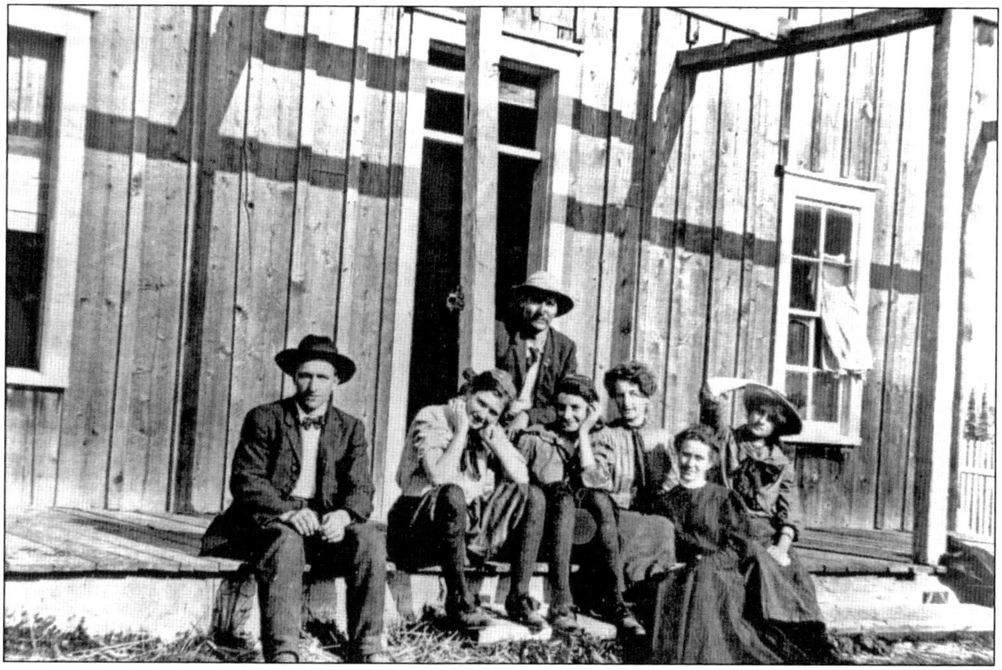

Stopping to take a rest at the Summit House near Summit Meadows in 1907 are, from left to right, Otto Meinig Nell Forrester, Elijah Coalman (at the rear), Clara Mitchell, Minna Hoffman, Mary Mitchell, and Mary Waespe. From 1866 to 1871, the Barlow Road toll was collected at Summit House, built by Perry Vickers, where wagons would pause and rest before descending the treacherous Laurel Hill.

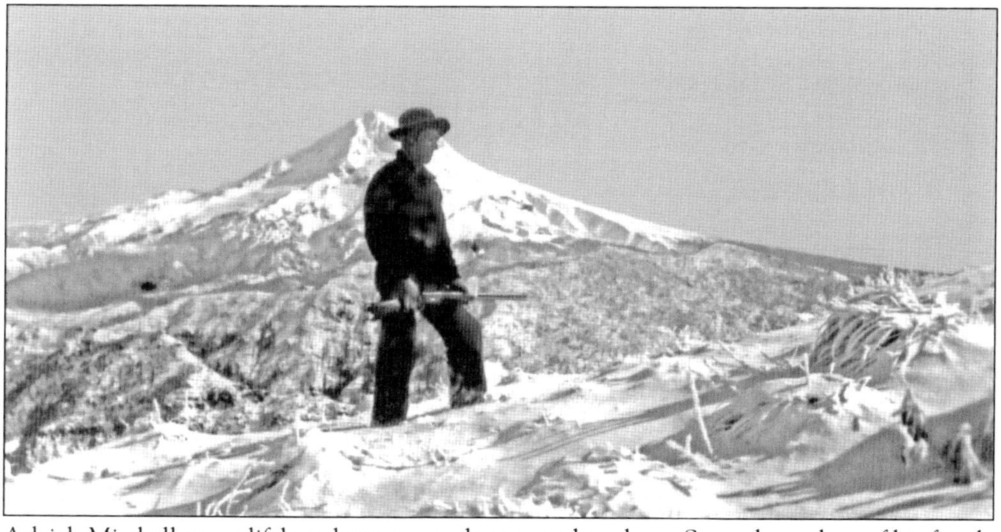

Arleigh Mitchell was a lifelong hunter, woodsman, and explorer. Several members of his family were tollgate keepers for years, but he still found time to hunt all over the mountains above Sandy. He is seen here on the top of Zig Zag Mountain, with Mount Hood in the background. (Courtesy of SHS and the Mitchell family.)

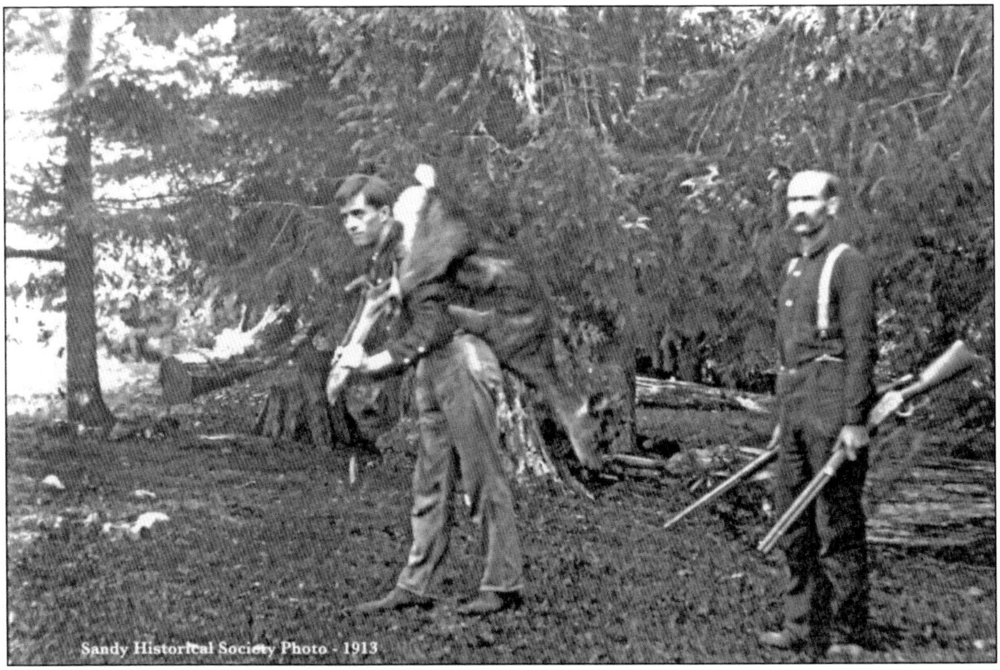

Arleigh Mitchell (left) displays his hunting prowess, accompanied by Marshall Davis near the Barlow Road tollgate in 1907. Arleigh's father was Steven Overton Mitchell, who had nine children and raised famed mountain man Elijah Coalman as his own after Elijah's mother died when he was only 18 months old. (Courtesy of SHS and the Mitchell family.)

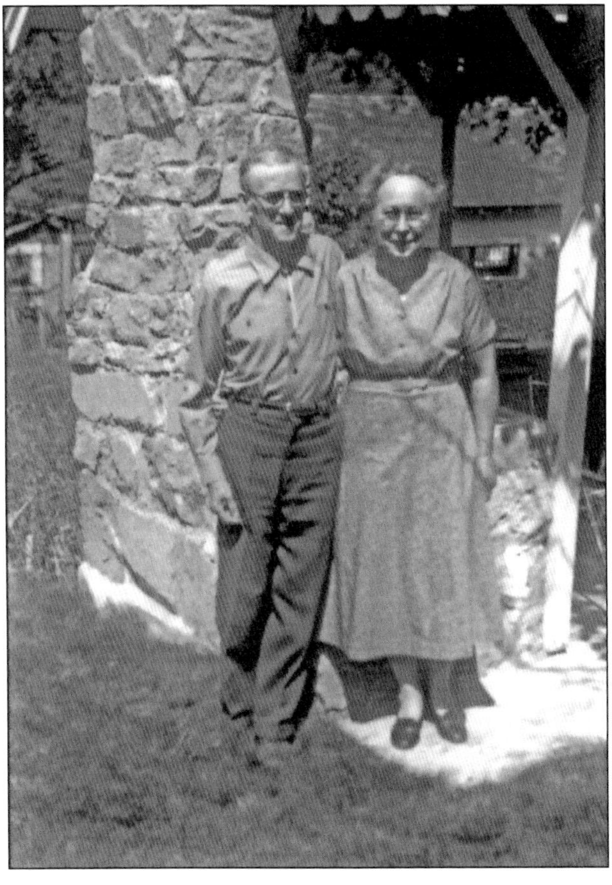

In their retirement years, Arleigh and Anna Mitchell still enjoyed the woods in their rustic home in the hills above Sandy, but perhaps did so a little less actively. During World War I, he had made 11 round-trips over the Atlantic as a member of the US Navy and served eight months of shore duty overseas. (Courtesy of SHS and the Mitchell family.)

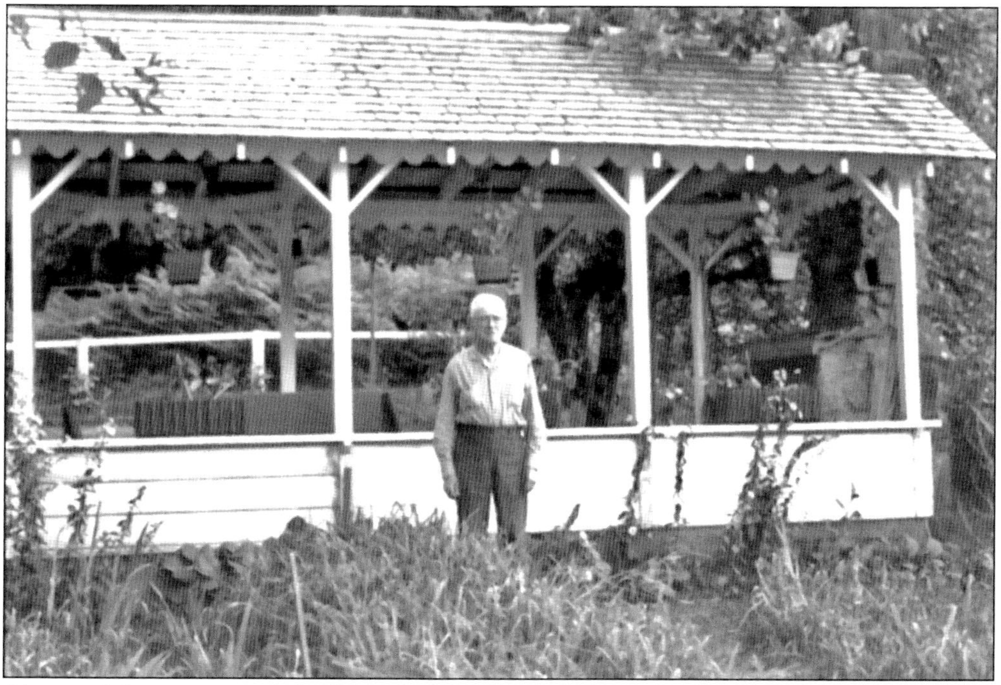

Alone with his memories, Arleigh Mitchell lived out his life in the woodland setting he had grown up in and learned to love so well. He and his brother reminisced how, as children, they would stop at "old man Clark's" barn and listen to him tell stories of the Civil War.

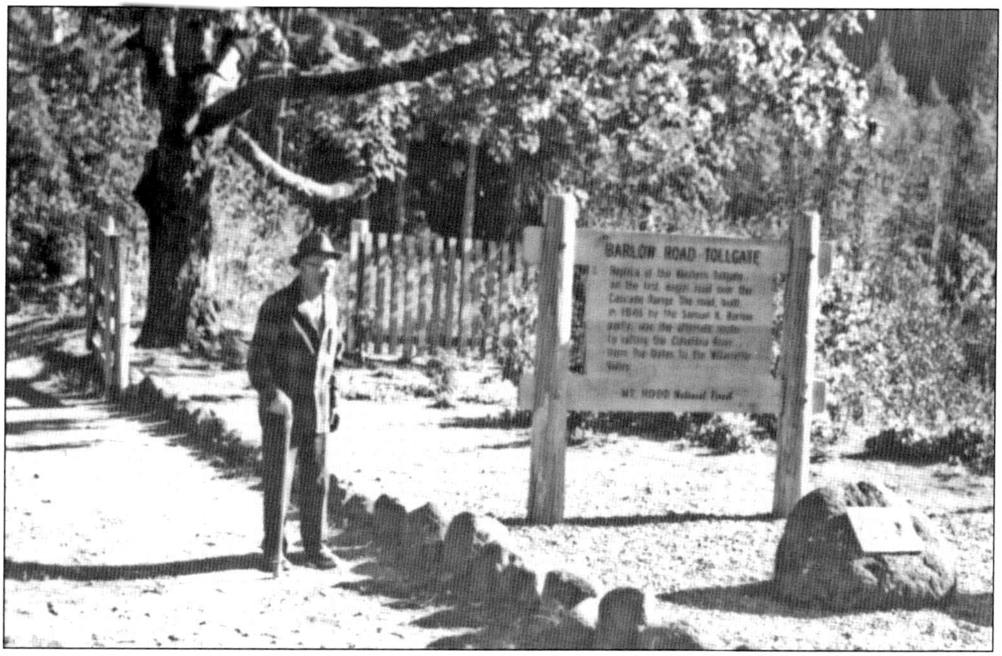

It was highly appropriate for Arleigh Mitchell to dedicate the replica of the Barlow Road tollgate when it was restored. The work was undertaken by 77 clubs comprising Portland, Multomah, and Clackamas Districts of the Oregon State Federation of Garden Clubs, with the cooperation of the US Forest Service on a two-year landscaping project. (Courtesy of SHS and Arleigh Mitchell.)

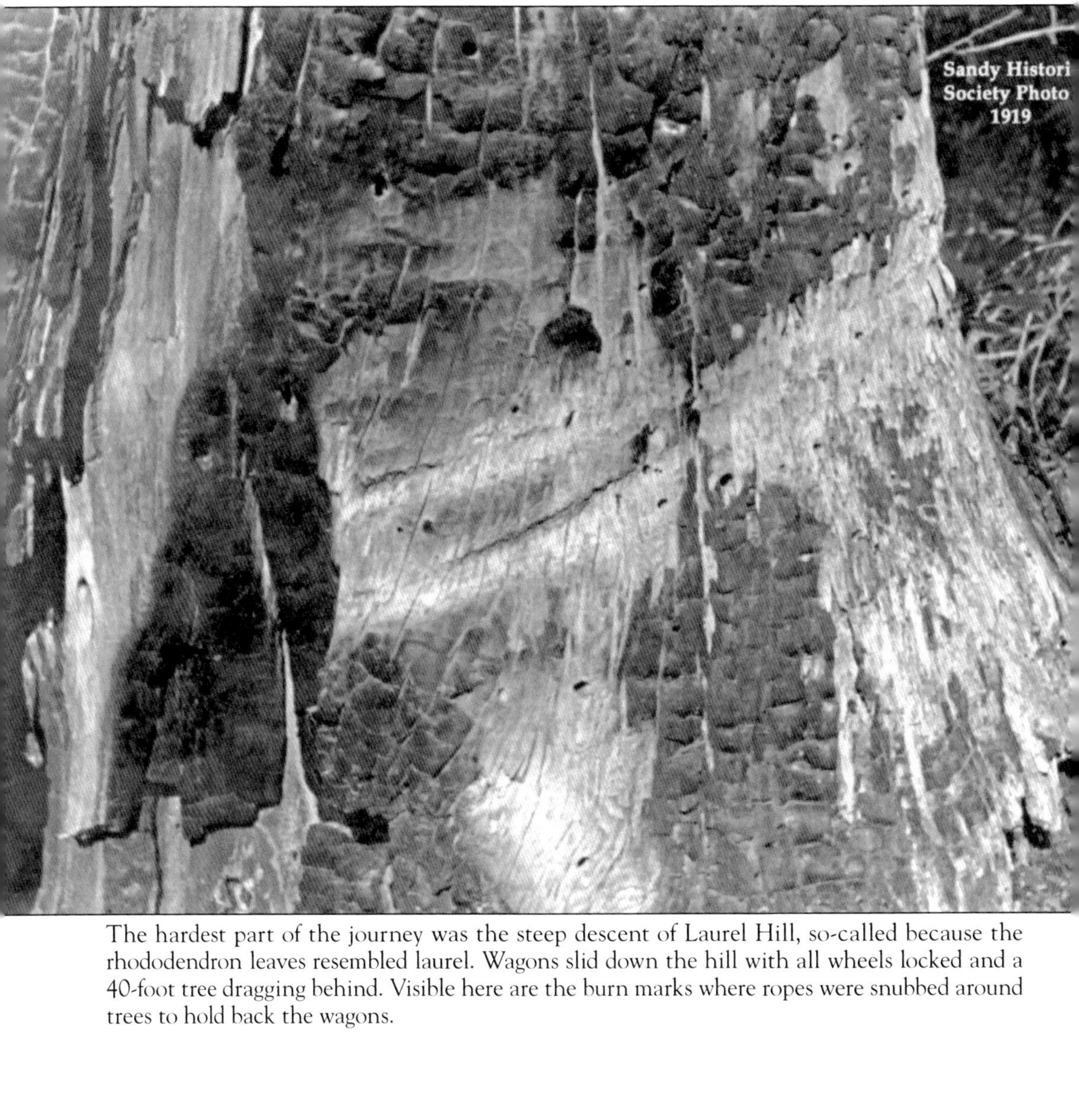

The hardest part of the journey was the steep descent of Laurel Hill, so-called because the rhododendron leaves resembled laurel. Wagons slid down the hill with all wheels locked and a 40-foot tree dragging behind. Visible here are the burn marks where ropes were snubbed around trees to hold back the wagons.

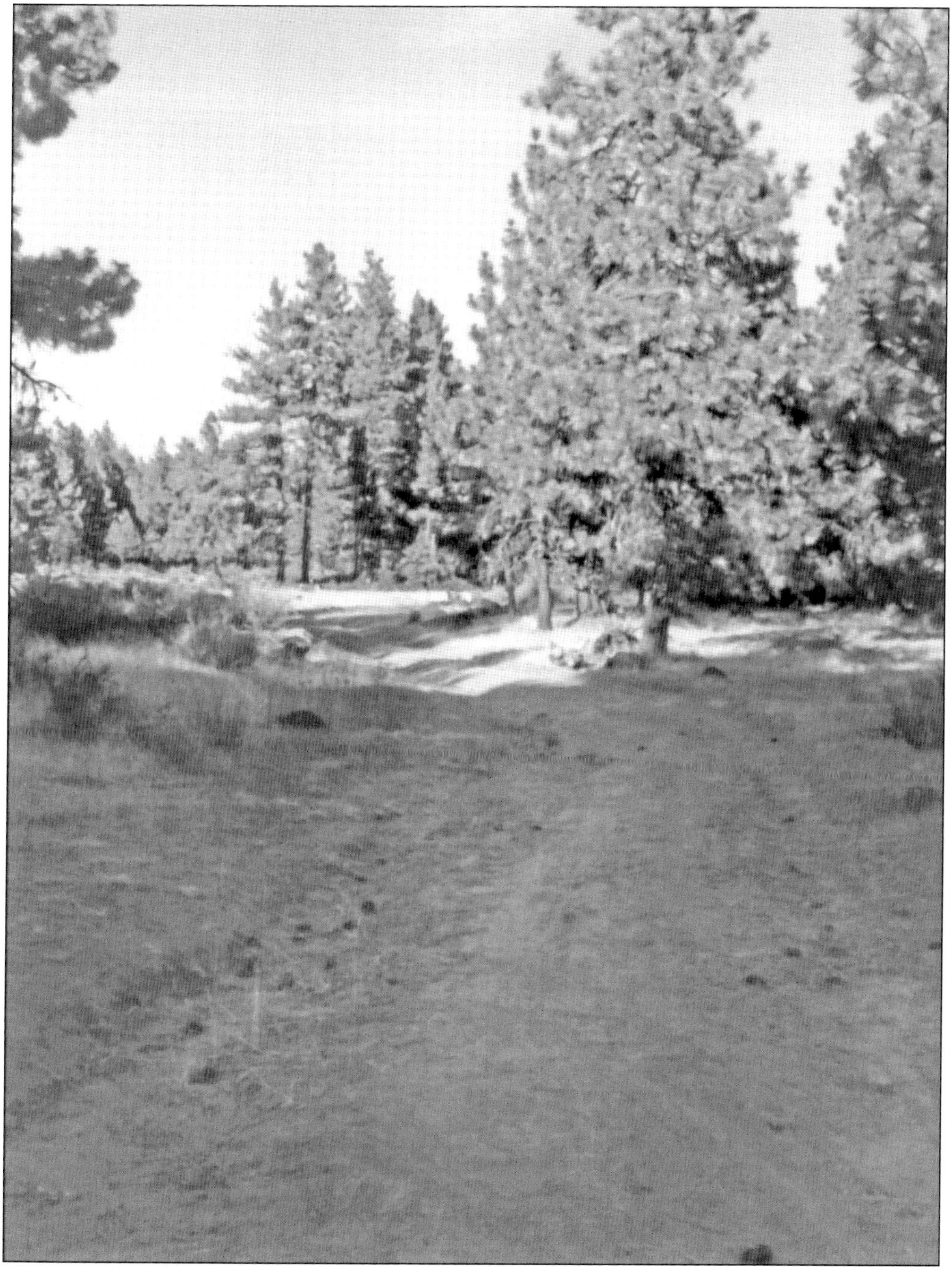

In 1993, an estimated three million people walked or rode portions of the Oregon Trail, many in covered-wagon replicas, to celebrate the "great migration" to Oregon beginning in 1843. Gov. Barbara Roberts declared passionately, "I knelt and put my hands in those tracks." These wagon-wheel ruts still remain on the Barlow Road. (Courtesy of SHS and Philip Jonsrud.)

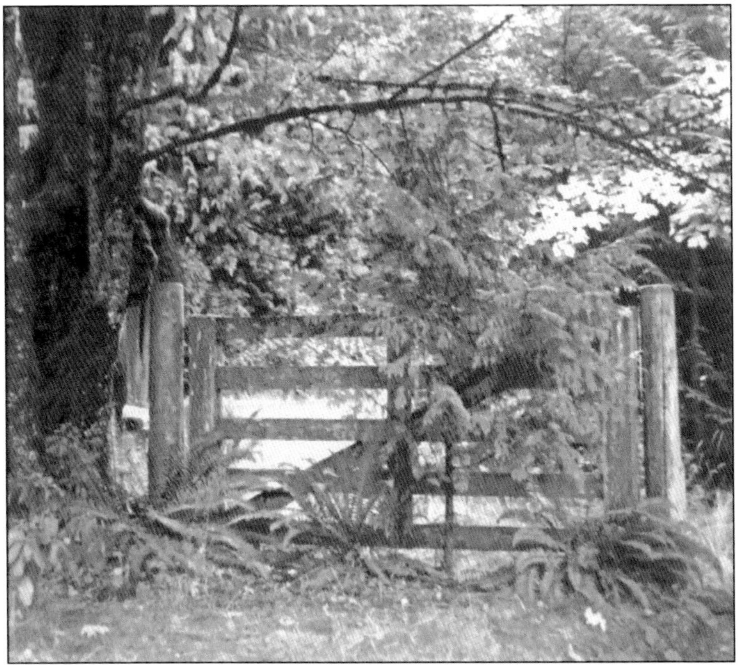

Of the five different locations for the Barlow Road tollgate, this was the one used longest and latest. The gate and the house associated with it have long since decayed, but this replica and the campground nearby keep it in the memory of Oregonians. The maple tree on the left is all that remains of the two planted on either side of the gate so long ago.

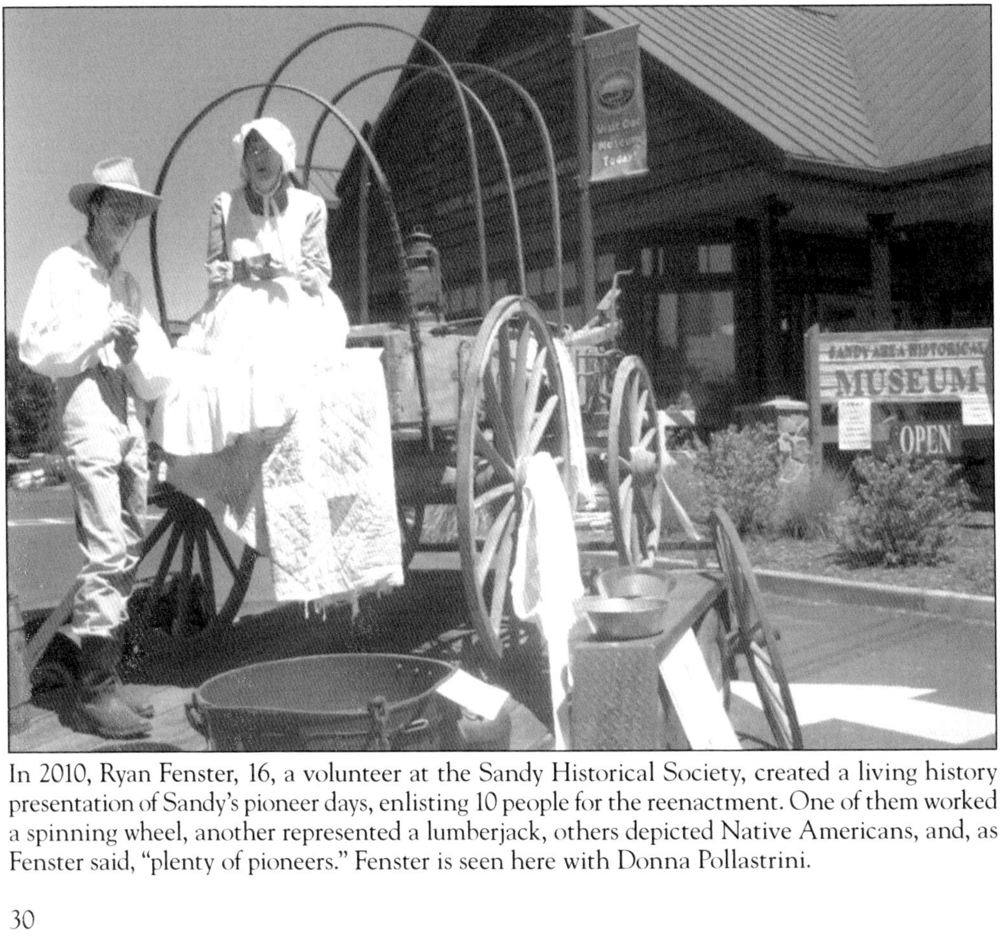

In 2010, Ryan Fenster, 16, a volunteer at the Sandy Historical Society, created a living history presentation of Sandy's pioneer days, enlisting 10 people for the reenactment. One of them worked a spinning wheel, another represented a lumberjack, others depicted Native Americans, and, as Fenster said, "plenty of pioneers." Fenster is seen here with Donna Pollastrini.

Three

FOUNDING FAMILIES

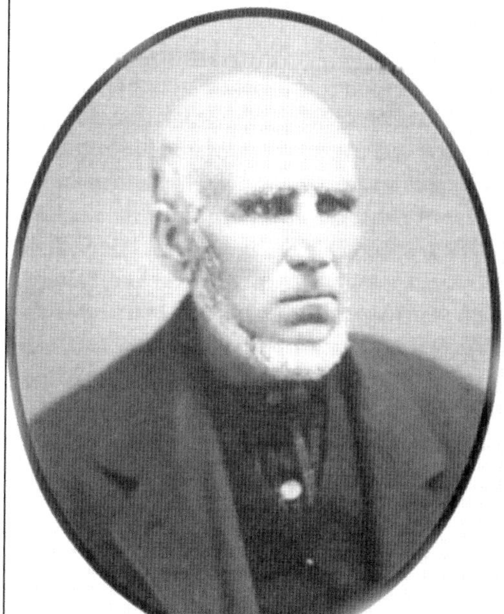

Francis Revenue

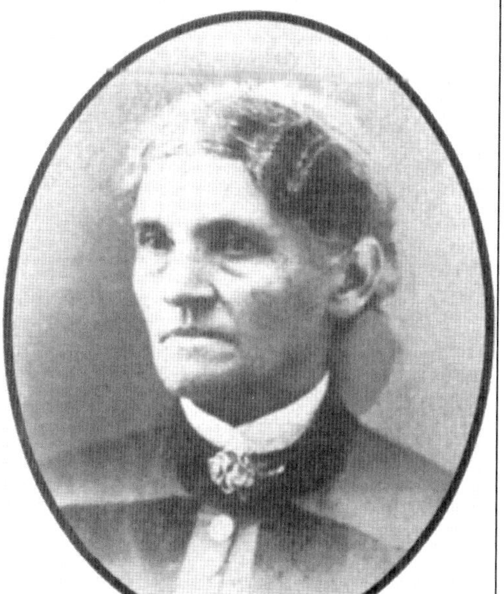

Lydia Revenue

Francis and Lydia Revenue were the first settlers in the Sandy area, which was called Revenue's before there was a post office. When they arrived, they had one child, Mary. John, the second of what would be nine children, was born three years later, the first non-Native child born in the area and an ancestor of many people still calling Sandy their home.

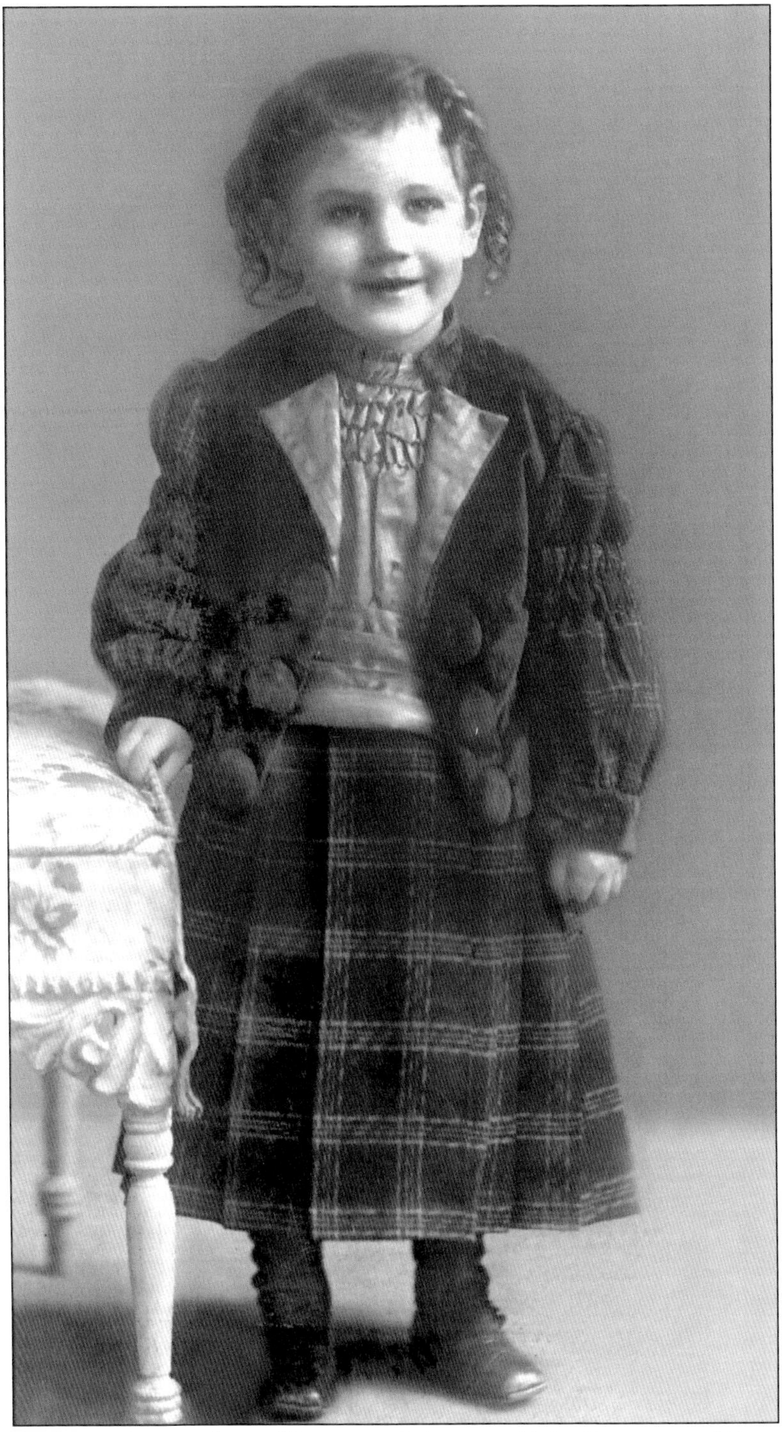

Homer Revenue was the grandson of Francis and the son of John Revenue and Parmelia Weed, who were married in 1884. He is seen here, like many little boys of his day, in long curls and a long dress. He wears more masculine attire in later photographs, which show him handling draft horses on his farm, near the county road named for his family.

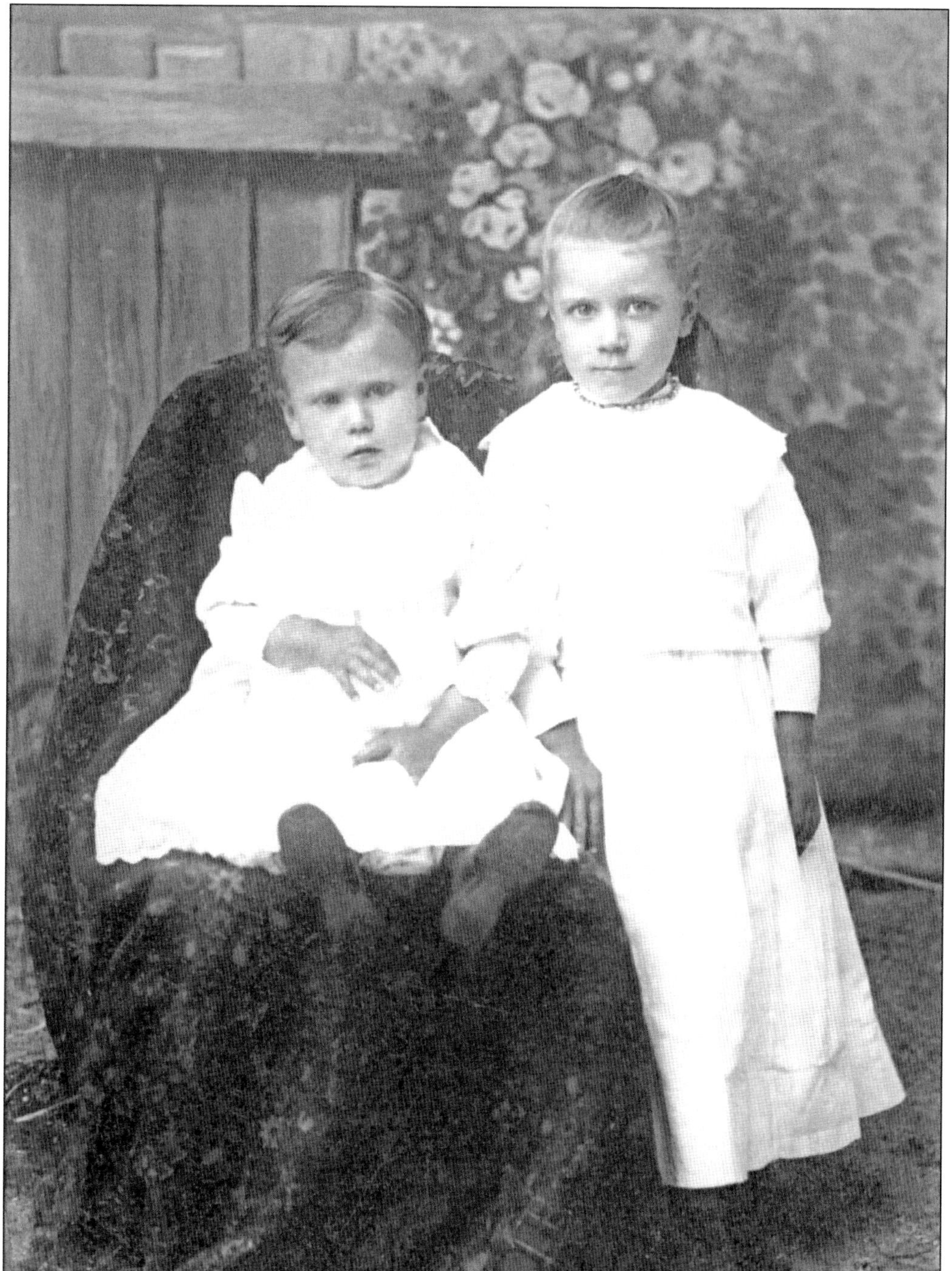

John Revenue fathered two other children. Emma was born in 1885, and Raymond was born in 1889. They are shown here in what seems to have been their Sunday best. Like Homer, Raymond is wearing a long, flowing dress, fairly common among families at the time when they wanted to show their young sons in the best light.

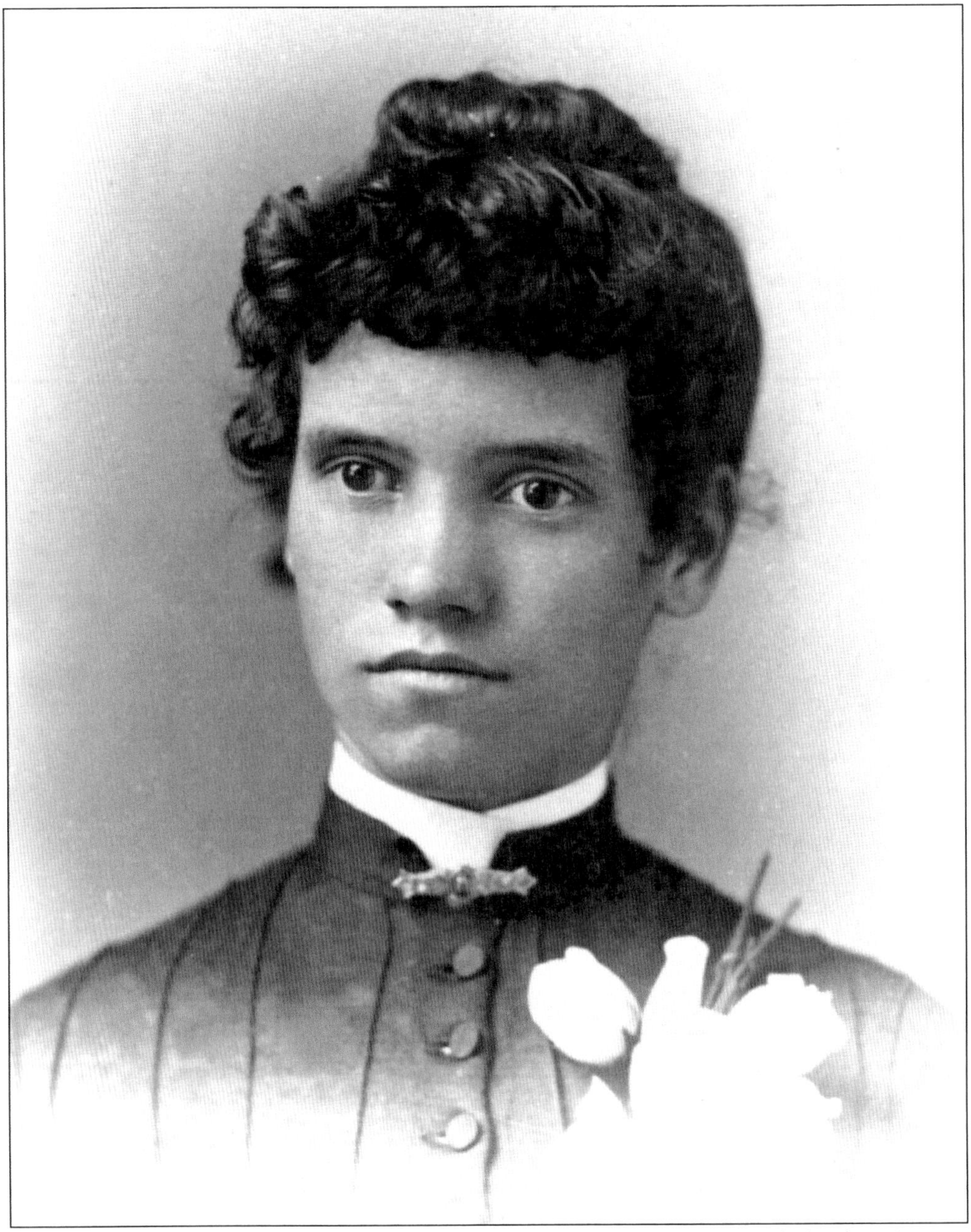

Cordelia Revenue was the eighth child born to Francis and Lydia, and the fifth daughter. Francis hired "Noyes Smith," whose real name was Egbert Alcott (or Olcott), to teach his children in the home. After Francis and John built a log school on the Revenue property, they hired Harvey Cross to teach in School District 6. The district was 50 miles wide and 50 miles long.

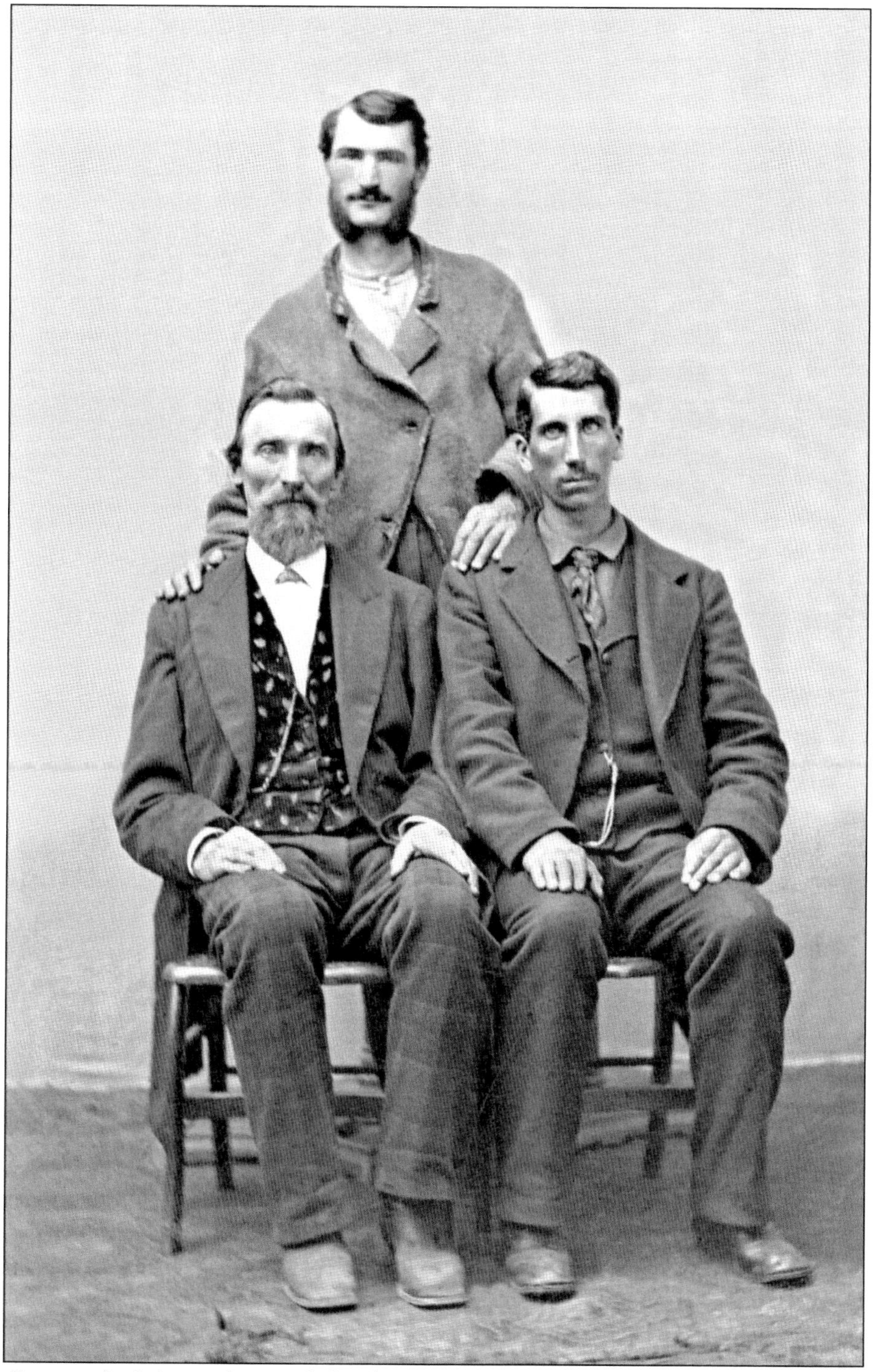

John Revenue (right) poses here with Stephen Coalman (left) and Roy Ward. John was one of the nine pupils attending the first term of the school his father, Francis, had built with logs hauled by John with his father's oxen. In 1884, John married Parmelia Weed, who left him when their son Homer was five.

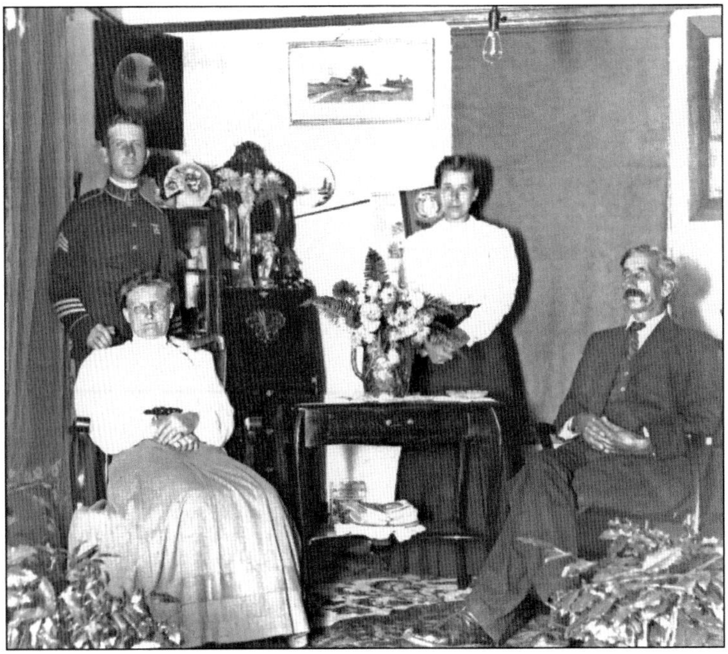

Emma Revenue grew up and married William Miller. Here, they are visiting her parents, John and Eliza Revenue. The Millers, who had no children, are buried in El Paso, Texas, at the Fort Bliss Military Cemetery. The pitcher holding the flowers came with Francis and Lydia on the Oregon Trail and was donated to the Sandy Historical Society by Connie Revenue Selzler.

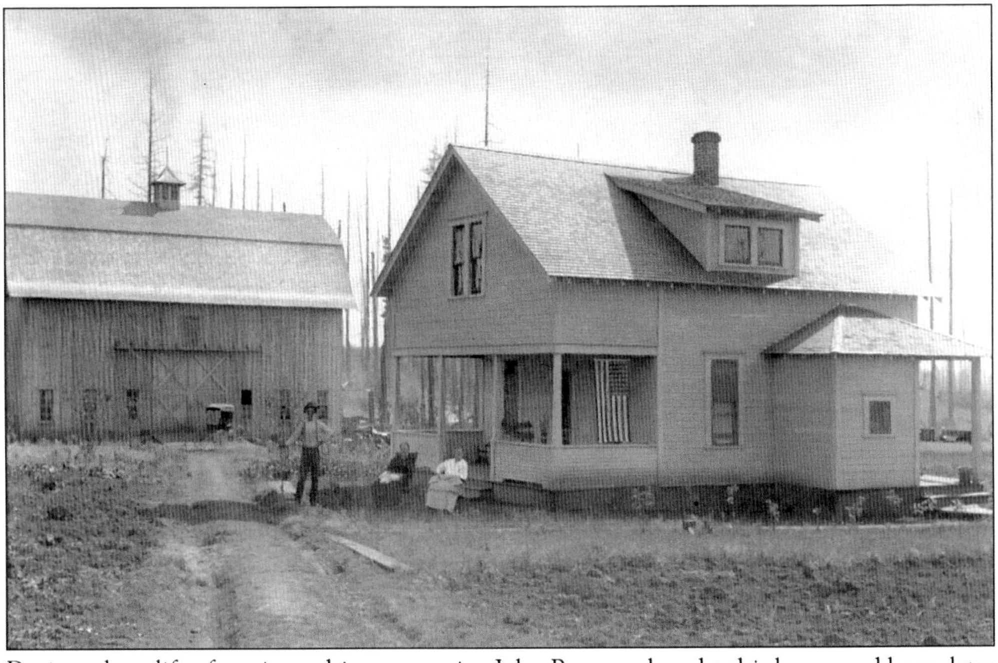

During a long life of service to his community, John Revenue bought this house and barn, later owned by his son Homer, at Dunn Road and 357th Avenue. The buggy in the background in front of the barn now rests in the lobby of the Sandy Historical Museum. (Courtesy of Connie (Revenue) Selzler and SHS.)

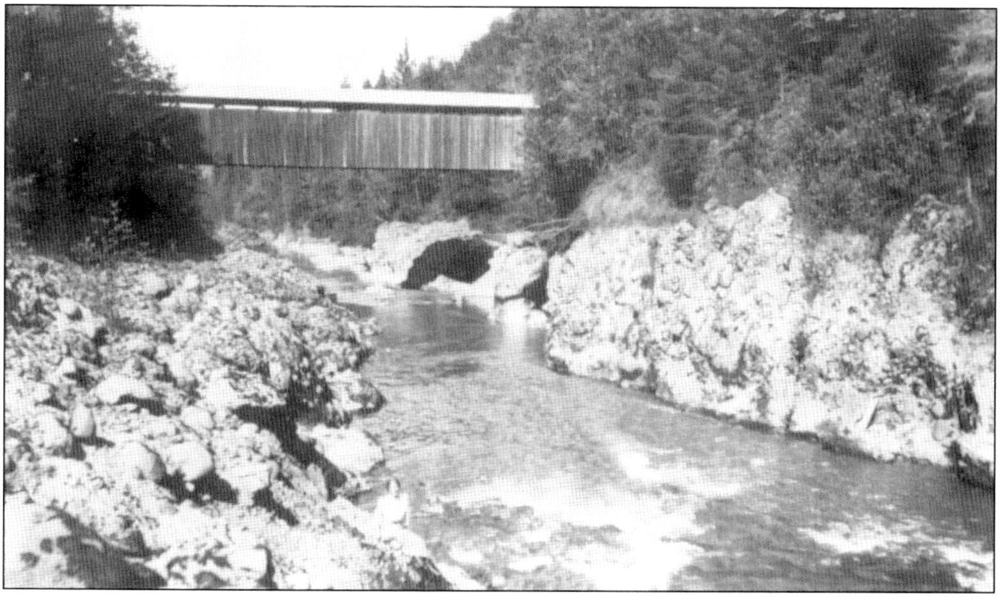

No photographs exist of the original Revenue bridge. It was washed away in a flood in 1884, as was the one built to replace it. This is the third bridge, which was torn down in 1929 to build a "modern" highway bridge, which itself was replaced to accommodate heavier traffic. (Courtesy of Connie Revenue Selzler.)

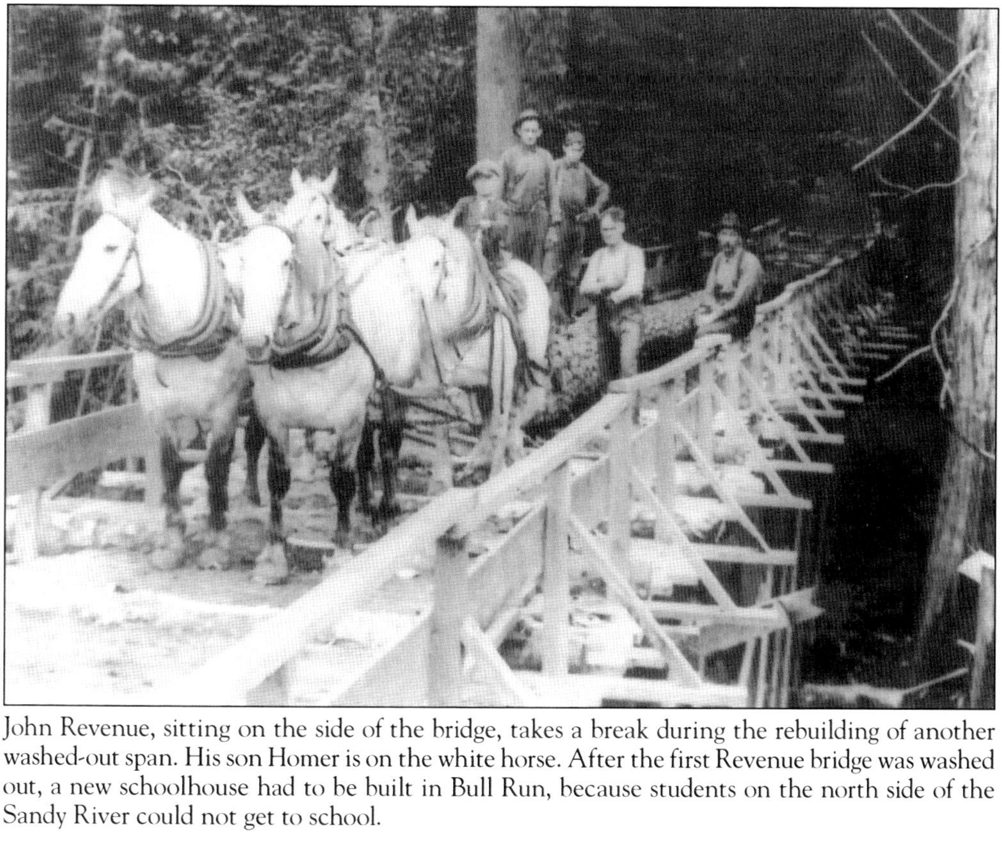

John Revenue, sitting on the side of the bridge, takes a break during the rebuilding of another washed-out span. His son Homer is on the white horse. After the first Revenue bridge was washed out, a new schoolhouse had to be built in Bull Run, because students on the north side of the Sandy River could not get to school.

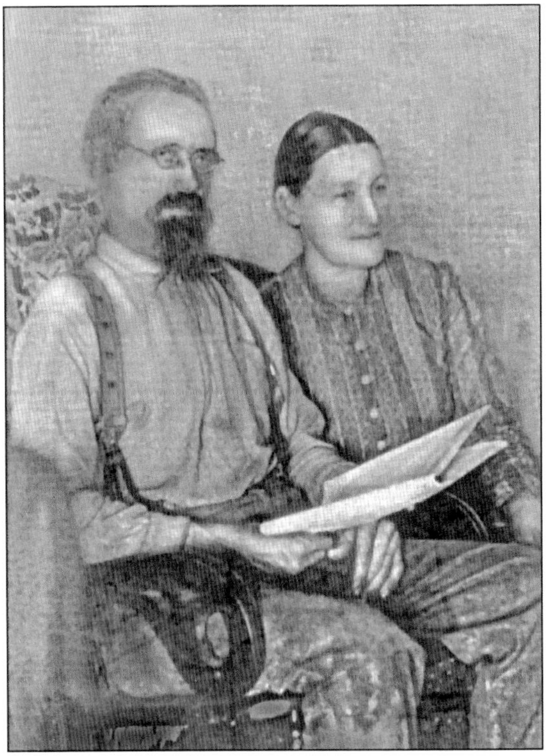

Torkel and Kari Jonsrud came to Oregon in 1877, after Torkel had served in the Minnesota Legislature. He operated his farm between Kelso and Sandy and was soon appointed justice of the peace. Torkel died in 1925, leaving a whole tribe of Jonsruds, including grandson Philip, who wrote several reminiscences of Sandy.

Herman and Ernestine Fischer were German immigrants who settled first in Missouri and then in Oregon. Their children were Ernest, Theodore, Anna, and Wilhelmina "Minnie." Shown here are Theodore and Marie Fischer and their daughters Selma (left) and Anna. (Courtesy of SHS and the Fischer family.)

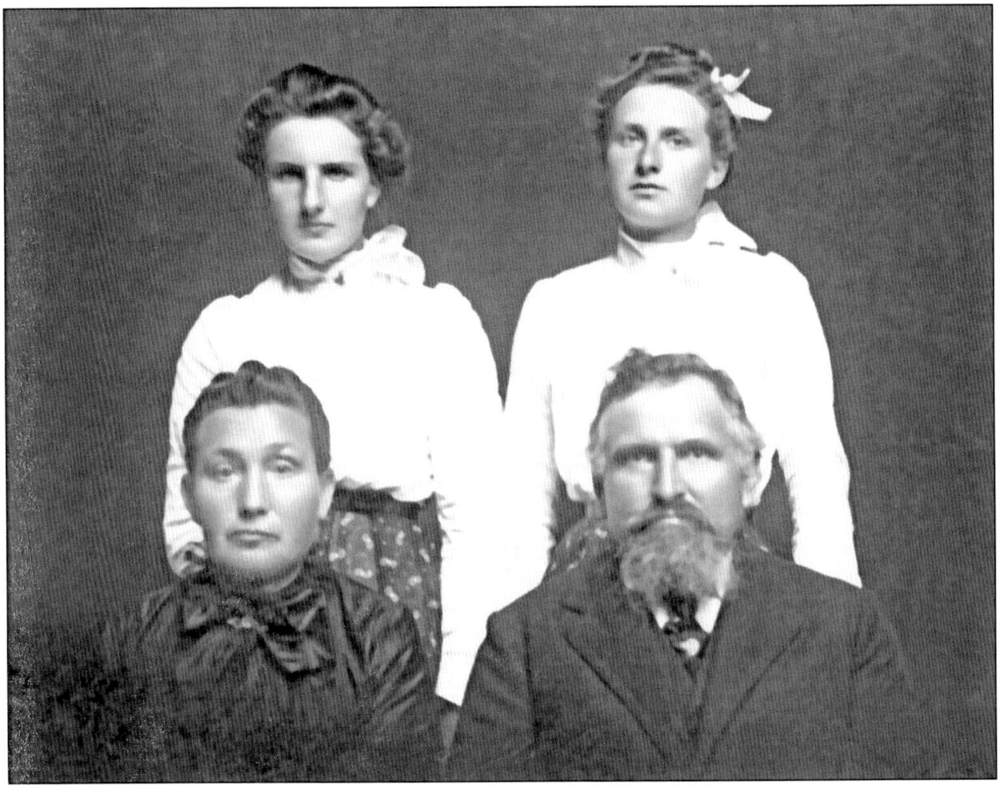

Richard Ten Eyck rode into Marmot, east of Sandy, on horseback in 1883, and the Ten Eyck name has been prominent ever since. He married Rosa Belle Hoffman, and they had eight children. The couple poses here in 1888 with baby George. Richard's father, Miles Ten Eyck, served as an aide-de-camp to Gen. Ambrose Burnside in the Civil War. (Courtesy of SHS and the Ten Eyck family.)

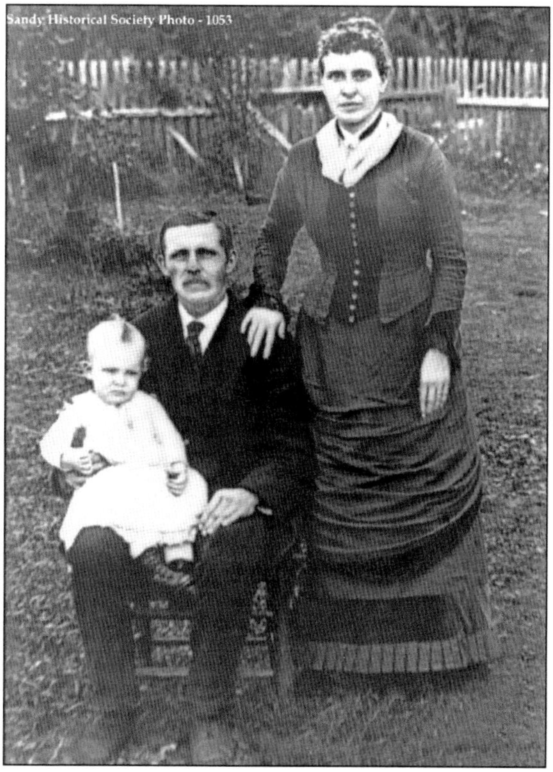

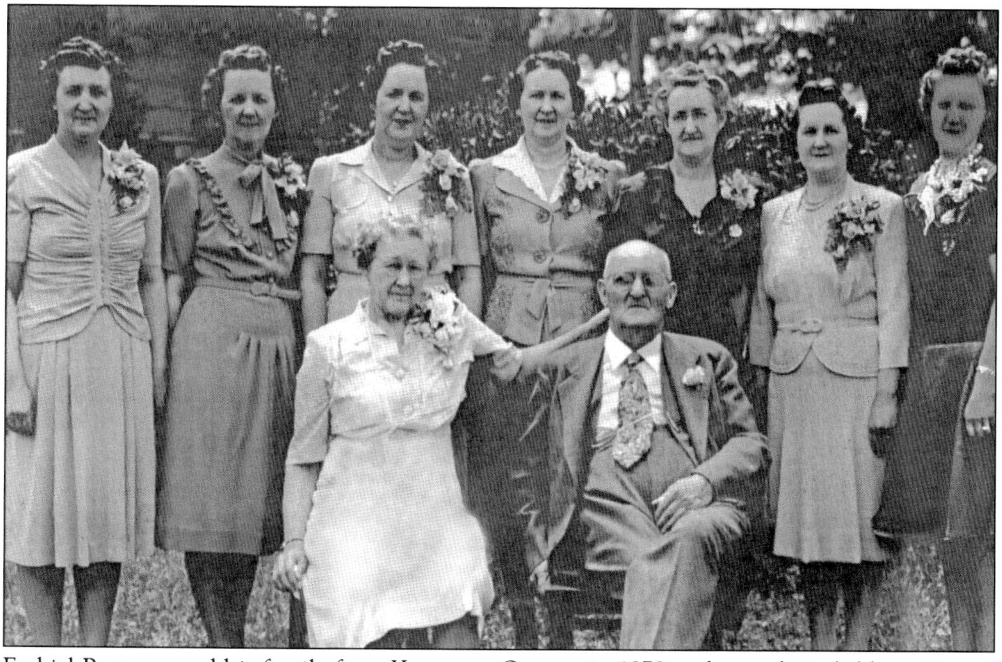

Ezekiel Beers moved his family from Kansas to Oregon in 1878 and reared 11 children. One of them was Frank Beers, a farmer and sawmill man who also operated a general merchandise store in partnership with Walker A. Proctor. Frank is shown here with his wife, Lillian, and their seven daughters. They are, from left to right, Florence, Rose, Rena, Eva, Alta, Edna, and Jessie.

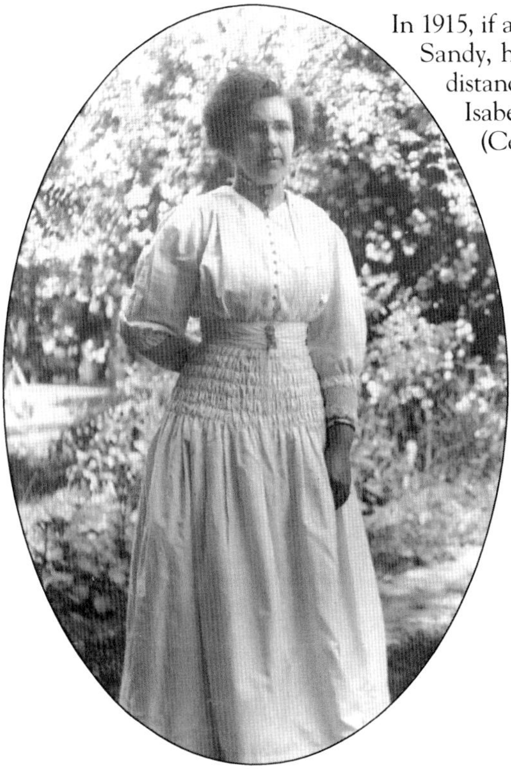

In 1915, if a resident wanted to talk with someone outside Sandy, he or she had to call the operator for a long-distance connection. That meant getting in touch with Isabel Gray Wolf, Sandy's noted telephone operator. (Courtesy of SHS and Dennis Gray.)

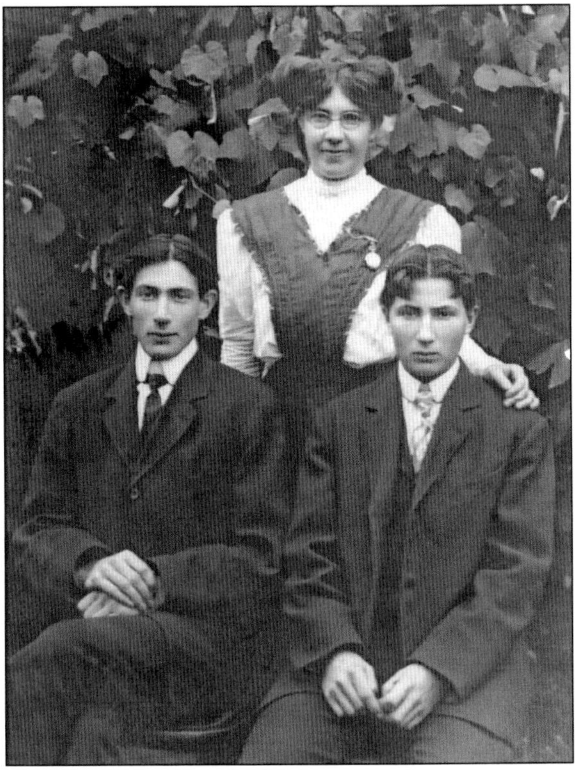

Before she could enter the field of telephone operating, Isabel Gray Wolf needed some practical experience. She wrote to her friend Della, "I am working in the Sandy Hotel and get $25 a month but I have to earn it just the same." Here, she poses with her brothers Raymond (left) and Alex. (Courtesy of SHS and Dennis Gray.)

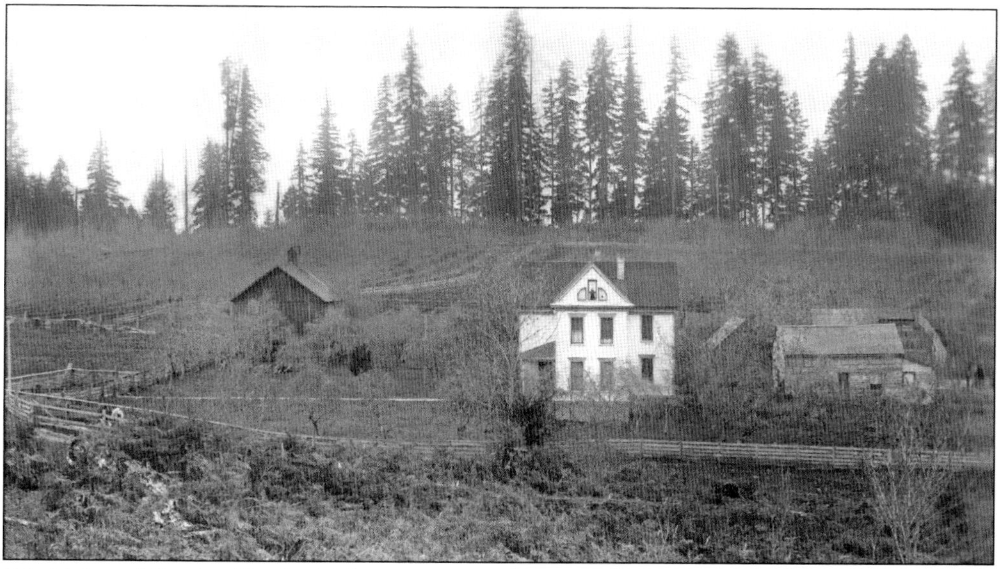

Friedrich and Bertha (Fischer) Meinig came to America from Germany in 1871 and to Sandy four years later. Shown here is their home, built in 1890. It was destroyed by fire in 1965. The house stood near the edge of the bluff on "Meinig's Hill," just north of the intersection of Ten Eyck Road and the Mount Hood Highway. (Courtesy of SHS and Richard Meinig.)

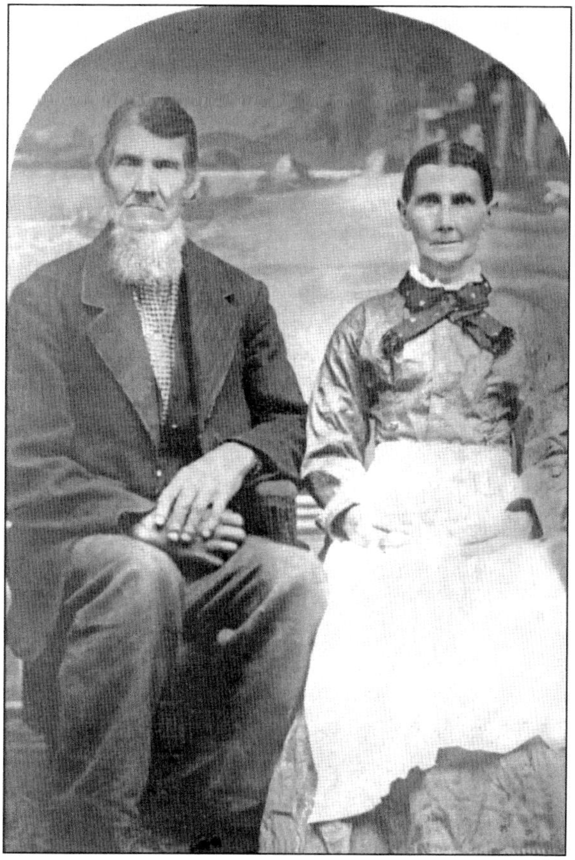

In 1863, Gilbert Epperson and his son Marion determined to join the Iowa Volunteers and fight for the Union, but Catherine Epperson persuaded them to move to Oregon instead. Gilbert and Catherine are shown here in 1864, about the time they settled near Eagle Creek, in the area now known as Sandy Ridge. (Courtesy of SHS and the Epperson family.)

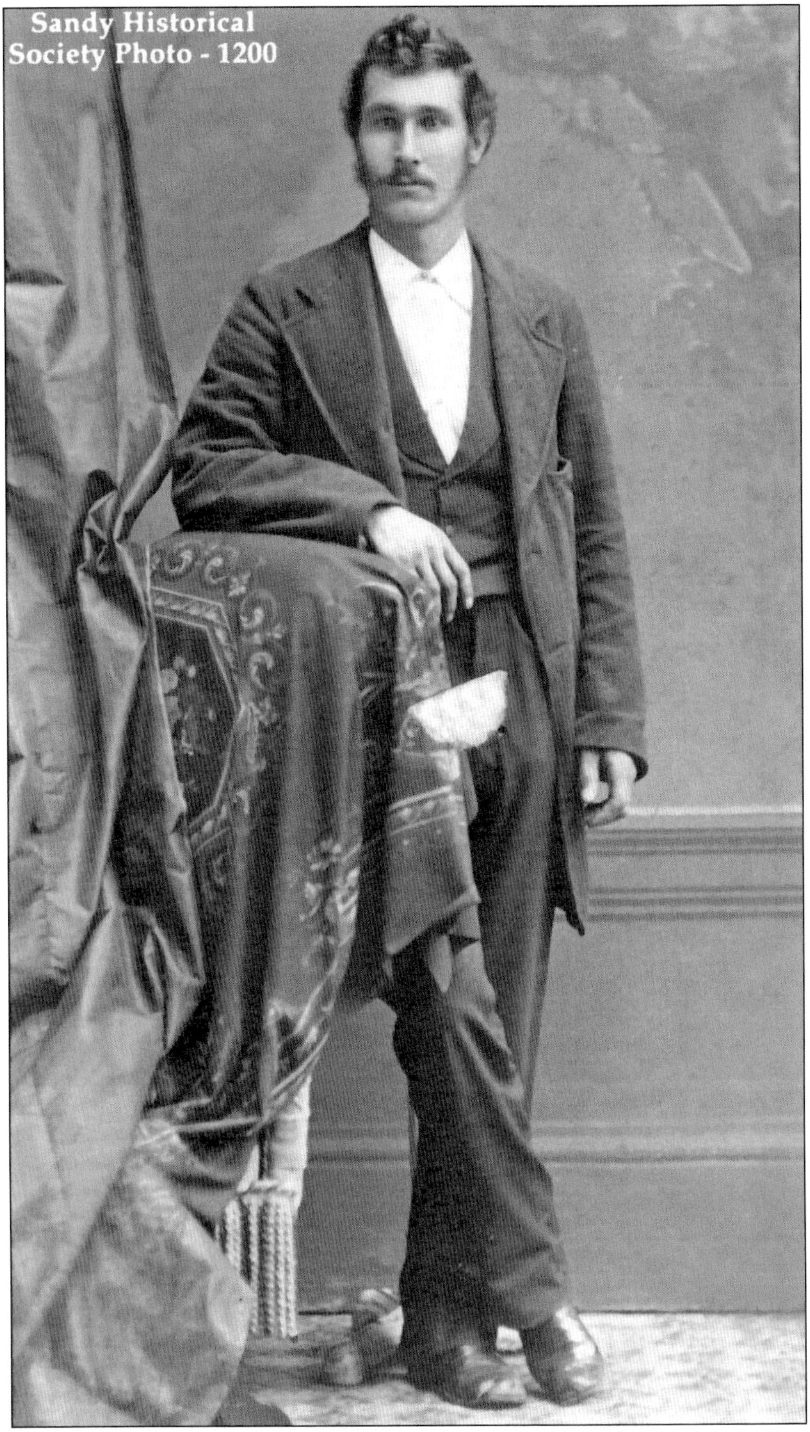

George Epperson's parents were the fifth homesteaders on Sandy Ridge. In the old Forrester mill there, George had installed the saw that was used as a dinner gong at the 1927 meeting of the Sandy Pioneer Association, later named the Sandy Historical Society. The author of this book lives on what was then called Epperson Road. (Courtesy of SHS and the Epperson family.)

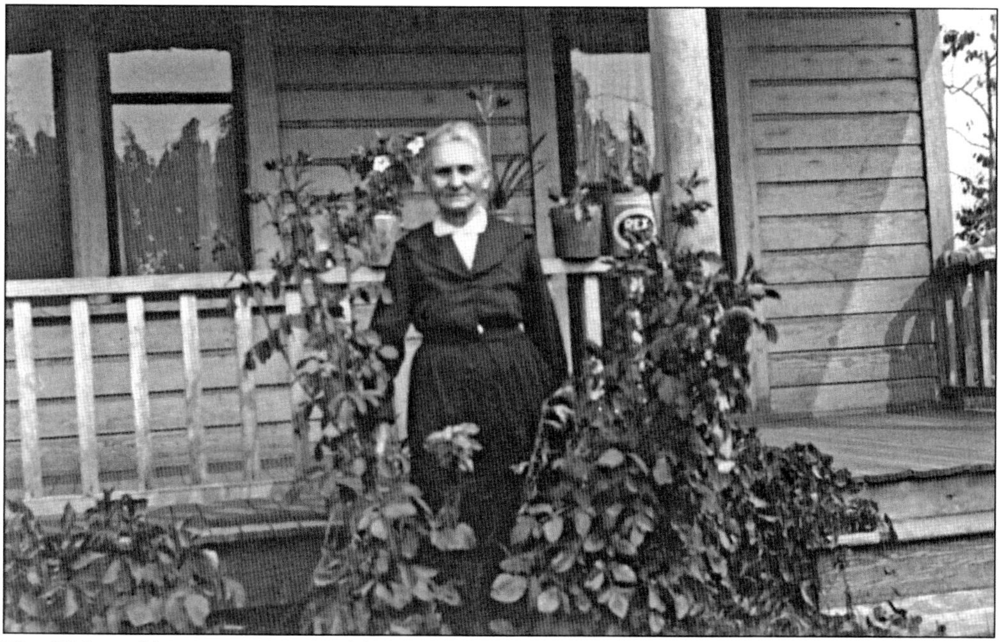

The 50th wedding anniversary celebration for Henry and Katherine Koch was held at the Caspar Junker home, which is now the home of Sandy Country Florist on Pioneer Boulevard. Katherine is shown here surrounded by the flowers that make her home's present use seem so appropriate. (Courtesy of SHS and the Koch family.)

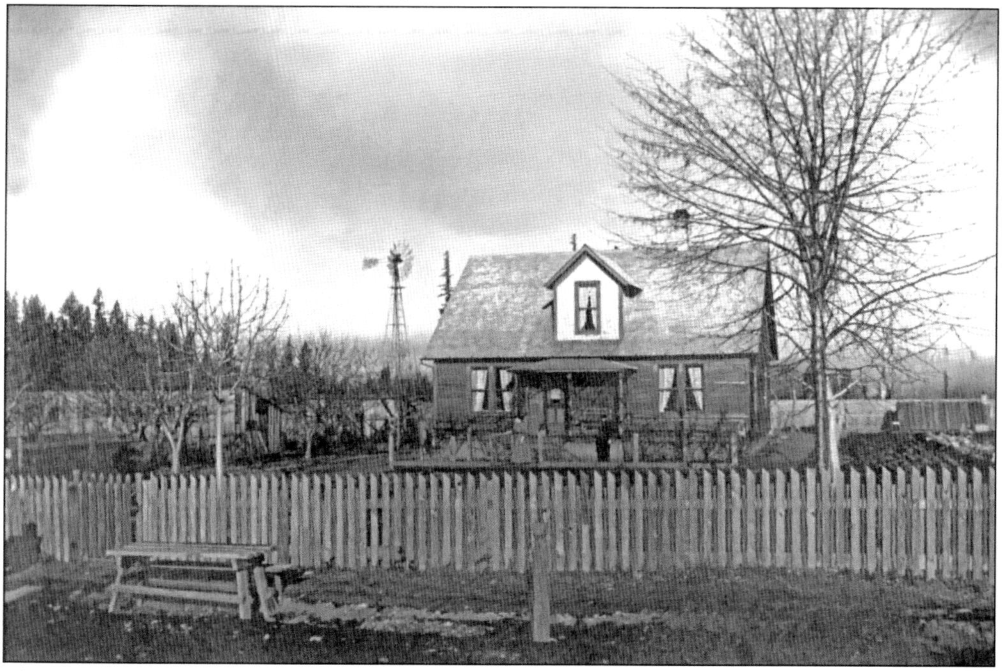

The farm windmill of the American West was invented in the United States in the late 19th century. In 1889, there were 77 windmill factories in the United States; by the turn of the century, windmills had become a major American export. Shown here is William Waespe's ranch on Coalman Road. (Courtesy of SHS and Grant DeShazer.)

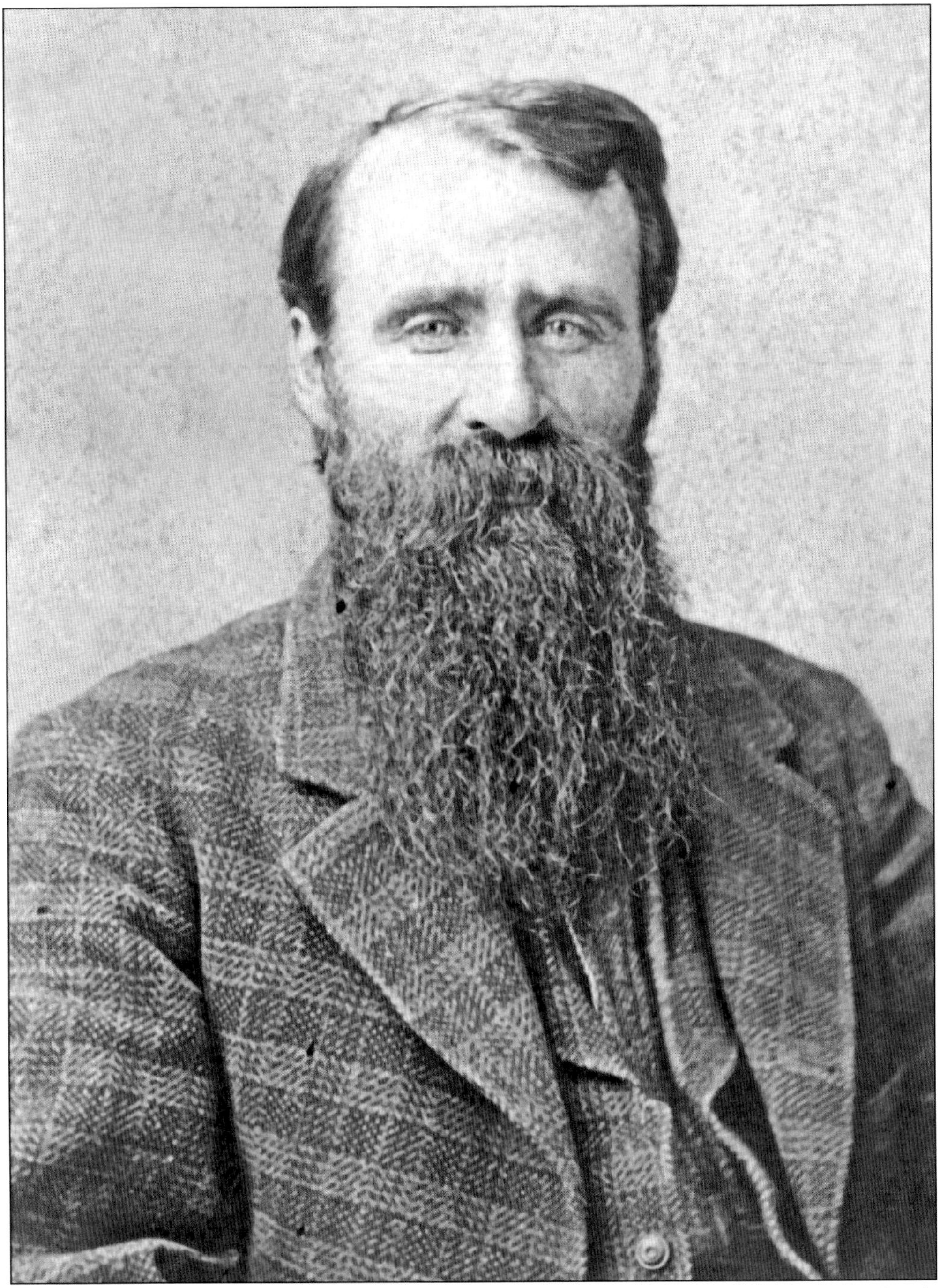

Troy Shelley wrote in his diary in 1869 while camping at Laurel Hill, "I thought of the hardy pioneers . . . and that mother, my dear mother who lies cold in the ground, had carried me down that long weary hill in her arms." Troy is shown here when he was Wasco County school superintendent. (Courtesy of SHS and W.H. Gilhousen.)

In 1915, long after Troy Shelley had retired from teaching and preaching, he and his wife, Annie, settled on the northern slopes of Mount Hood near Odell, Oregon. Their son Percy Troy Shelley was born in 1878 behind a barricade in Canyon City, Oregon, during the last Oregon Indian uprising.

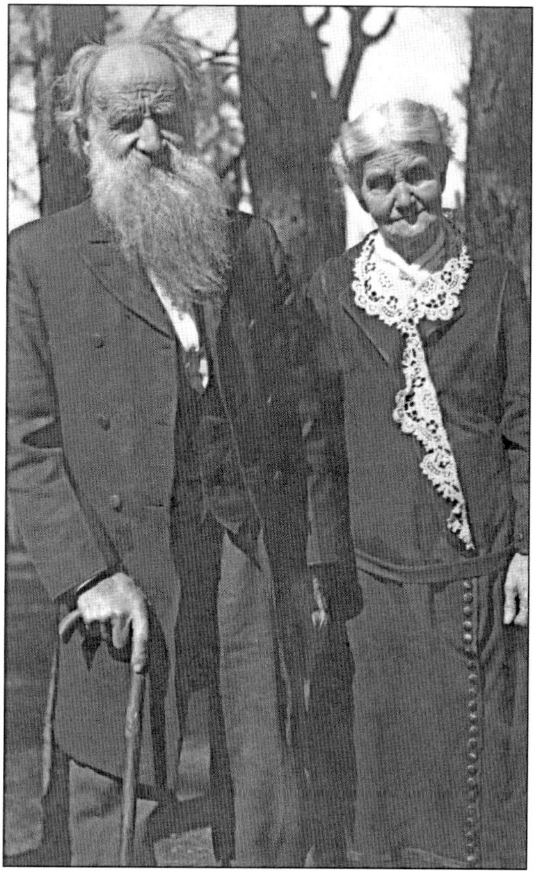

As an infant, Percy Shelley was taken to The Dalles, where he attended school. In 1906, he was assigned to the Sandy Ranger Station in the Mount Hood National Forest. Later, he operated a livery stable and had the mail contract for Boring and Sandy. He poses here with his dog Gyp.

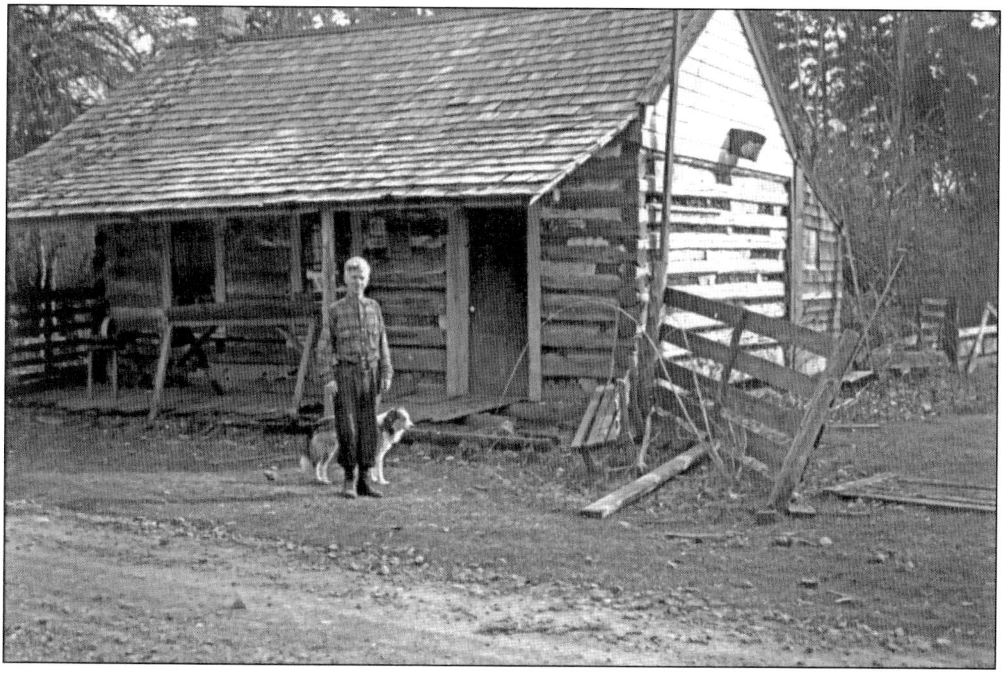

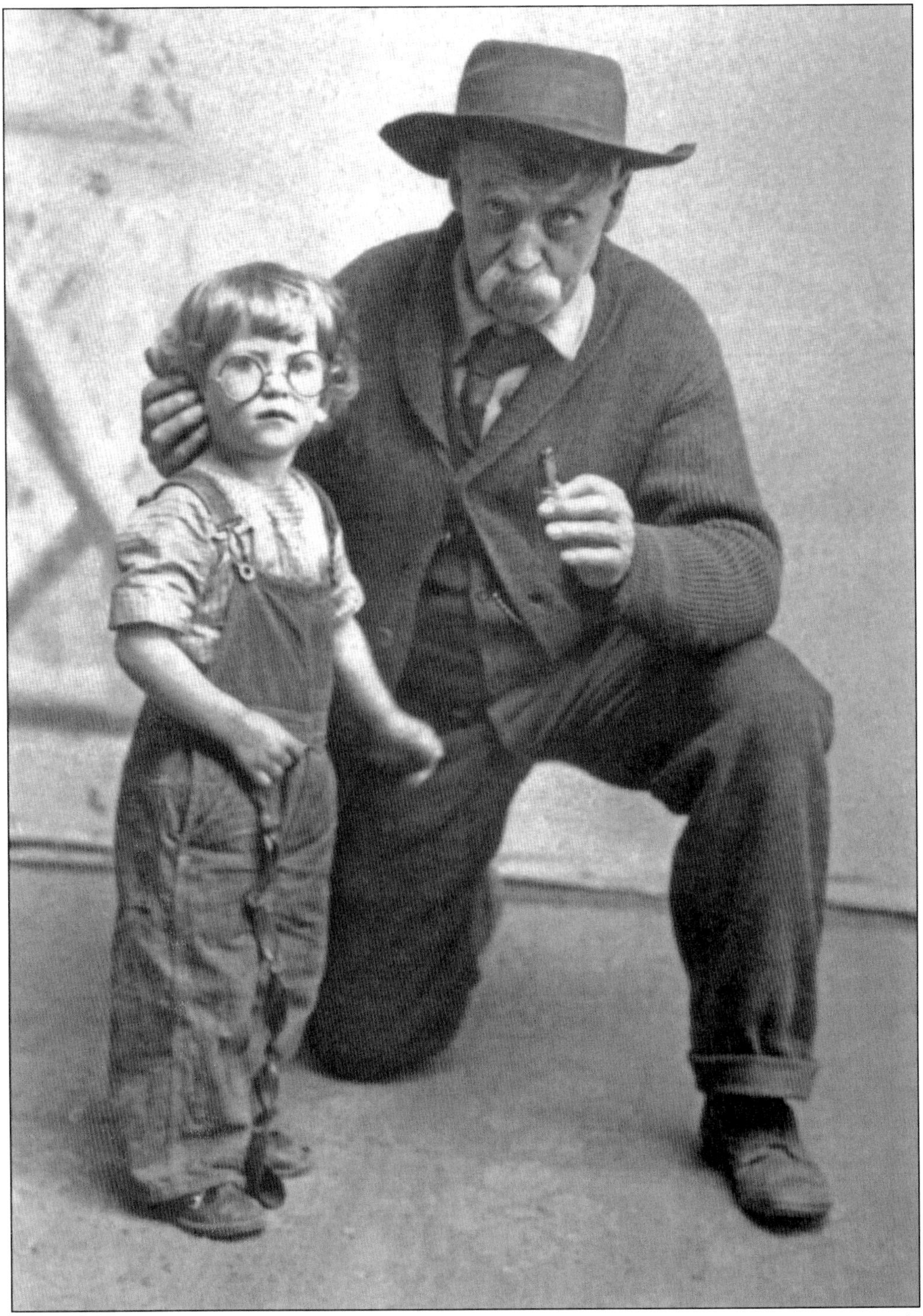

Troy Shelley's grandson Joseph is shown here in 1923 with his other grandfather, L.M. "Dad" Wilson. Joseph's mother, Blanche Rue Wilson Shelley, was to become Sandy's first female mayor and justice of the peace. Grown up and retired, Joseph Shelley provided much of the funding for the Sandy Historical Museum.

When John Bacon came across the plains with Samuel Barlow in 1845, he left behind an elder brother, Francis, who came to Oregon in 1871 and settled in the Bull Run area with his wife, Sarah Hanson Bacon. They offered a part of their donation land claim for the Bull Run School and another part for the Cliffside Cemetery, where many Sandy pioneers are buried. (Courtesy of Jean Bacon Rolli.)

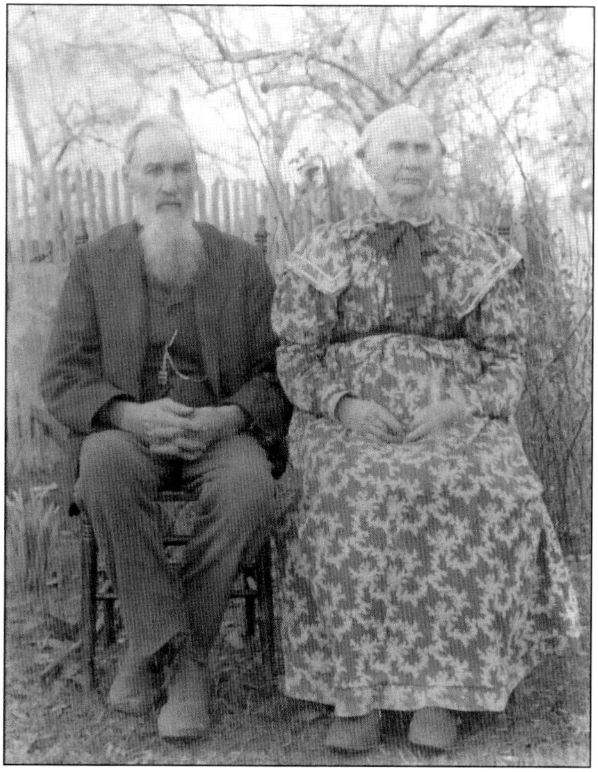

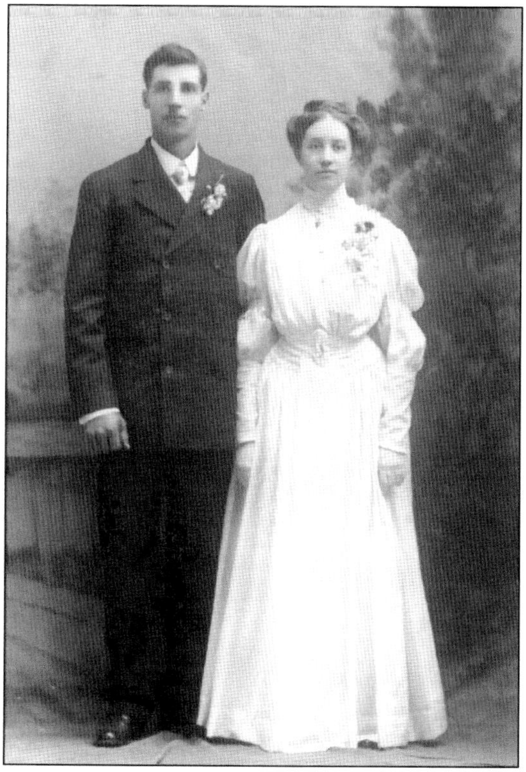

Francis and Sarah Bacon had a son, Samuel, who married Mary Wilson when she was 12 years old. The State of Oregon would not issue a marriage license for someone that young, so they had to cross the Columbia River to Washington. Shown here are Samuel and Mary's son Wesley and his bride, Jessie Gibbons Bacon. (Courtesy of Jean Bacon Rolli.)

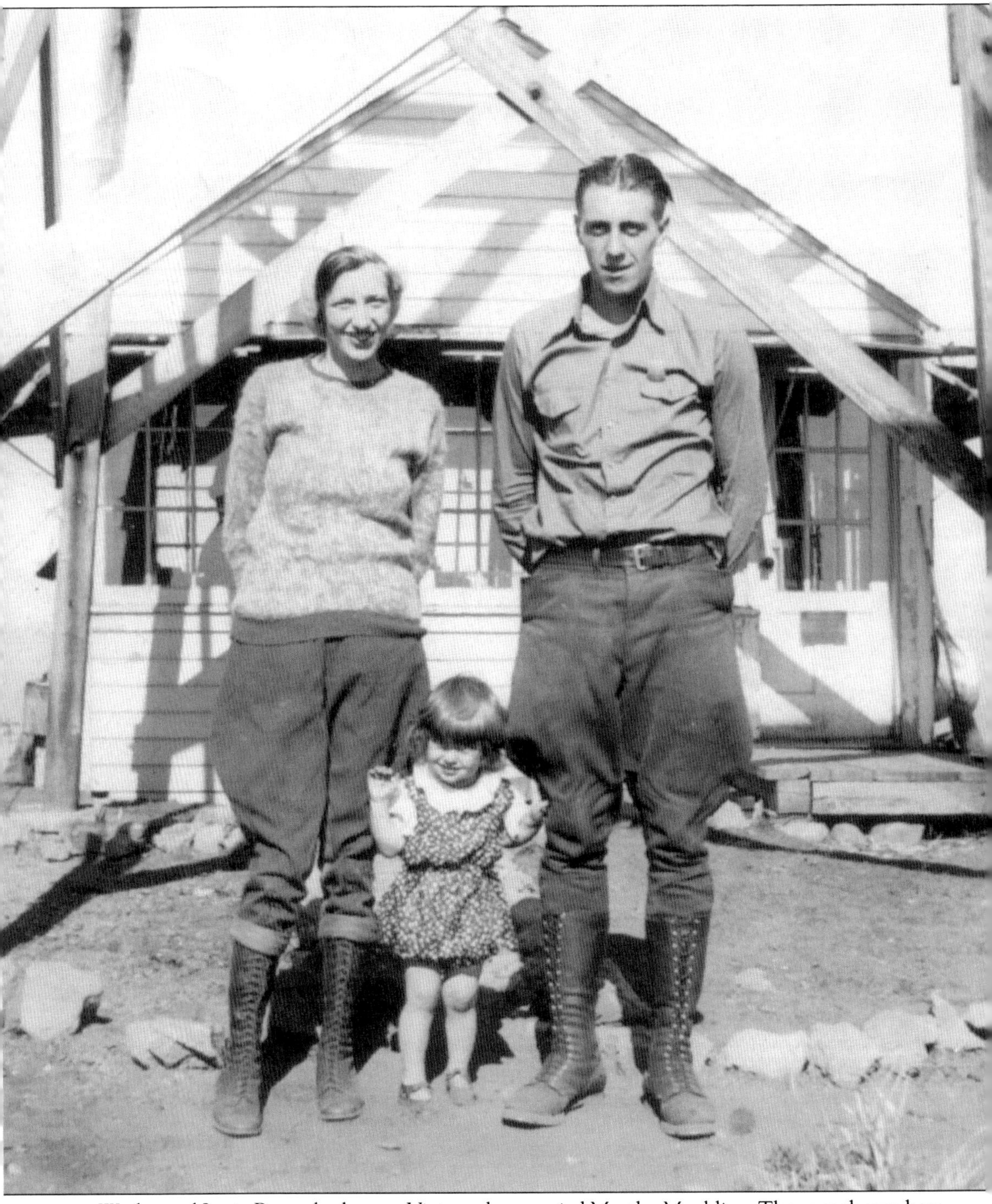

Wesley and Jessie Bacon had a son, Victor, who married Martha Maulding. They are shown here with their daughter Jean, who still lives in nearby Boring, Oregon, where she was the postmistress for many years. Victor worked for the US Forest Service, and they pose here at the base of the forest fire lookout tower on Hickman Butte. Victor left a generous donation for the Sandy Historical Museum. (Courtesy of Jean Bacon Rolli.)

Four

BUILDING A TOWN

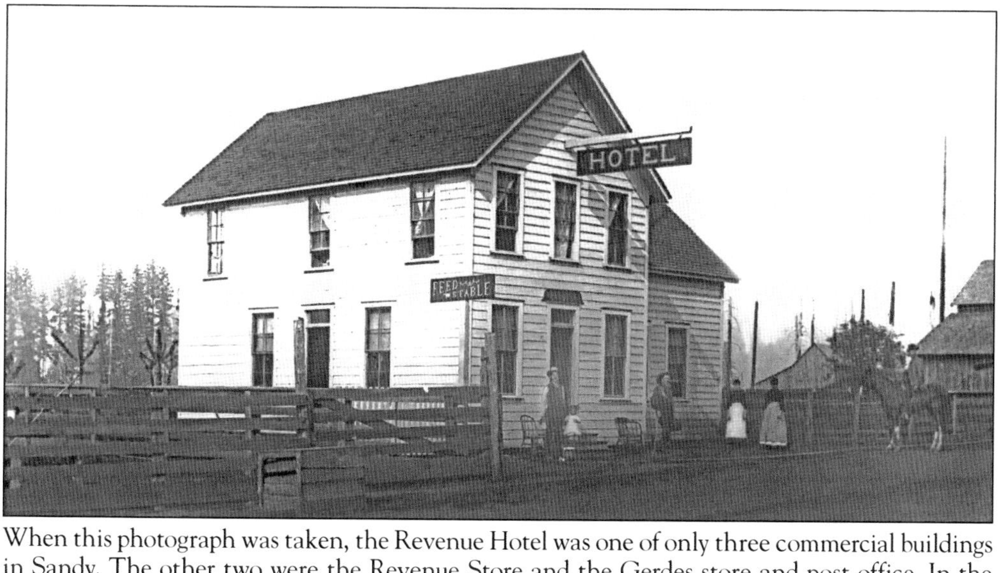

When this photograph was taken, the Revenue Hotel was one of only three commercial buildings in Sandy. The other two were the Revenue Store and the Gerdes store and post office. In the early 1900s, Percy and Blanche Shelley bought the hotel and moved it one block north to Proctor Boulevard and turned it into their home. Later, it was the notorious Dew Drop Inn, and it is now the Sandy Family Restaurant.

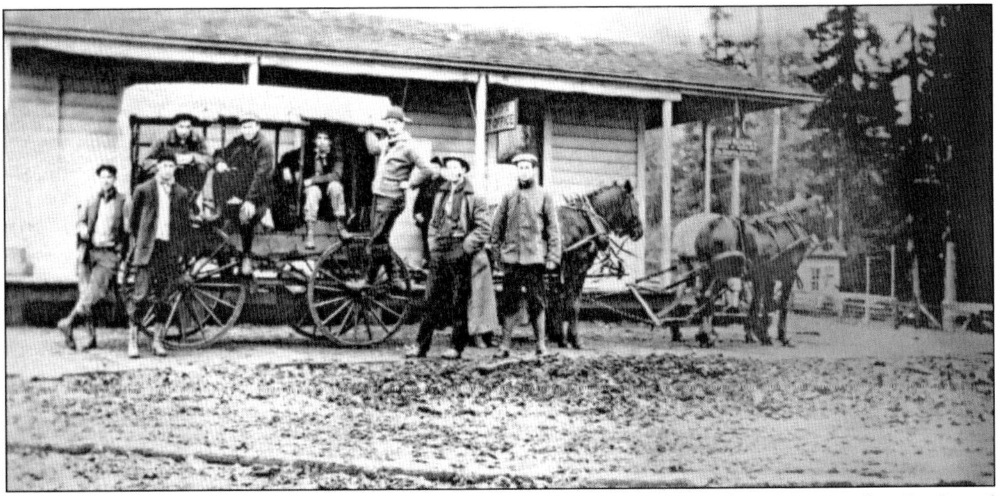

Richard Gerdes applied for a post office after he built his store. Until that time, settlers had paid a carrier to bring mail once a week from Oregon City by way of Eagle Creek. It took some time to get authorization for an official post office, because 200 citizens were required, and it was said that every time a baby was born, a man left town.

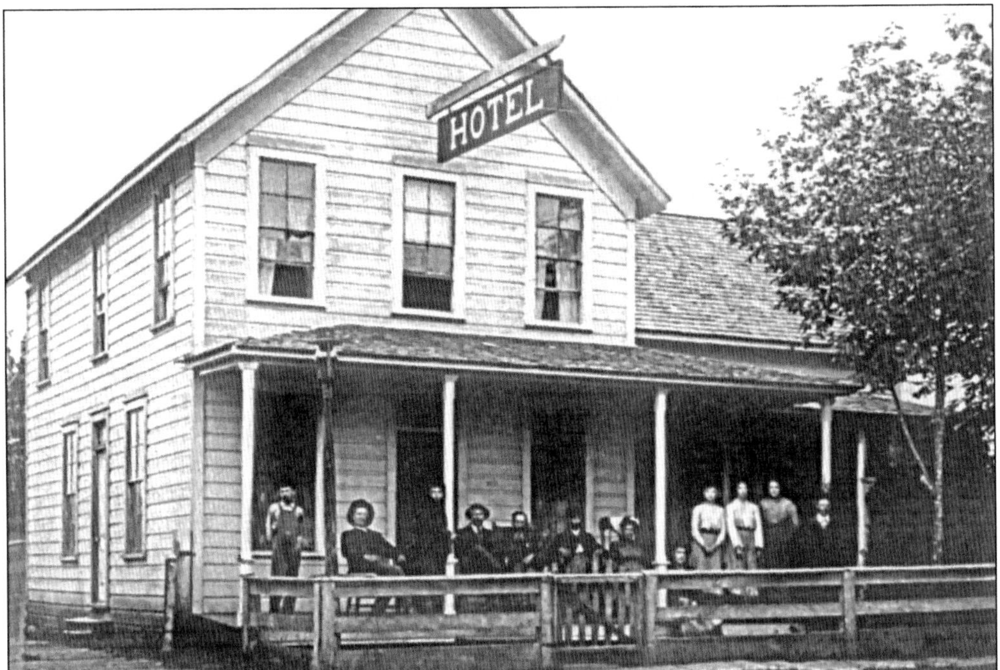

One of the sales of the Stulke property was to John Revenue. He poses here (second from left) in 1890 with friends and guests on the porch of the Revenue Hotel, built by him and his father in 1874. (Courtesy of SHS and Connie Revenue Selzler.)

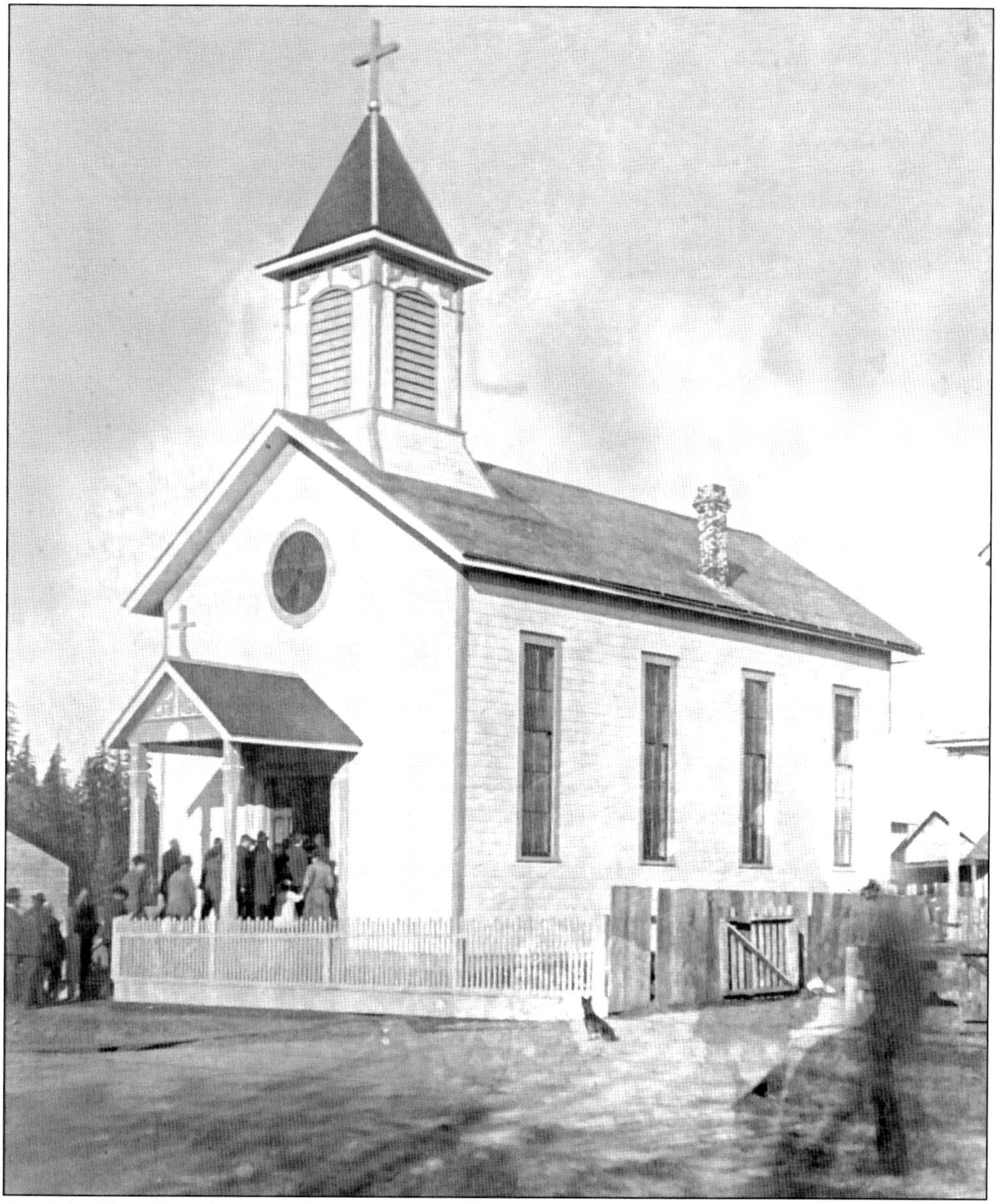

Sandy's oldest church, St. Michael's, opened its doors on December 18, 1894, with Father Anselm, Order of St. Benedict, as minister. Among the 40 founding families were Mr. and Mrs. Luis Vaeretti and Thomas Phelan. Located at the northwest corner of Shelley Avenue and Main Street (now Pioneer Boulevard), the church was destroyed by fire on October 28, 1917.

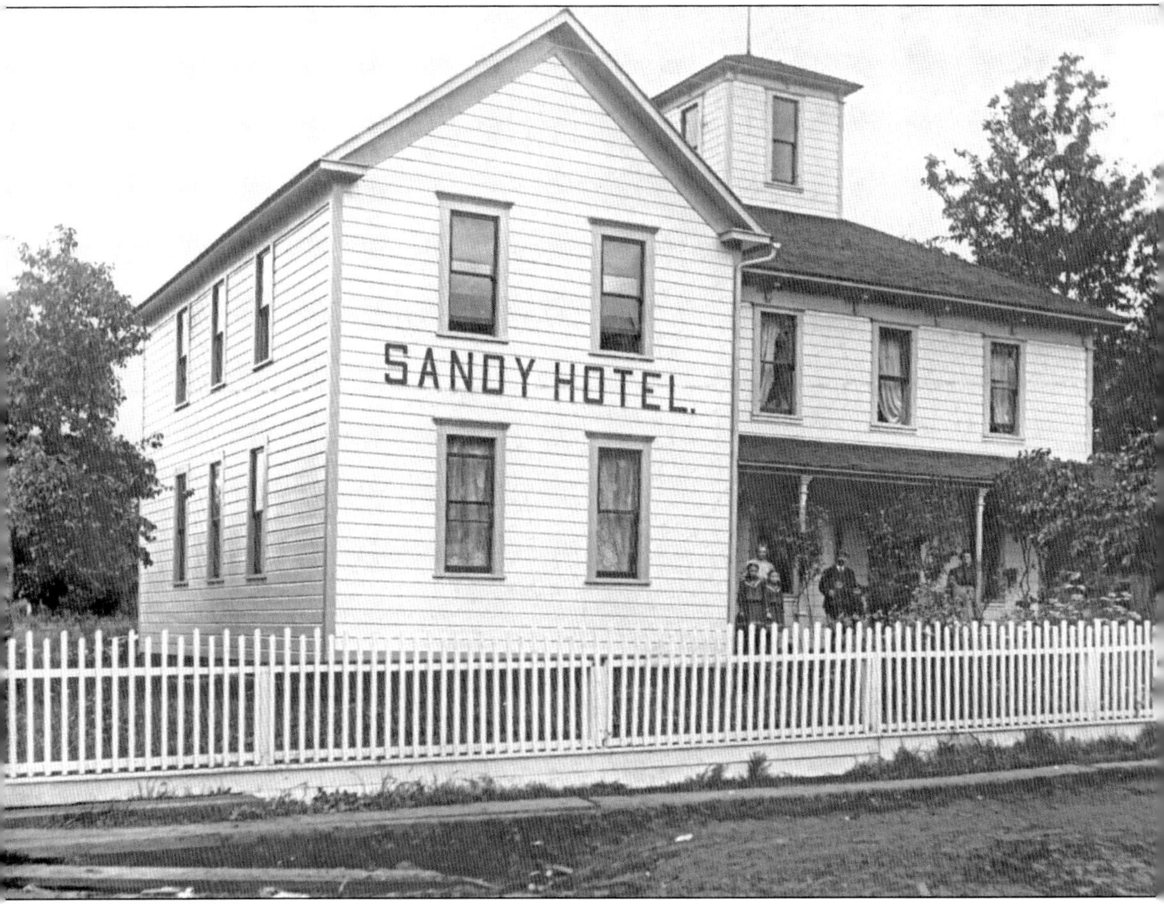

Built by Baron Otto von Scholley in 1890, this was Sandy's second hotel. The baron died of a stroke while the hotel's tower was being raised. In 1897, Caspar Junker purchased the hotel. It proved so successful that he added the wing on the left. Junker and his family are standing on the porch. (Courtesy of SHS and Florence Schmitz.)

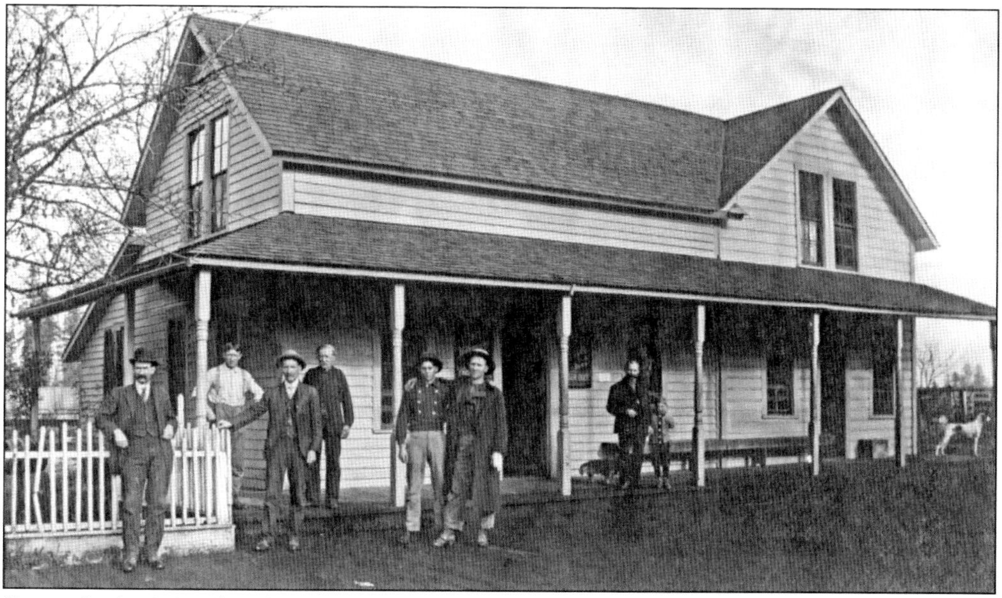

Caspar Junker's Sandy Saloon, across the street from the Sandy Hotel, is shown here in 1904. By all accounts, it was just as successful as the hotel. Caspar had moved to Portland and spent seven years learning the hotel trade before returning to Sandy. He and his son Henry are on the right. (Courtesy of SHS and Dean and Lucille Schmitz Schneider.)

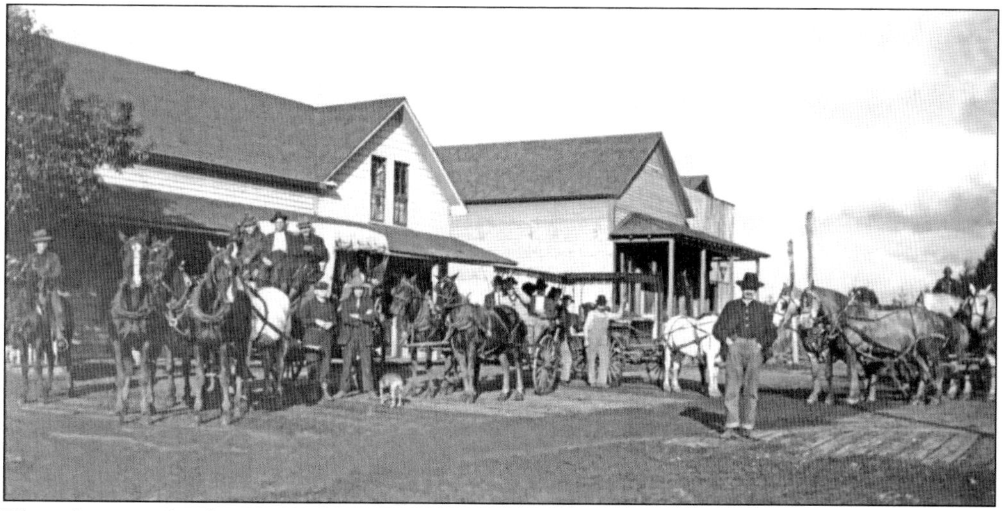

This photograph of Caspar Junker's Sandy Saloon is labeled "A Busy Day in Sandy, Oregon," possibly giving a clue as to why his hotel and saloon were so successful. Junker was an active member of Immanuel Lutheran Church and a leader in civic affairs. He occupied the office of mayor of Sandy for two terms.

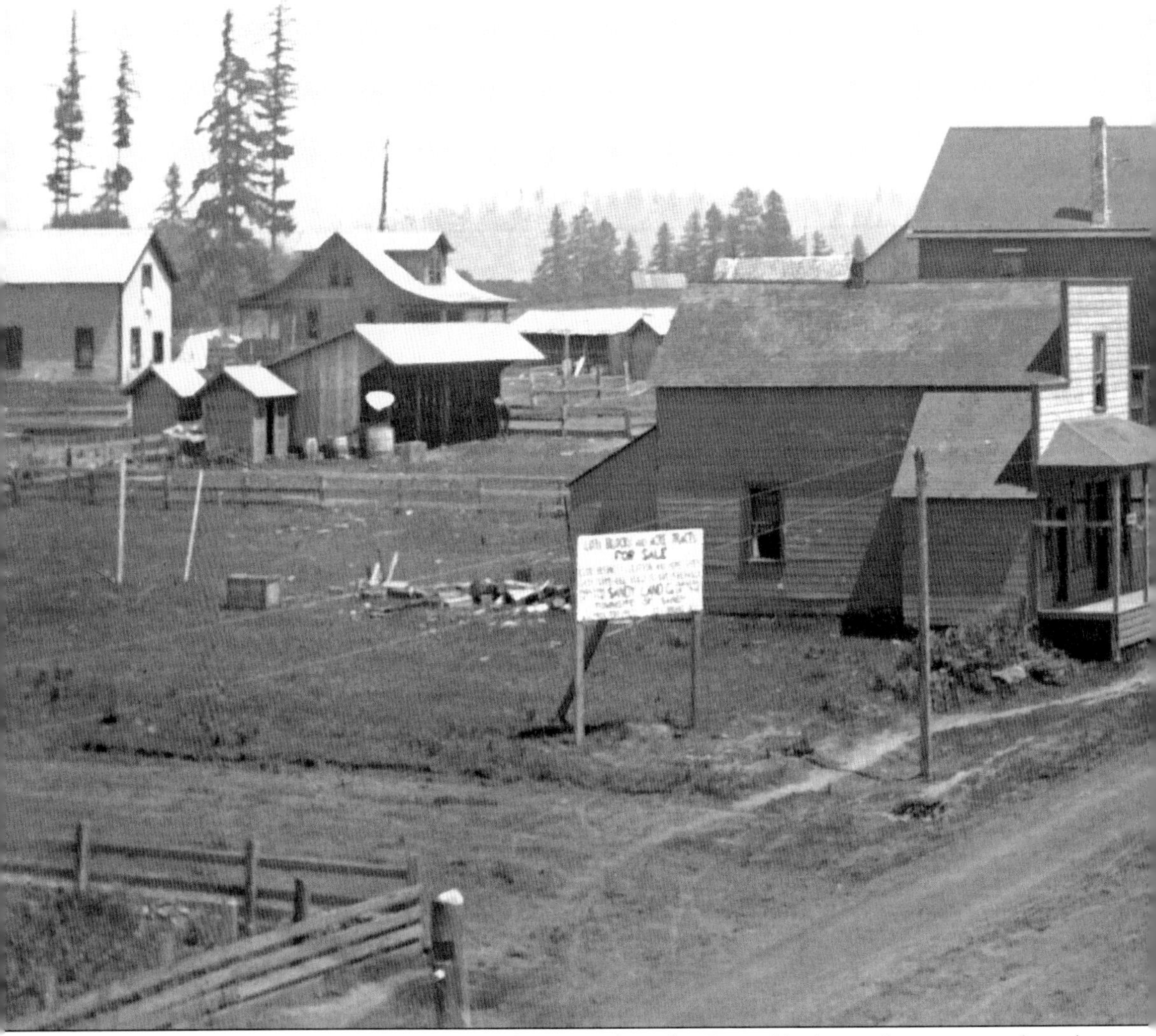

The poorly hand-lettered sign in the foreground reads, "Lots, blocks, and acre tracts for sale. Good business location and home sites. Easy Terms. Will build to suit purchaser. Inquire of the Sandy Land Co., owners of the townsite of Sandy. W. Proctor, Pres. Ed F. Bruns Sec." The Sandy

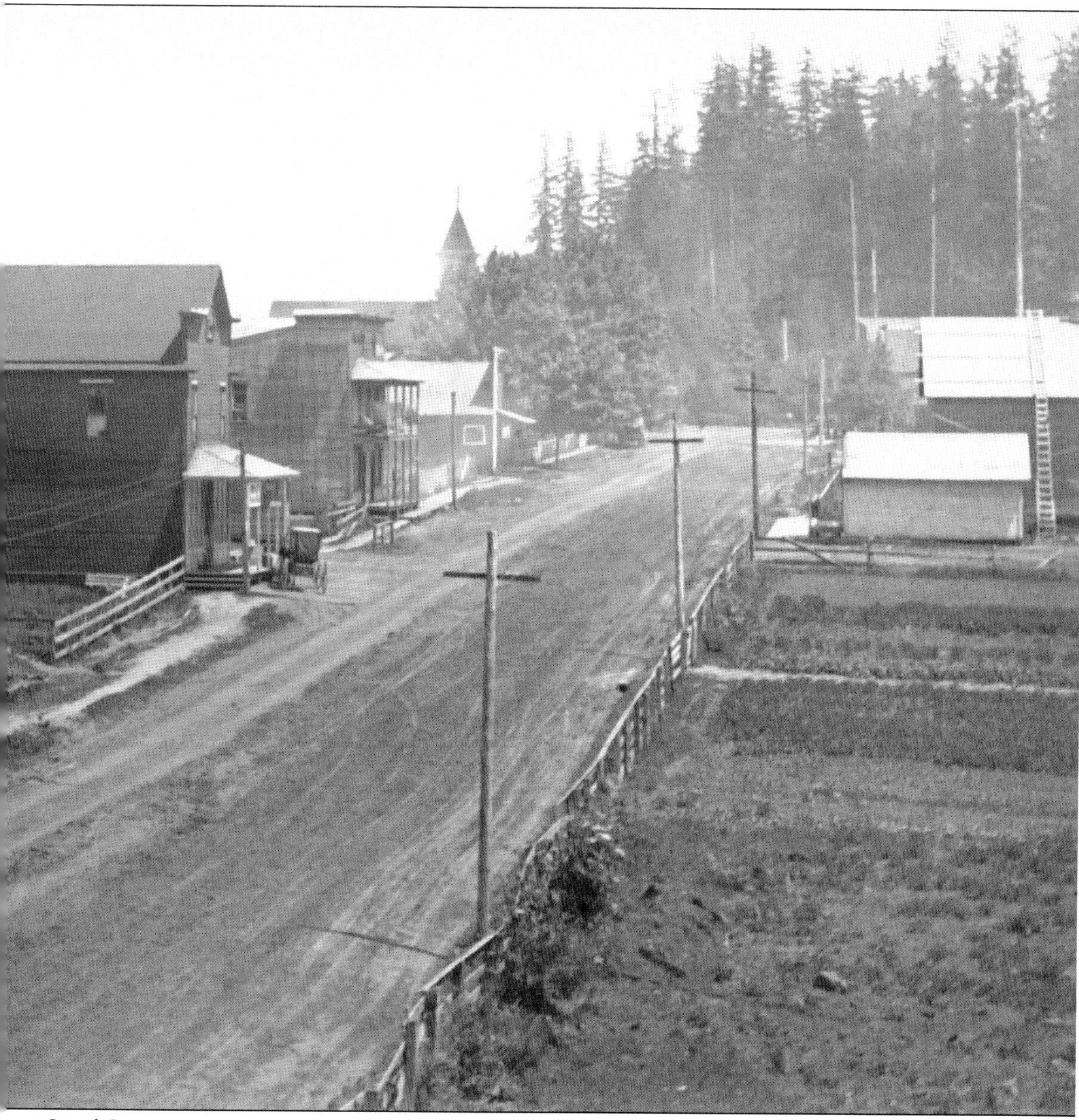

Land Company was incorporated in 1907 by Walker Proctor, Edward Bruns, Franklin Beers, and John Strauss.

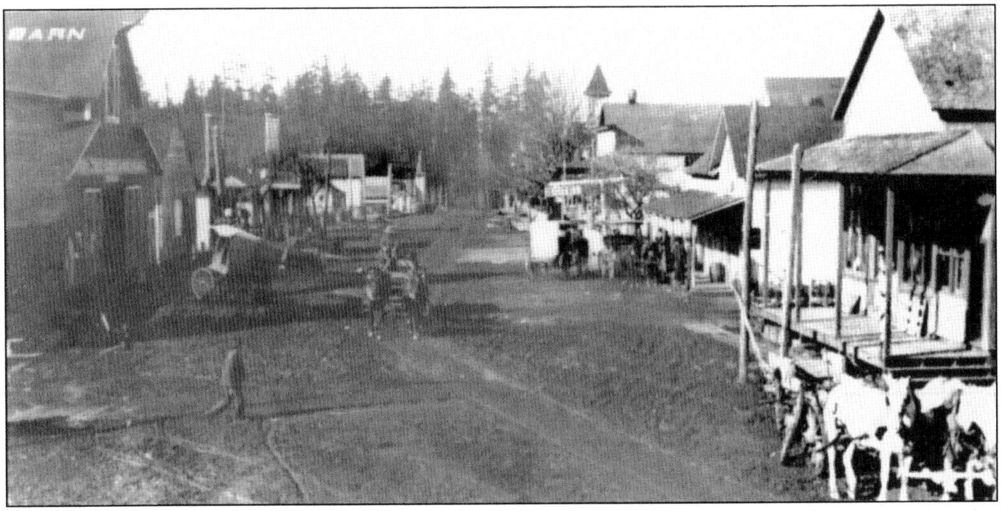

The view in this 1910 photograph looks west on Main Street (now Pioneer Boulevard). The spires of St. Michael's Catholic Church are on the right, and Immanuel Lutheran Church is in the distance on the left. On the immediate near side of St. Michael's is the Revenue Hotel, and next to it is the Sandy Hotel.

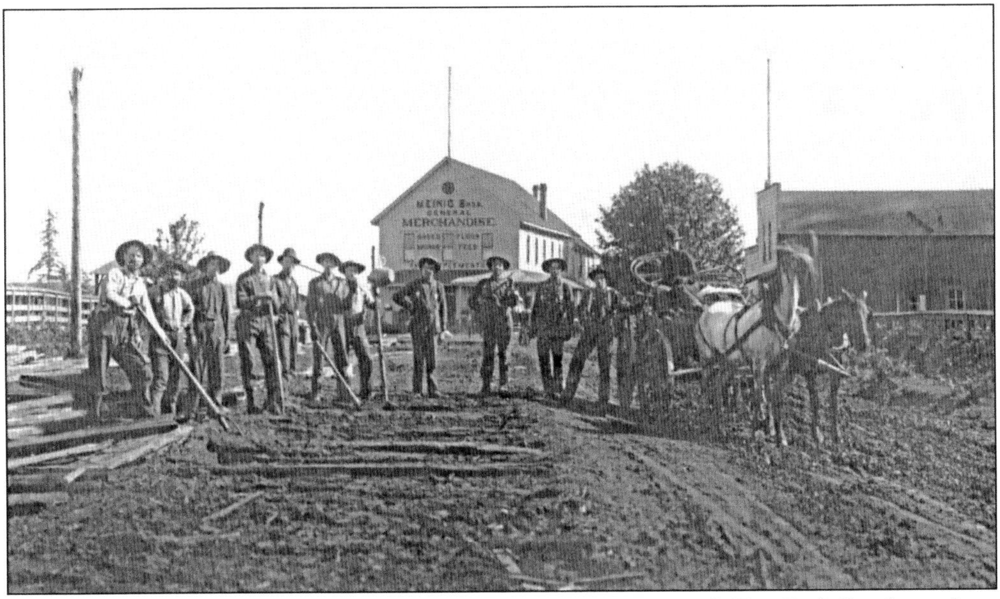

Repairing a section of Sandy's Main Street near its intersection with Ten Eyck Road are, from left to right, Albon Meinig, Fritz Kiesecker, Gustav Stucki, Fred Koennecke, Will Bosholm, three unidentified men, Milton Nelson, Albert Ridderbusch, and unidentified. The man in the wagon is not identified. Plank roads helped keep wagons from being stuck in the mud, but they wore out quickly.

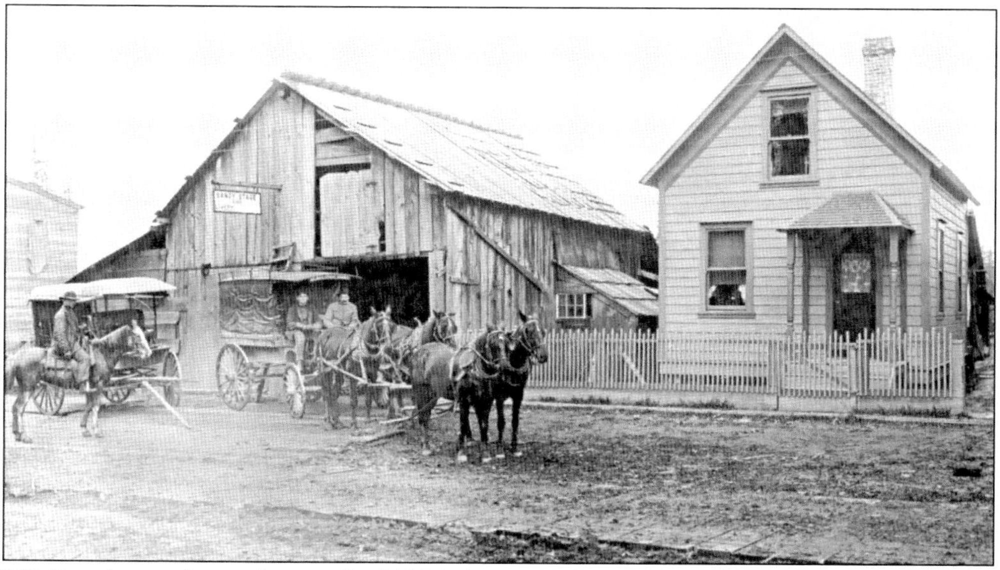

E.F. Donahue is shown driving the US Mail stage in front of his livery stable, one of the first in the area. The mail stage also transported freight and passengers. Even this primitive postal service was far superior to Sandy's first mail line: a pair of diminutive mules attached to a mountain buckboard.

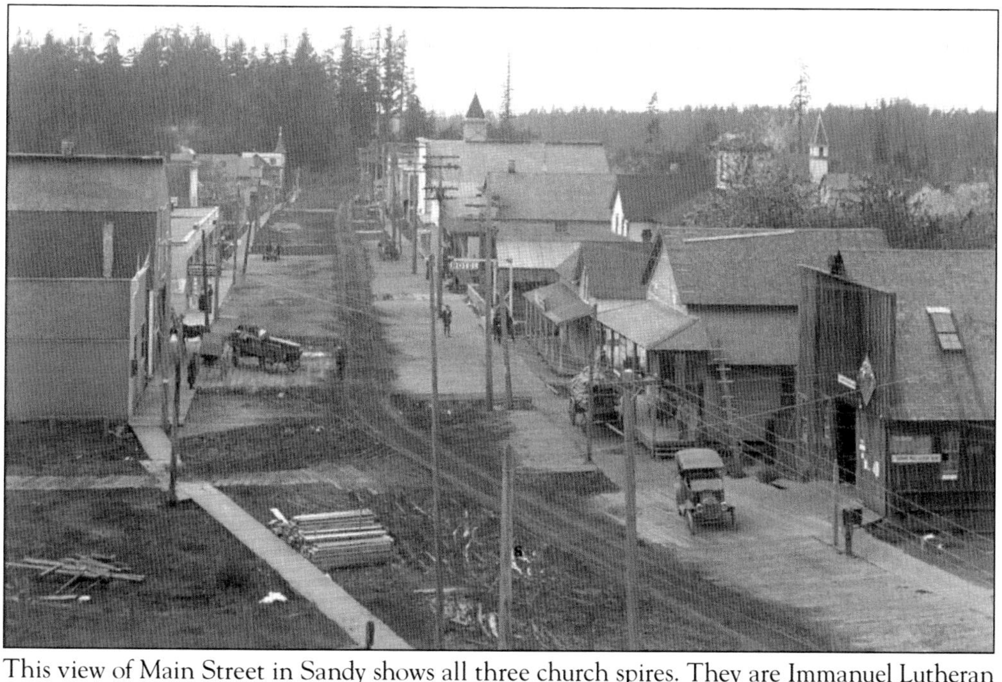

This view of Main Street in Sandy shows all three church spires. They are Immanuel Lutheran Church (in the distance at left), St. Michael's Catholic Church (center), and the Community Methodist Church (midblock at right). St. Michael's burned to the ground in 1917. The Methodist church has been torn down and replaced by commercial buildings. The Lutheran church building still stands, but it is used as a yoga center.

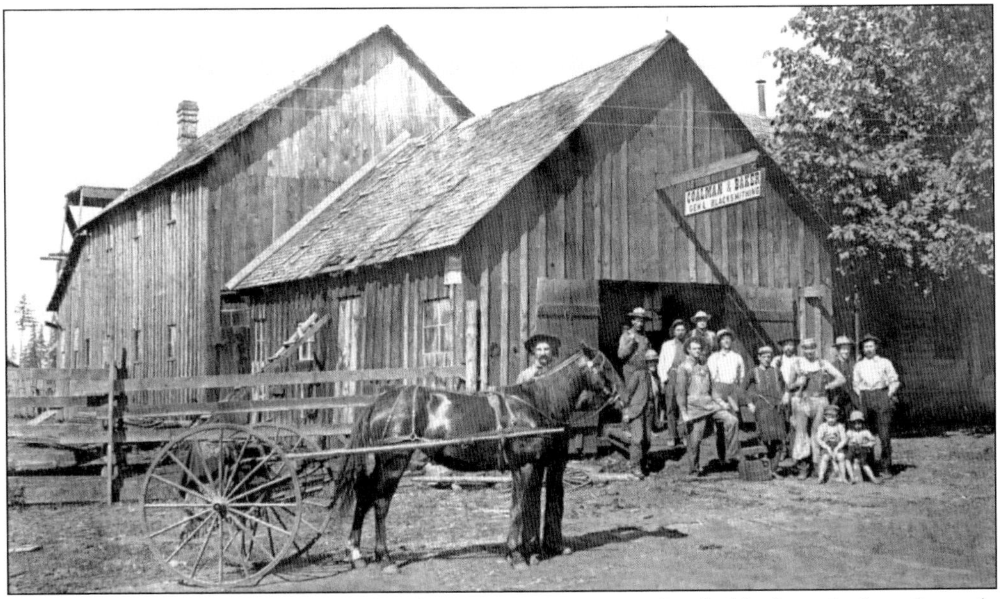

In 1902, Elijah Coalman and Lloyd Baker were partners in a Sandy blacksmith shop formerly owned by Robert Jonsrud. Standing in the front row in the group at right are, from left to right, Alfred Williams (later a Sandy doctor), Herman Bruns, Lee McCabe, Oswald Rambow, Lloyd Baker, John Maronay, Lige Coalman, Sam Miles, and George Maronay. All others are unidentified. (Courtesy of SHS and the Coalman family.)

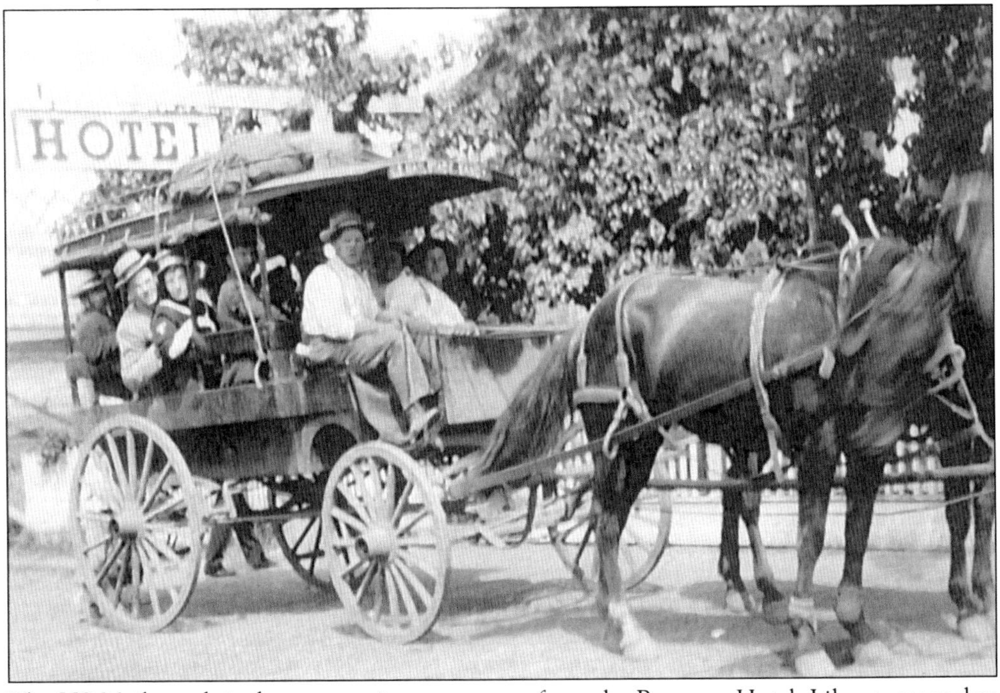

The US Mail coach is shown carrying passengers from the Revenue Hotel. Like stagecoaches in the Old West, mail coaches seldom were restricted just to mail deliveries, but were frequently relied upon for regular transportation from Portland, Oregon City, Eagle Creek, and even farther up the mountain.

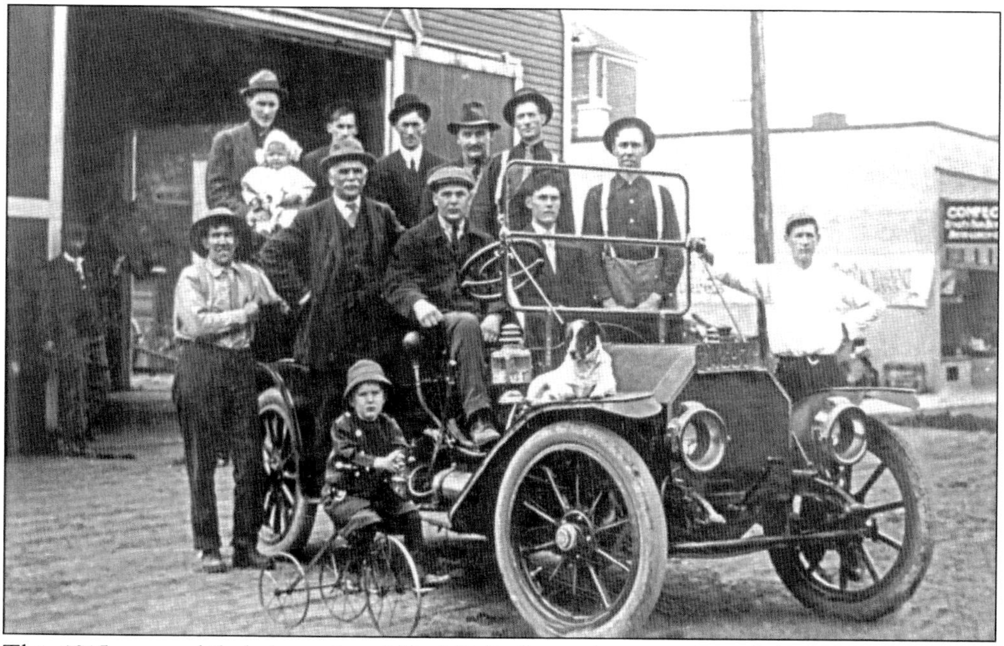

This 1915 automobile belonged to Alfred Bell. Posing here are, from left to right, (first row) Andrew Jackson (standing on ground), James Bell (standing on running board), owner Alfred (behind steering wheel), Bart Cline, John Bickford (standing on running board), and Frank Schmitz; (second row) unidentified, holding baby (also unidentified), Alex Schmitz, Jesse Hite, Clement Bartsch, and Dell Jadwin. Ellsworth Bell is on the tricycle. Ringer is lying on the fender. (Courtesy of SHS and the Bell family.)

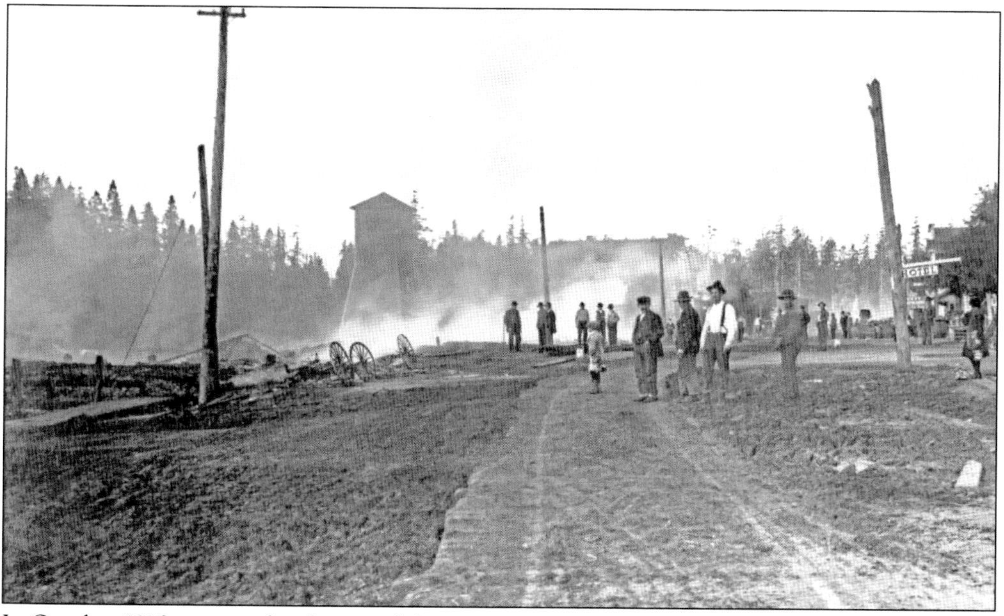

In October 1913, a major fire destroyed Goger's Restaurant, the Star Saloon, and George O'Dell's Sandy Livery Stable and Sandy Saloon, all on the south side of Main Street. Caspar Junker, who owned the restaurant and the saloon, went to work right away and put up the Junker Building, Sandy's first concrete structure. It is still in use today.

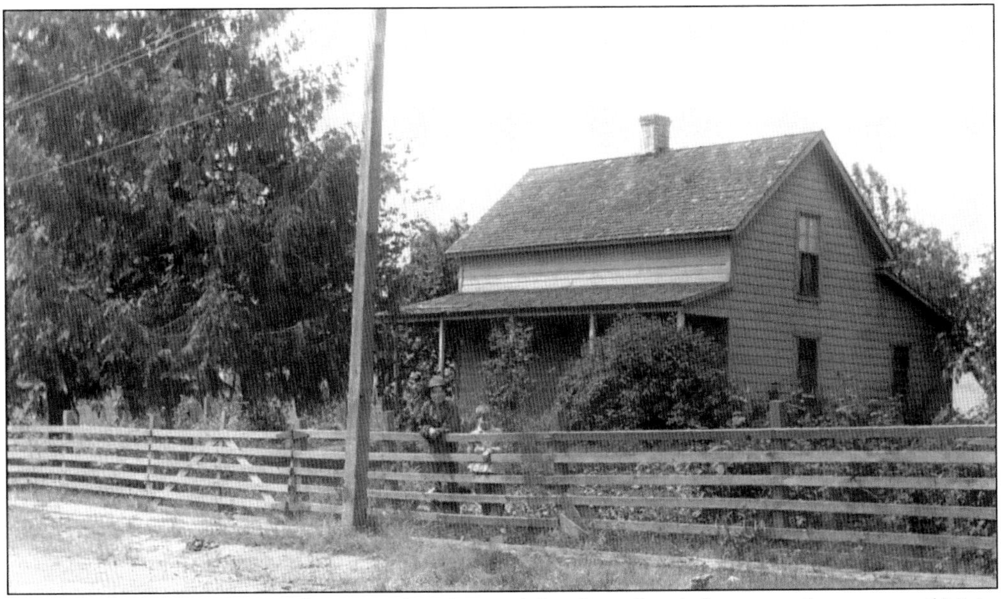

Patrick Gray and his son Milton stand in front of the Gray family home at the corner of Main and Center Streets (now Pioneer Boulevard and Scales Avenue). Patrick owned and operated a feed store and was Sandy's city recorder during and after its incorporation process. (Courtesy of SHS and Dennis Gray.)

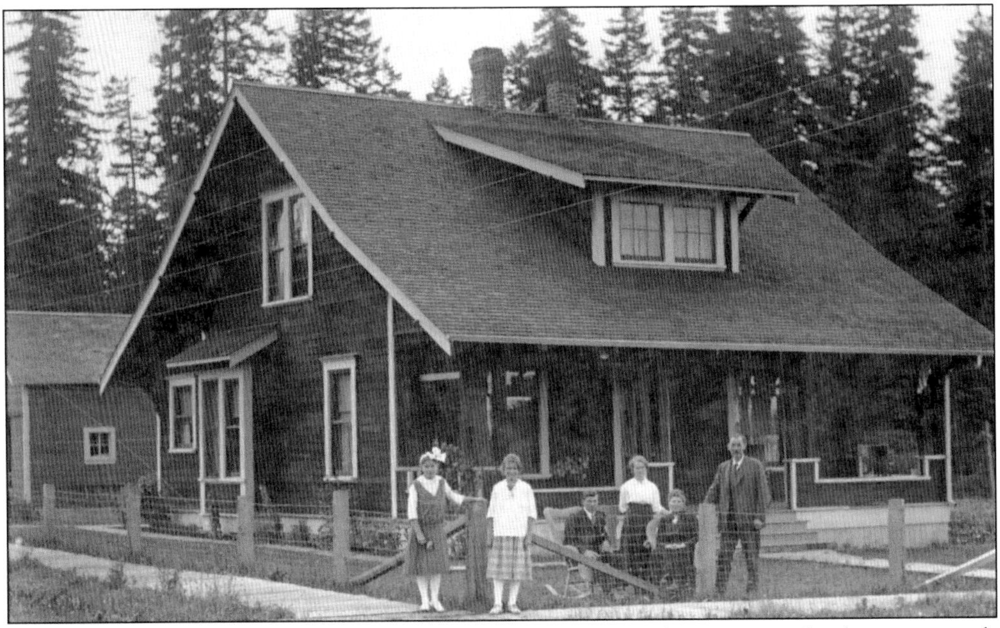

Martin Lennartz, foreman at the Sandy Fir Lumber Company and a prominent lumberman, stands with his family in the yard of their new home, located at the southwest corner of the intersection of Proctor Boulevard and Scales Avenue. It was moved across Proctor Boulevard and occupied by the Michael Lamb family in the 1940s, then was demolished when the US Bank was built. (Courtesy of SHS and the Lennartz family.)

Five

A Civilization—of Sorts

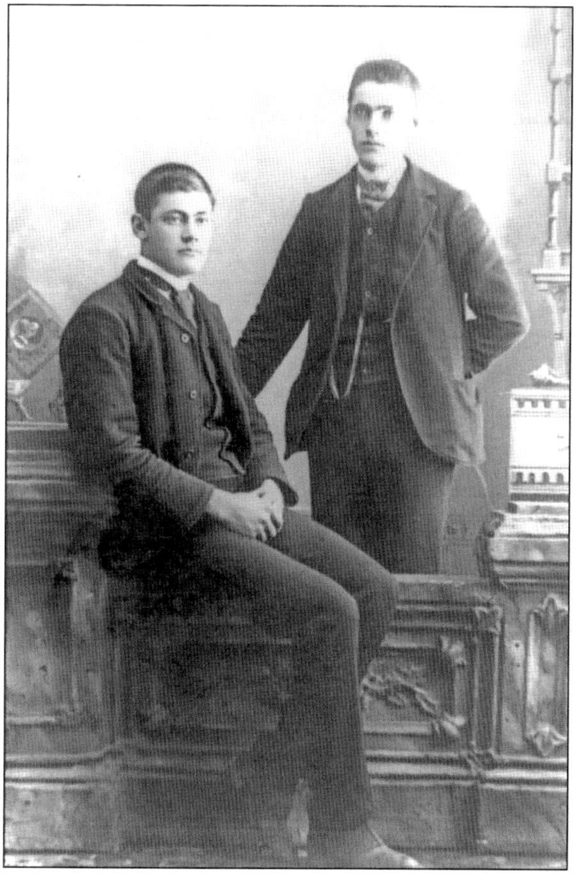

Berthol Jonsrud (left) and his brother Robert came with their parents to Kelso in 1877. Robert had a blacksmith shop in Sandy, but spent most of his time sawmilling. Berthol served as constable for eastern Clackamas County, extending from Damascus to Government Camp. Even so, during his free time, he worked his four-horse logging team, yarding logs for various mills.

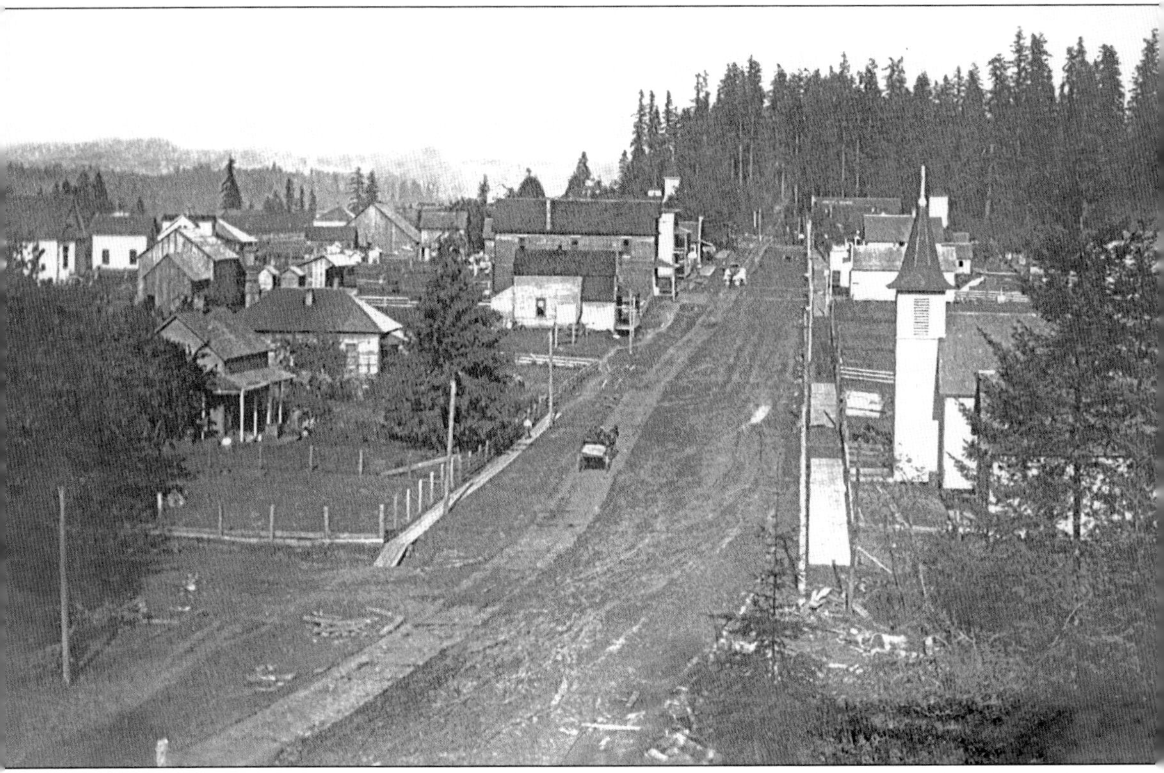

The Lutheran church, in the foreground on the right, was constructed in 1902 on land donated by Caspar Junker and was the second church built in Sandy. The first church, St. Michael's Catholic Church, was built in 1894. In 1959, the Lutheran congregation built a new church and this one became the Good Shepherd Episcopal Church. The structure is now a retail business and yoga center. (Courtesy of SHS and Dennis Gray.)

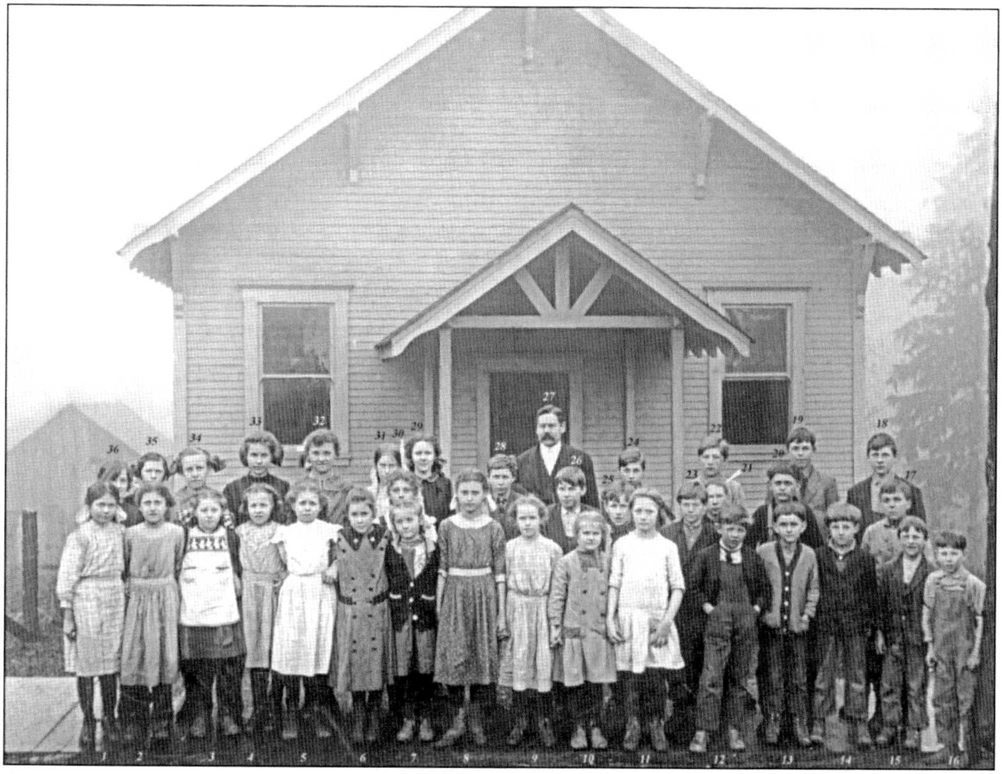

On one side of the Immanuel Lutheran Church building was the parsonage. On the other was the Lutheran Parochial School, shown here with its student body in 1915. Reverend Dobberfuhl, standing in the back, was the second pastor of the church, supervising the school since its opening on January 4, 1904.

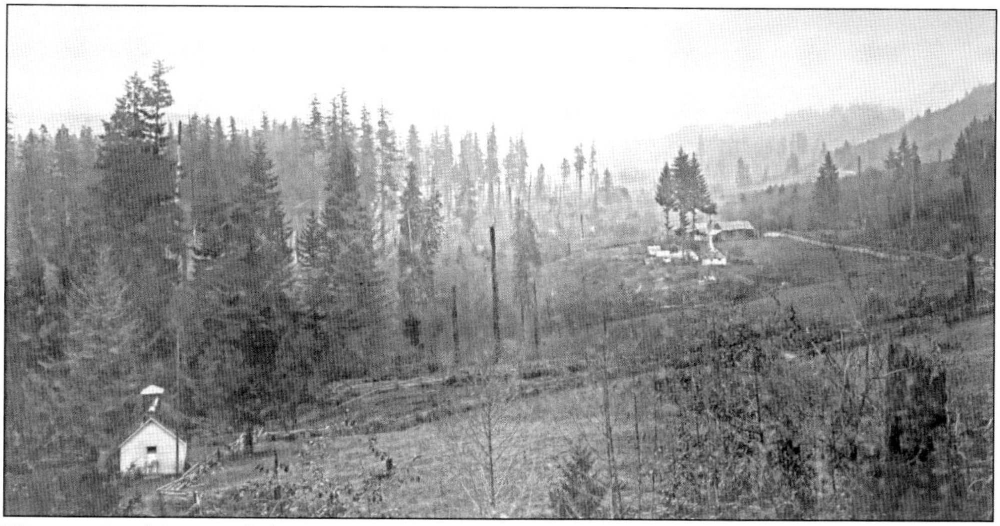

This was Sandy's second elementary school building, constructed about 1890 at the foot of Meinig Hill near Cedar Creek. Sandy's first log schoolhouse was a mile north of this one, on Francis Revenue's land, convenient for Sandy's earliest settlers on the north. As the town of Sandy grew, a larger building, closer to town, was needed.

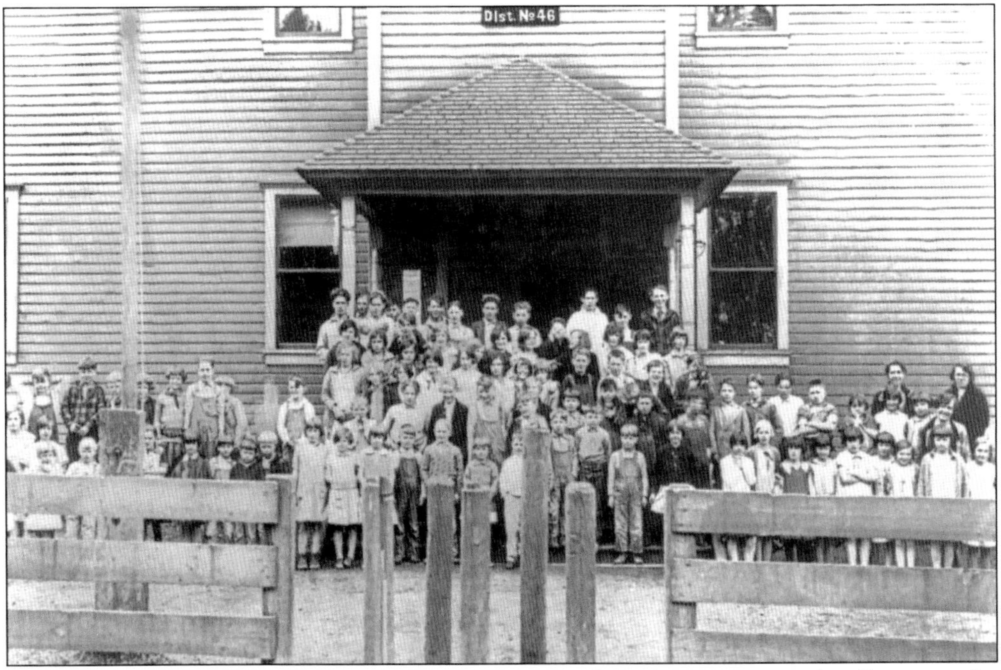

As the town of Sandy grew, it became necessary to replace the two-room schoolhouse at the bottom of the hill with one closer to the center of population. Built in 1908, this structure became a two-teacher school in 1909. In 1914, a second story was added, and one room was used as the high school.

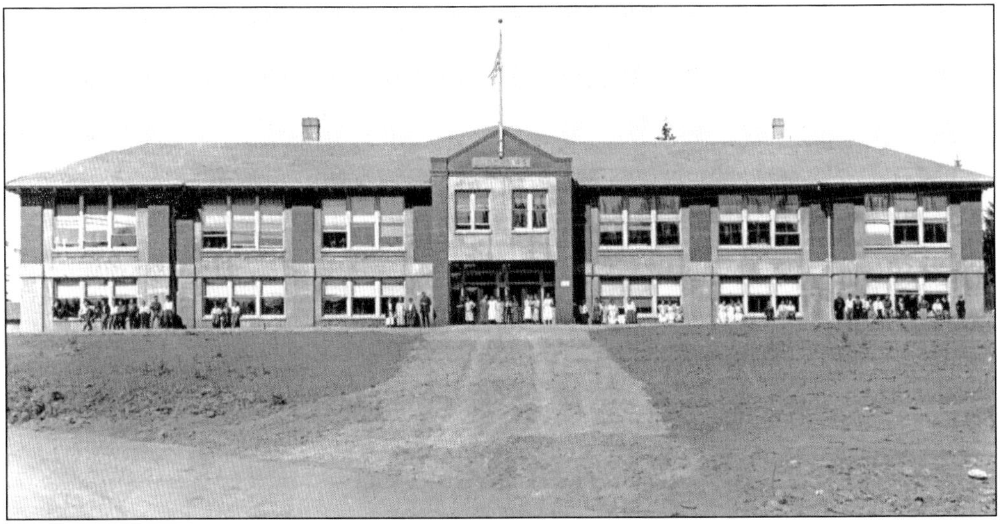

The first Sandy Union High School building, called the "Pioneer Building," was completed in 1923. It cost $30,000, including desks and furniture. There was an office, 12 classrooms, an assembly hall with a stage, and a "crackerbox" gym, all of which sufficed until 1936, when another building was added on land donated by Ed and Augusta Bruns. (Courtesy of SHS and Ruth Baumback.)

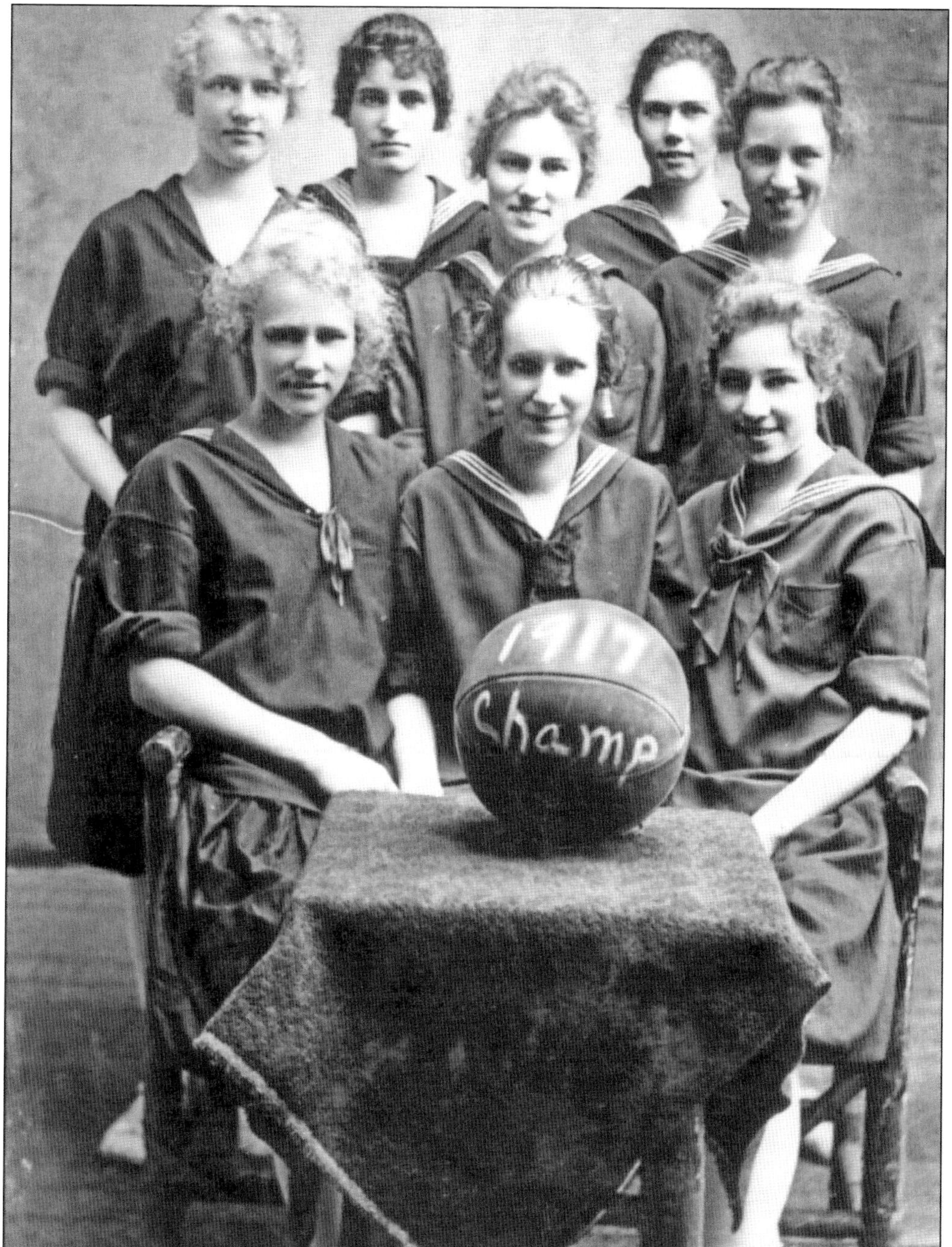

The Sandy High School championship girls' basketball team of 1917 includes, from left to right, (seated) Frances Meinig (Loundree), Bea Beers (Harris), and Mary Junker (Clinefelter); (standing) Gertrude Meinig (Alt), Ruth Revenue (Reed), Kate Junker (Schmitz), Sabra Deaton (Klingler), and Mary Klingler. Gertrude Meinig and Sabra Deaton made up two-thirds of the graduating class that year. Dorothy Couper was the third graduate.

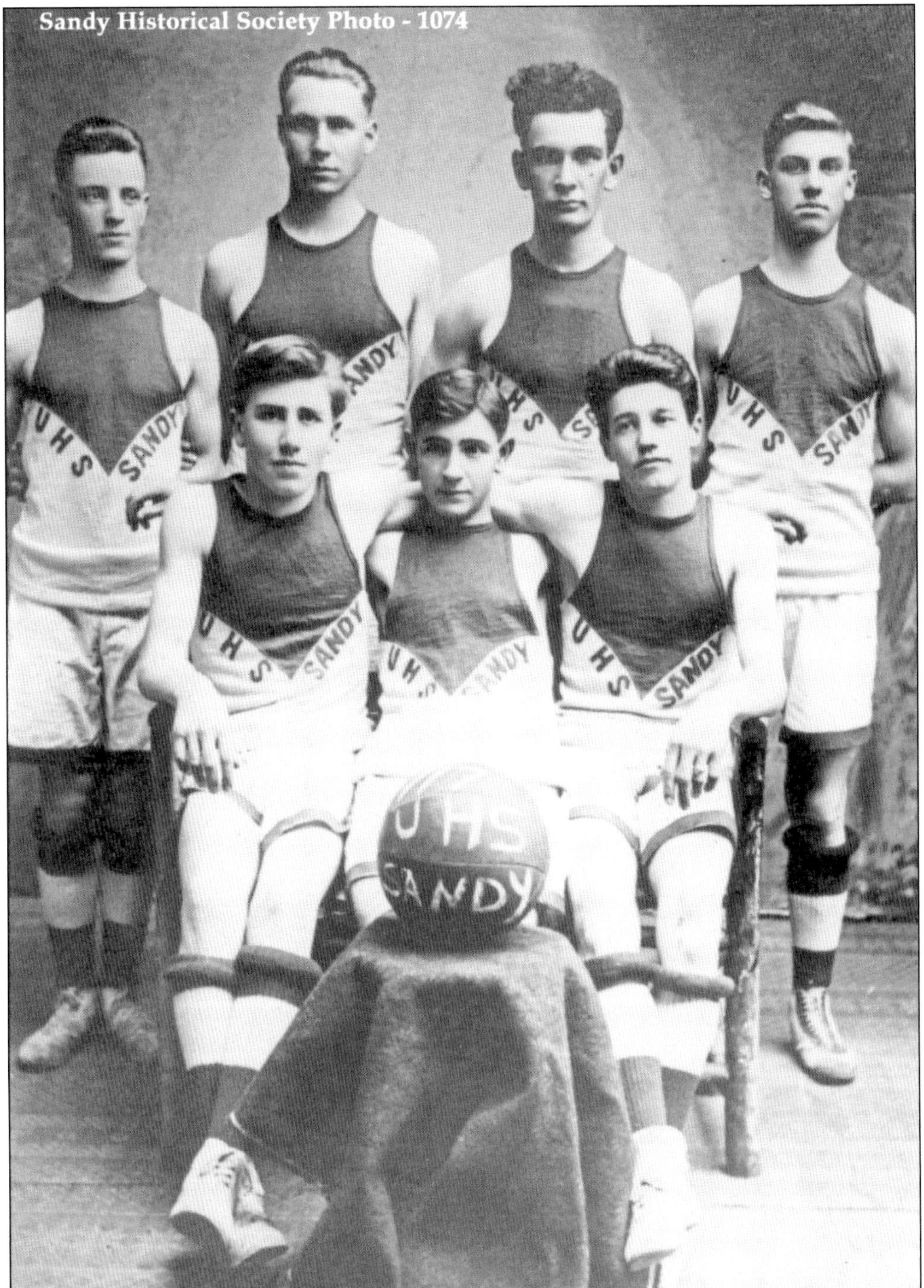

The members of the Sandy High School boys' basketball team of 1917 are, from left to right, (seated) Glenn Loundree, Aloysius Gray, and Bill Martin; (standing) Ralph Ganger, Ned Netzel, Walter Helms, and Henry Junker. The high school graduated its first class on May 21, 1917. No boys were included.

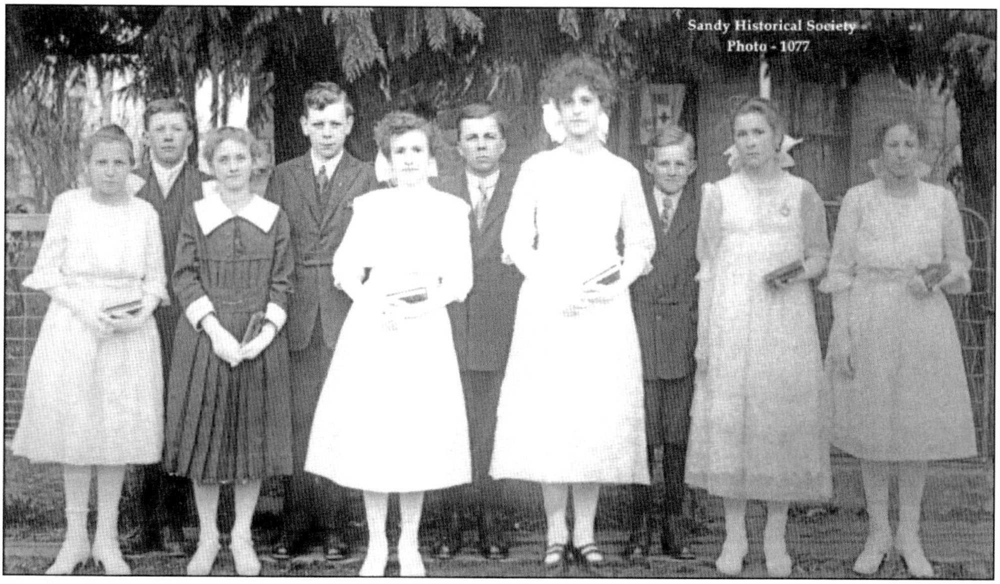

Students in the Sandy Lutheran Parochial School's eighth-grade class of 1918 are, from left to right, (first row) Amelia Krebs, Bertha Yabs, Ella Finger, Frieda Schwartz, Dorothy Trubel, and Ruth Krebs; (second row) Alex Heni, Henry Hazlander, Henry Schwartz, and Ruben Hoffman. Still used, the building where they attended school is known as the Schoolhouse Natural Medicine Building. (Courtesy of SHS and Ruben Hoffman.)

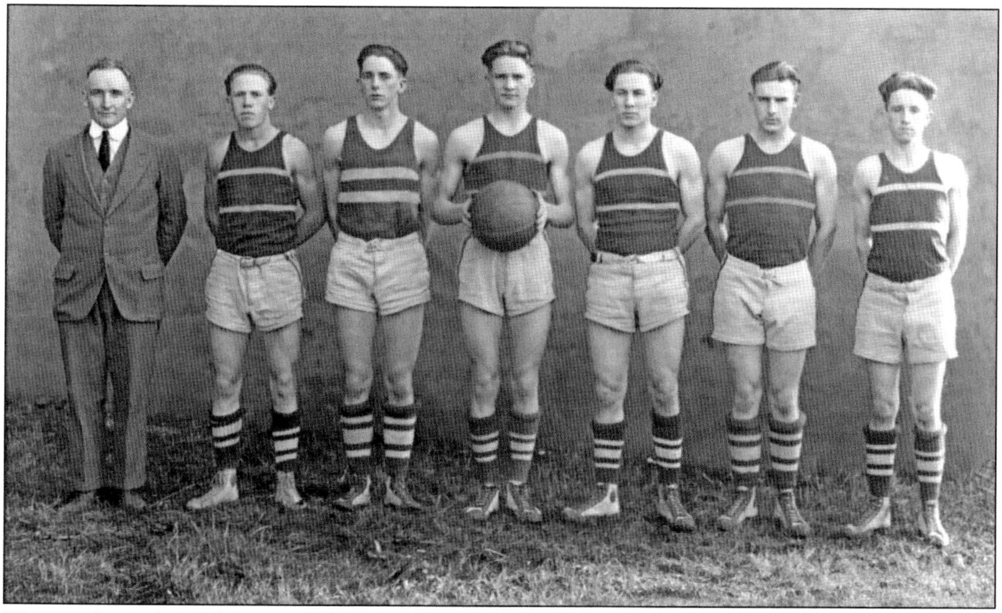

The 1925 Sandy High School boys' basketball team is seen here. Pictured are, from left to right, Coach McNulty, Edgar Hite, Thomas Scales, Kenneth Scales, Harold Krebs, Richard Suckow, and Lloyd Dunn. The school had begun furnishing transportation, and the enrollment grew from 73 students in 1925 to nearly 200 in 1926. (Courtesy of SHS and Lloyd Dunn.)

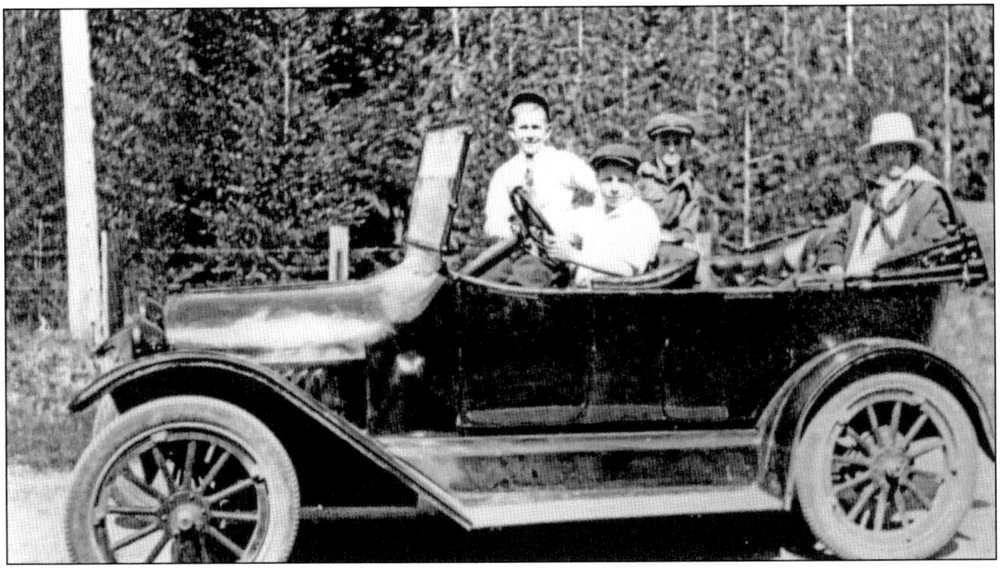

Lennis Edwards, at the wheel of his father's Chevrolet in 1920, is taking his teacher, Mary Jane Collier (in the backseat), and some friends for a ride. Edwards was 13 at the time and did not have a driver's license, but regulations were not strict in those days. The friends are Carl Loundree (left) and Ruben Hoffman. (Courtesy of SHS and the Edwards family.)

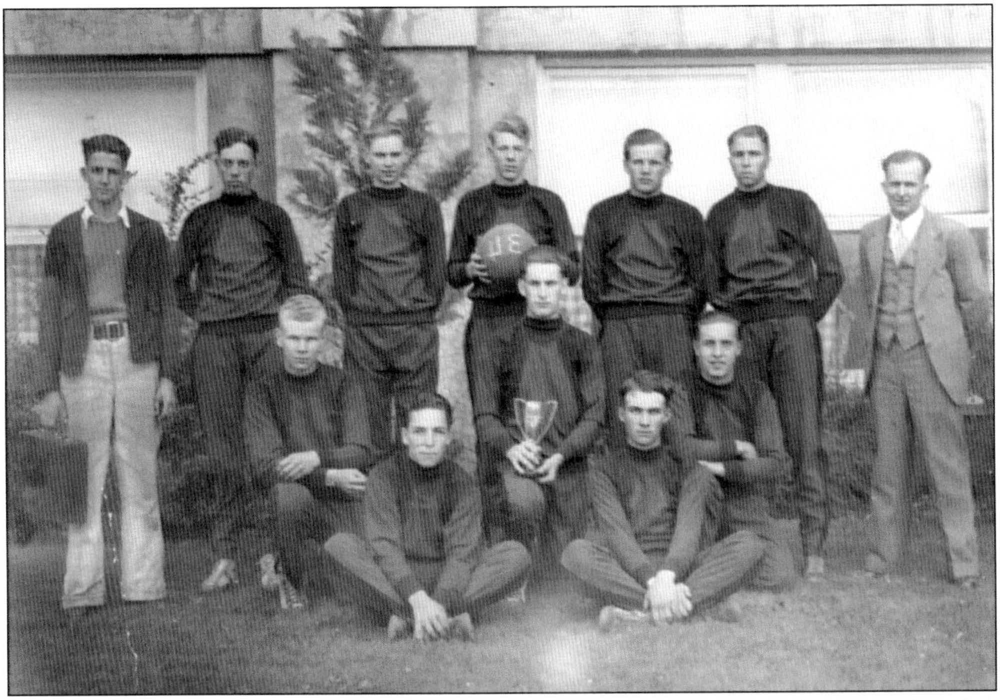

The 1934 Sandy High School boys' basketball team poses for a photograph. Shown are, from left to right, (sitting) Malcolm Marx and Ted Schoen; (kneeling) Larry Armstrong, Maurice Light (with trophy), and Earl Mills; (standing) Lawrence Aubin (equipment manager), Philip Jonsrud, Robert Bruns, Edward Maulding, Carl Westerberg, John Spooner, and coach L.E. Palmer. Yes, they finally won a trophy.

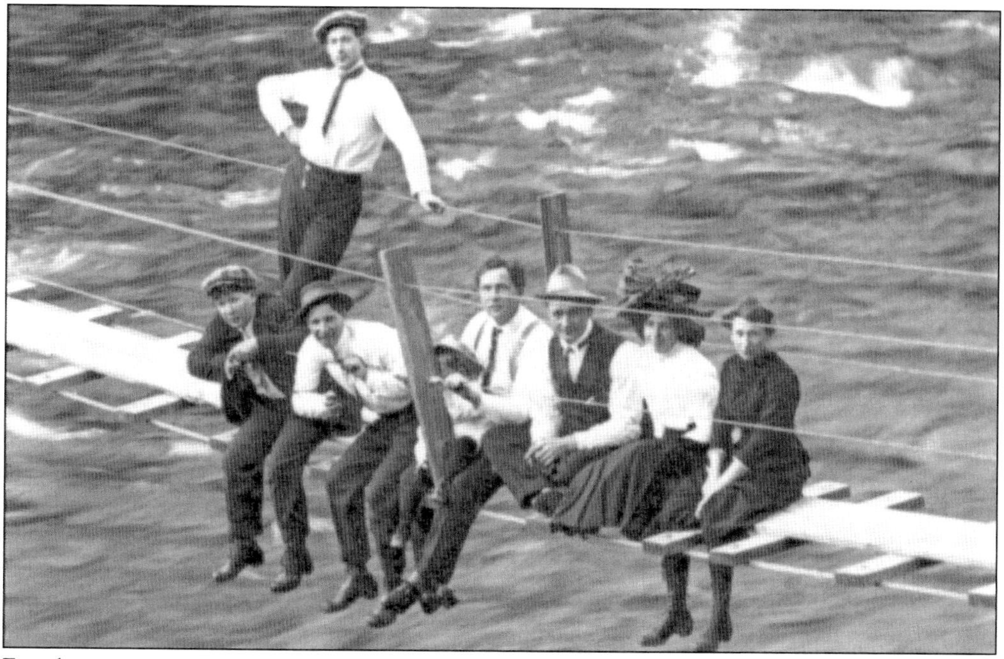

Family outings were common, especially when visitors came from the "faraway metropolis of Portland," 20 miles away. It was only a short distance to this swinging footbridge across the Sandy River. Shown here are, from left to right, (seated) Theodore Gray, Alex Gray, C.R. Kehres, a Mr. Weise, Isabel Gray, and an unidentified woman; (standing) Raymond Gray. (Courtesy of SHS and Dennis Gray.)

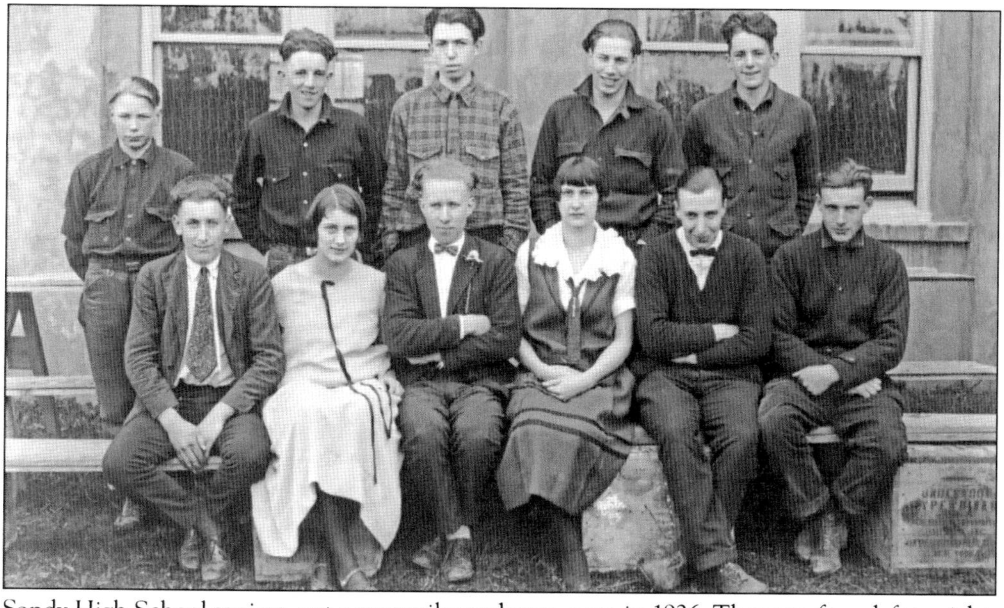

Sandy High School seniors, not necessarily graduates, pose in 1926. They are, from left to right, (first row) two unidentified students, Herbert Edwards, Ruth Revenue (Reed), Ken Proctor, and Richard Suckow; (second row) Roland Erickson, Lloyd Dunn, Milton Meinig, Harold Krebs, and Tom Scales. This was the year, following the Smith-Hughes Vocational Act, that home economics and agriculture were added to the curriculum.

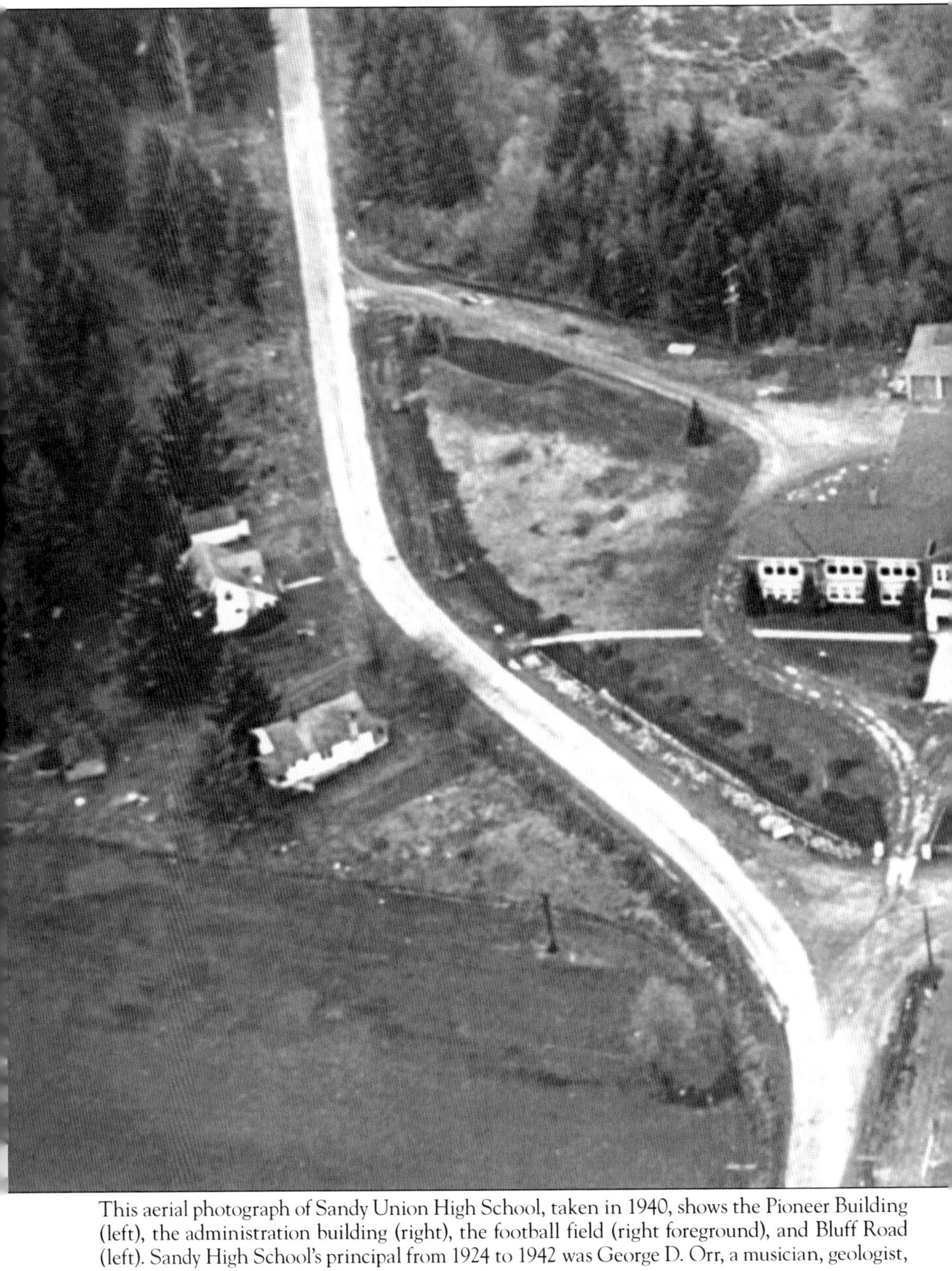

This aerial photograph of Sandy Union High School, taken in 1940, shows the Pioneer Building (left), the administration building (right), the football field (right foreground), and Bluff Road (left). Sandy High School's principal from 1924 to 1942 was George D. Orr, a musician, geologist,

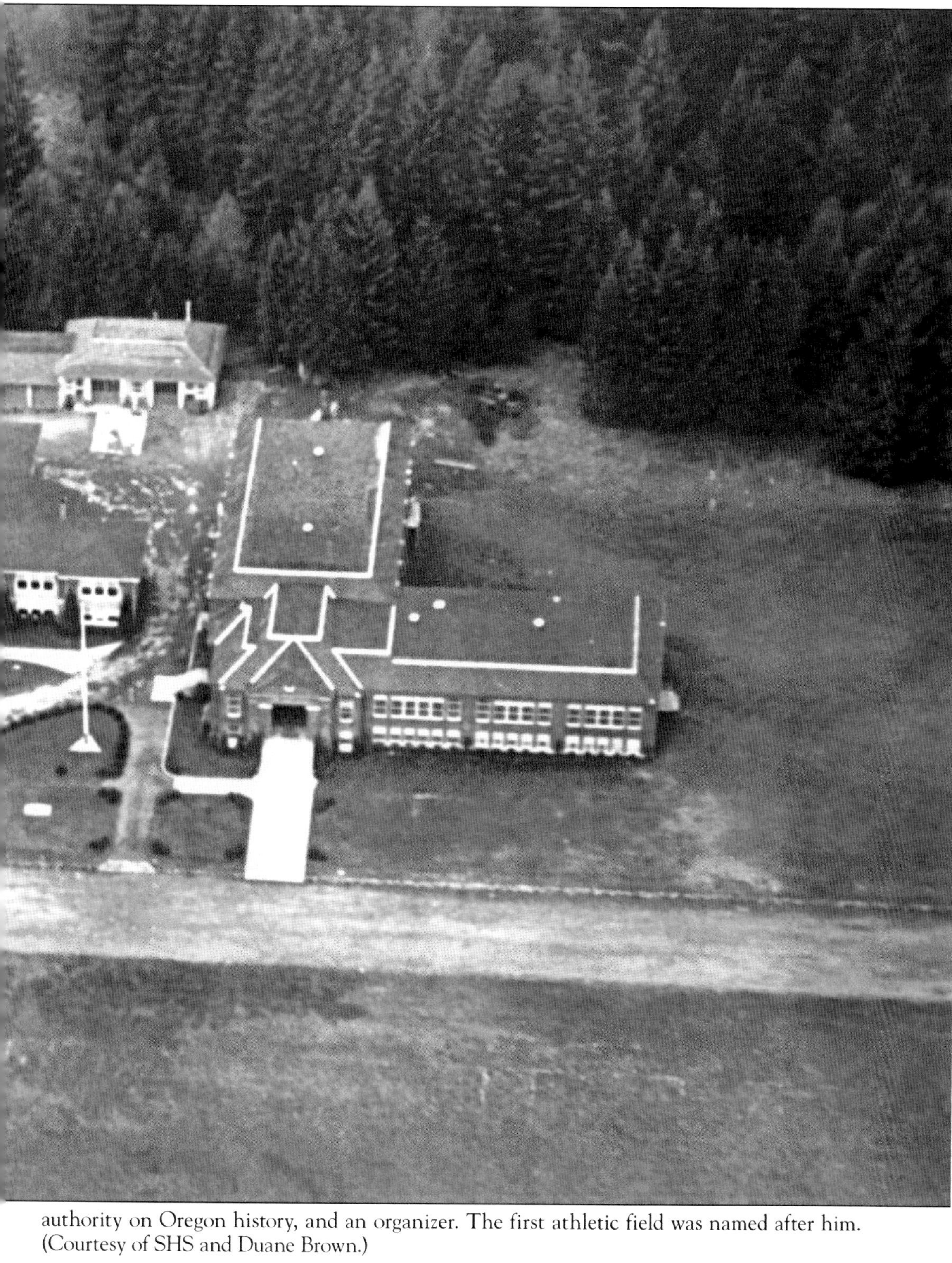

authority on Oregon history, and an organizer. The first athletic field was named after him. (Courtesy of SHS and Duane Brown.)

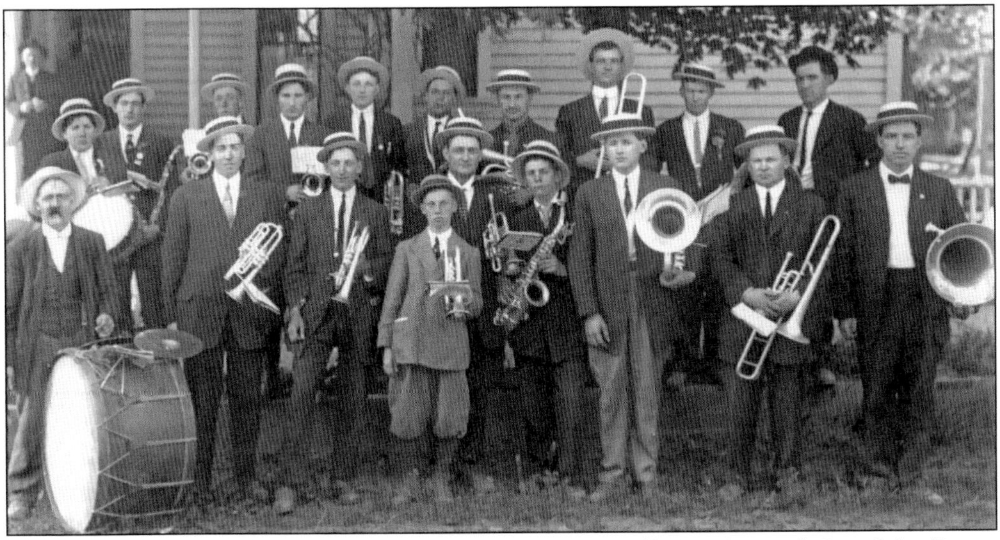

Members of the first Sandy Booster Band are, from left to right, (first row) Patrick Gray, John Dunn, George Hennessy, Henry Junker, instructor Edward Weiss (behind Junker), Ervin Earl Radford, Clarence Kehres, Ronald Esson, and Robert Smith; (second row) Theodore Gray, Raymond Gray, Jack Staley, Alex Gray, Edward Hoffman, Henry Wewer, Clement Bartsch, Melvin Smith, Gustav Dahrens, and unidentified. The man standing on the porch is unidentified. (Courtesy of SHS and Dennis Gray.)

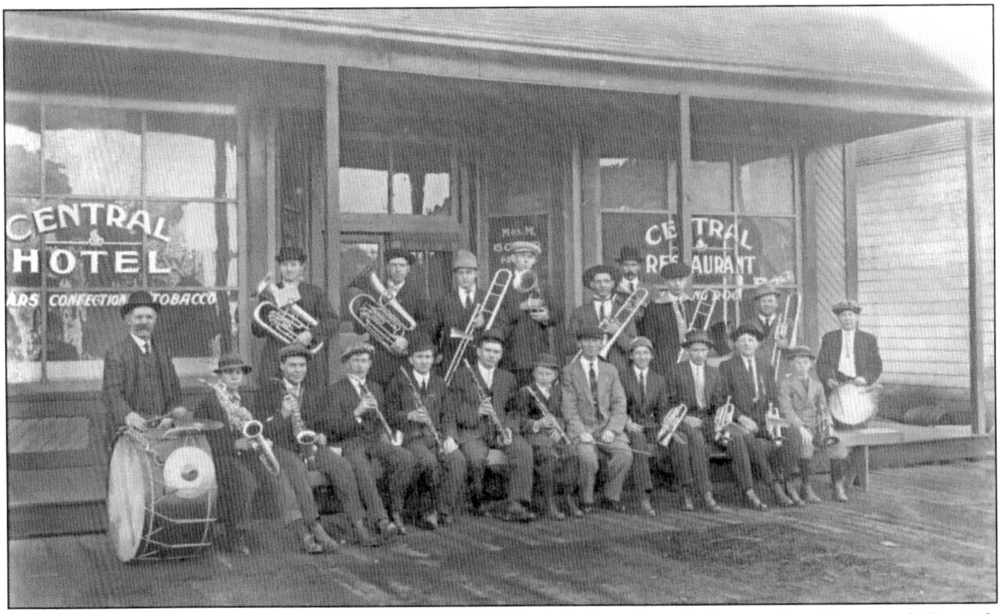

The Sandy Booster Band, more organized in 1907, includes, from left to right, (first row) Patrick Gray, Ervin Earl Radford, Henry Wewer, Raymond Gray, F.E. Beckwith, Gustav Dahrens, Alfred Meinig, conductor ? Robart, George Hennessy, Alex Gray, Edward Hoffman, and Henry Junker; (second row) Clarence Kehres, Robert Smith, J.E. Pomery, Merle Deaton, Melvin Smith, Henry Perret, Edward Grunert, Ronald Esson, and Theodore Gray (drums).

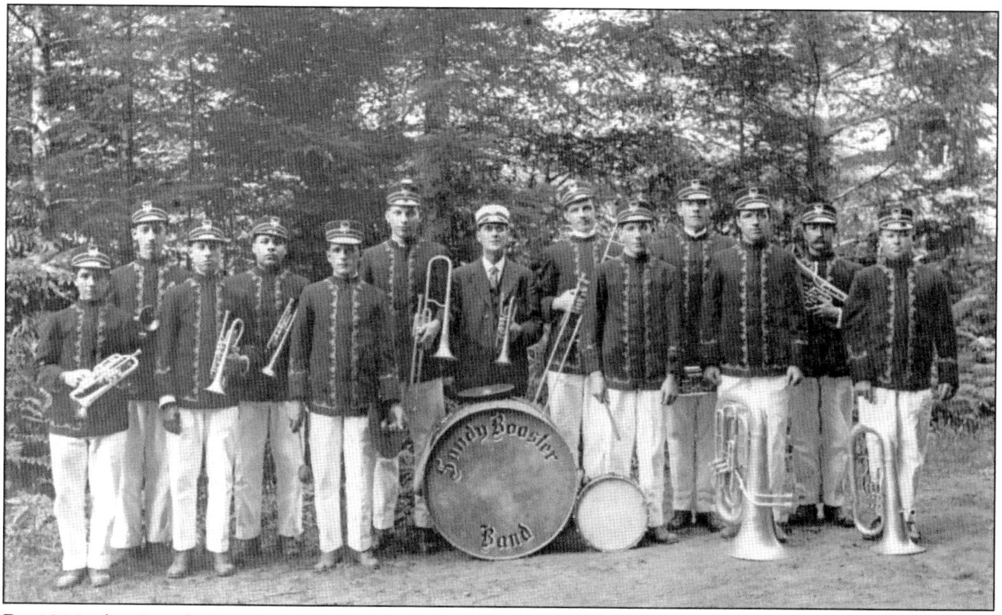

By 1914, the Sandy Booster Band had progressed to the point that it could afford uniforms and assemble in a fairly straight line. The members are, from left to right, Alex Gray, George Hennesey, Henry Junker, Henry Wewer, Theodore Bornstedt, William Fischer, E.V. Nye (instructor), Melvin Smith, Theodore Gray, unidentified, Robert Smith, Clement Bartsch, and Ronald Esson. (Courtesy of SHS and Dennis Gray.)

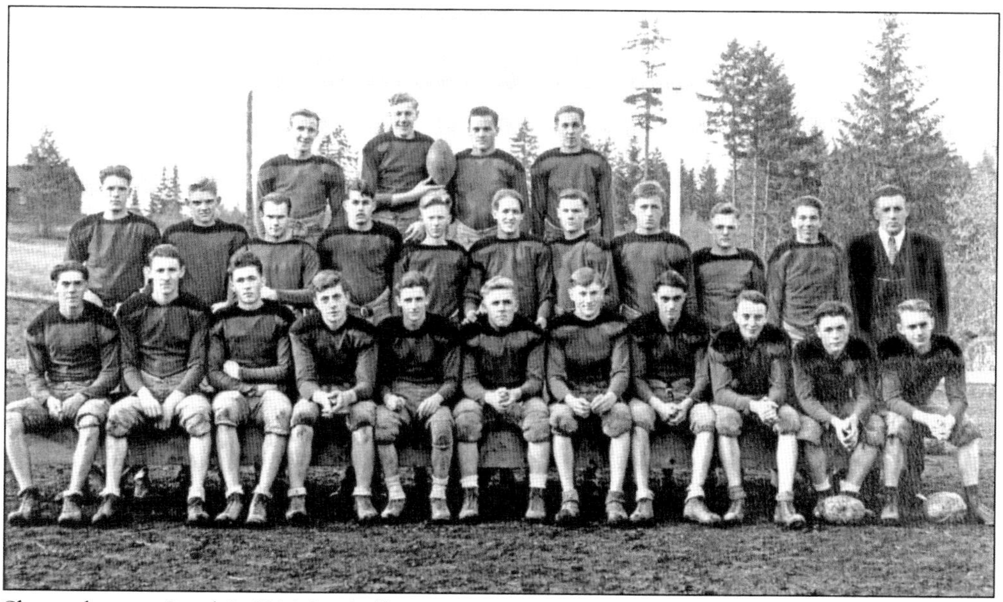

Shown here is Sandy's 1936 football team. Pictured are, from left to right, (first row) Charles Steinke, Raymond Wilcox, John Orr, Gearhart Schwartz, Lawrence Aubin, Lester Gant, James Howard, John Apa, James Kealiher, Donald Marx, and John Furby; (second row) Louis Reich, Lester Bruns, Vernon Dahrens, Charles Bettis, Glen Benedict, Emmett Mills, Clifford Rich, Kent Price, Loyal Rich, Wilbur Butts, and coach William "Pop" Rannow; (third row) John Price, Edward Maulding, Lawrence Guthu, and Robert Burdette.

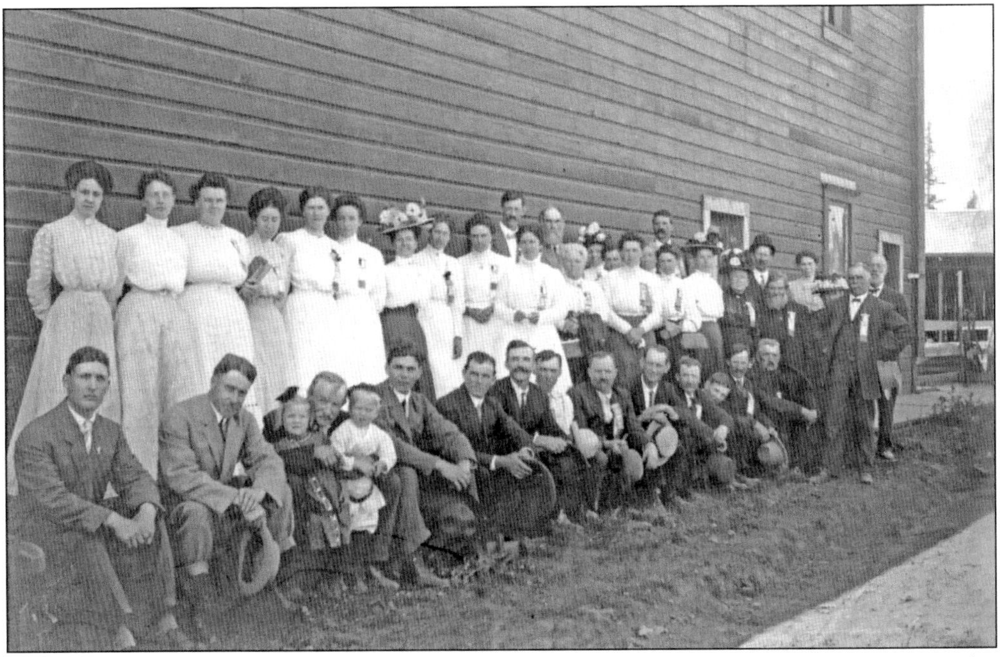

The Sandy Odd Fellows Hall was built in 1908 with lumber donated by Michael Donahue, who had a mill on Bluff Road. Elijah Coalman was in charge. Others who helped with the building were Arleigh and John Mitchell, Edward Bruns, and Arthur Baumback. When Sandy Grange No. 392 was instituted in 1908, it held its installation and subsequent meetings in the Odd Fellows Hall.

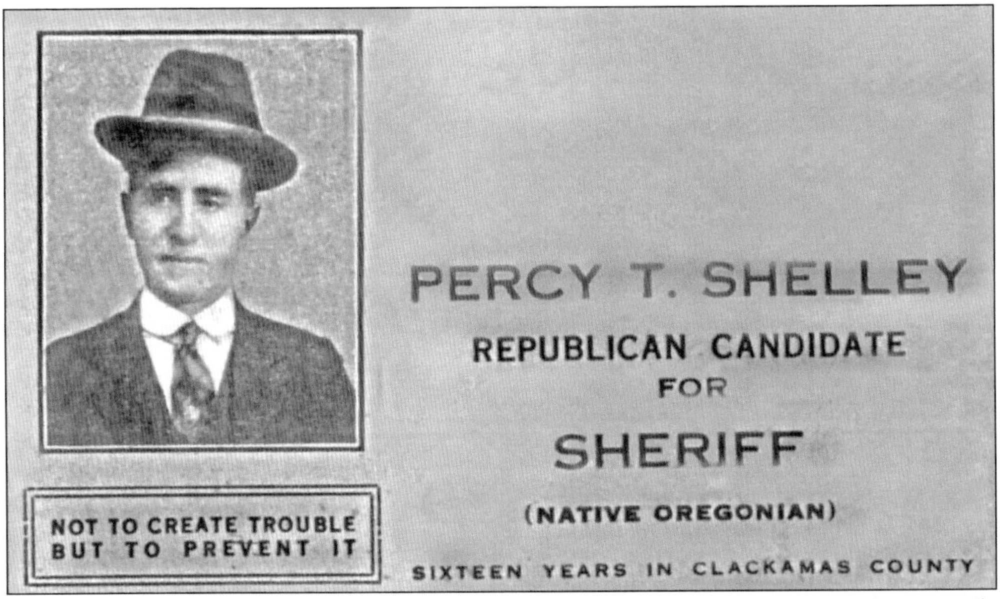

When Percy T. Shelley, Republican candidate for sheriff, ran as a native Oregonian, he certainly had credentials. His father, Troy Shelley, was carried as an infant down Laurel Hill by Percy's grandmother in 1848. Percy was born in Canyon City in 1878 and eventually was assigned to the Sandy Ranger Station in Mount Hood National Forest. He married Blanche Rue Wilson, who became Sandy's first female mayor.

Six

The Women of Sandy

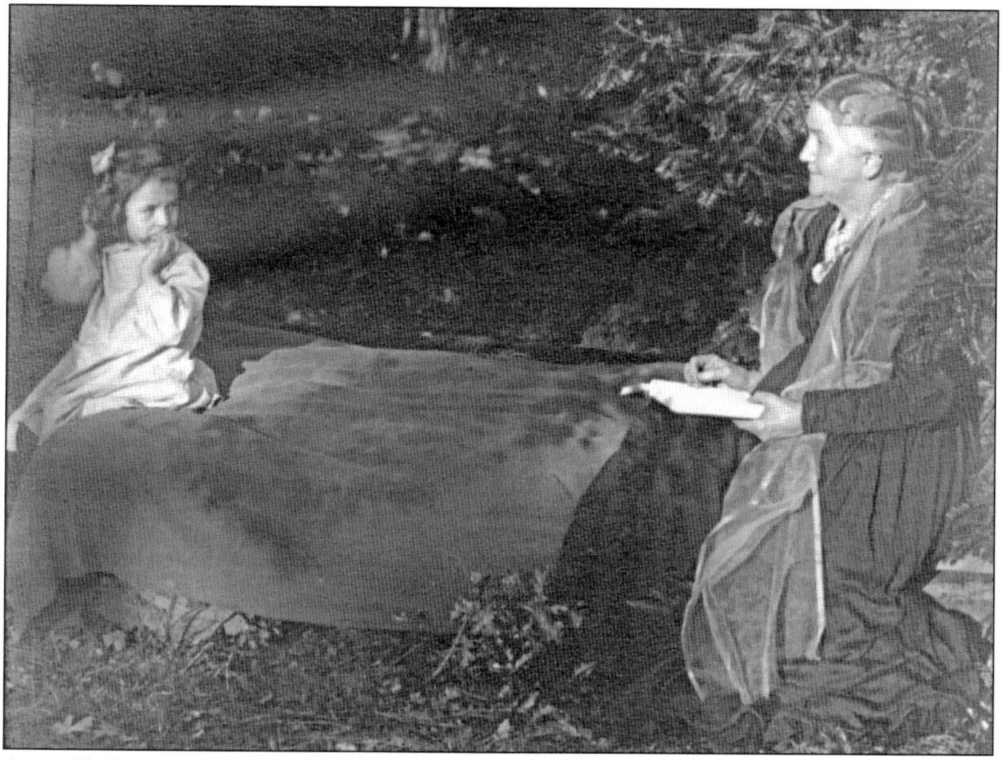

Anne Shelley, grandmother of Joseph Shelley, is on the right, and her daughter Nell Shelley is at left. A ribbon with a gold ring is attached to the frame of the picture. An inscription on the back reads, "This ribbon was part of little mother's sash she wore on her wedding day. She was married on the Rickreall Green 7-5-71." (Courtesy of SHS and Joseph Shelley.)

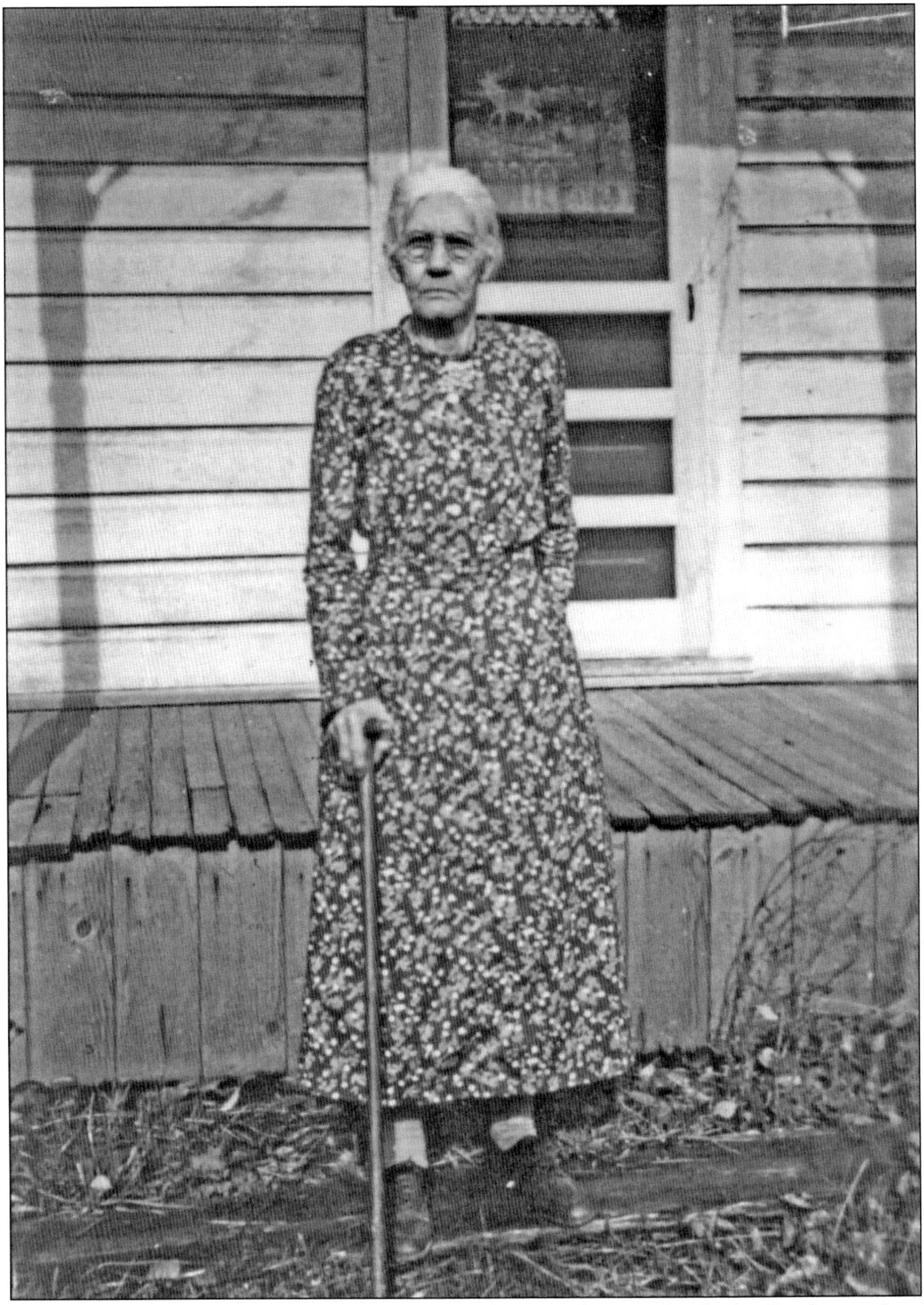

"Grandma" Wilson, mother of Blanche Shelley and practical nurse of early-day Sandy, stands in front of her home on her 92nd birthday in 1951. She had just returned from a party given for her by Agnes Barker. For many years, Wilson lived in this house on the corner of Proctor Boulevard and Smith Street. It was built for her by Elijah Coalman.

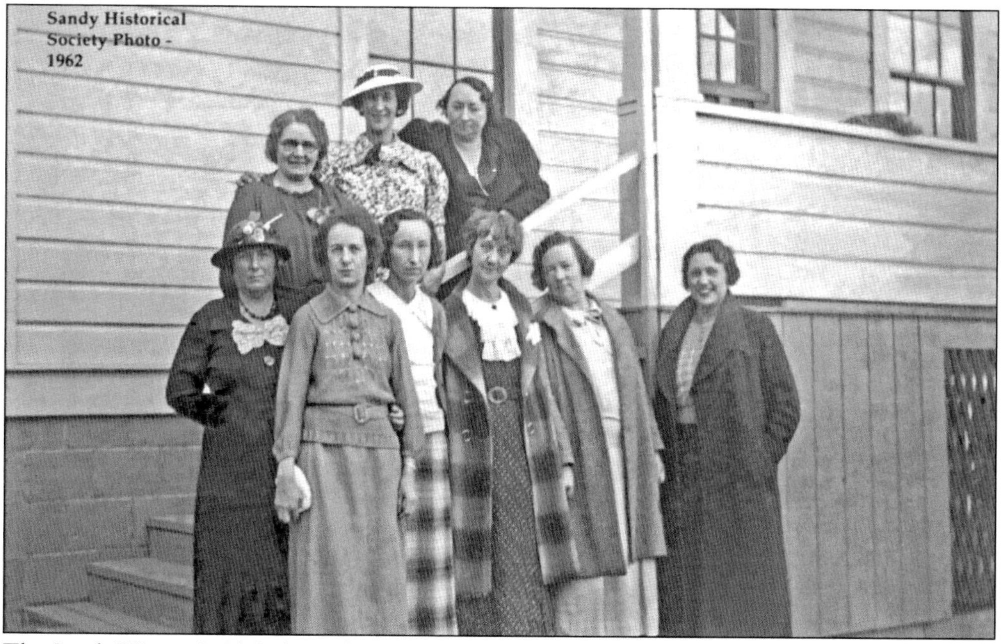

The Sandy Women's Club, formed in 1912, completed its new building, including a library, in 1936. Shown here are, from left to right, (first row) Lyda Bartsch, Minnie Proctor, Georgia Gunderson, Mathilda Jonsrud (president), Hazel Murray (secretary), and Hazel Brown; (second row) Augusta Bruns, Agnes Barker (vice president), and Margaret Dittert. All were on the building committee, except Bartsch and Proctor.

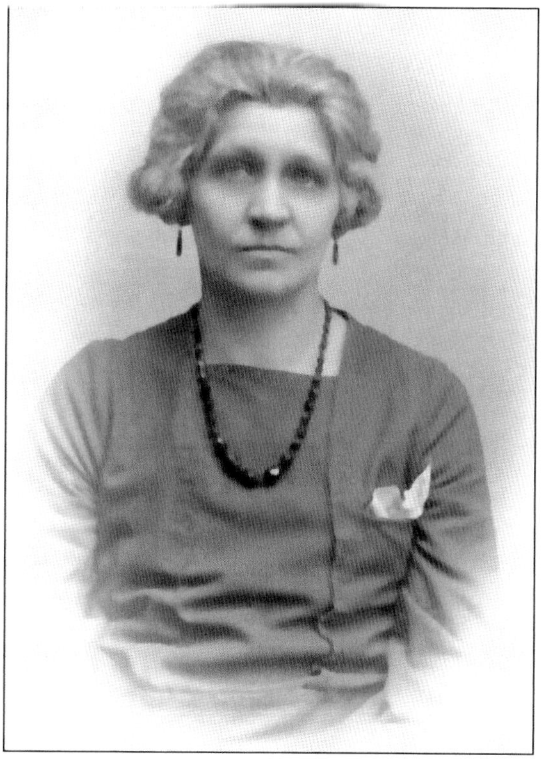

Blanche Rue Shelley was born in Chehalis, Washington. She taught school in The Dalles and Hood River before marrying Percy Shelley in 1906. After they moved to Sandy, she was a charter member of the Sandy Rebekah Lodge and the Sandy Women's Club. She was Sandy's first female mayor, before national women's suffrage, and served as justice of the peace. (Courtesy of SHS and Joseph Shelley.)

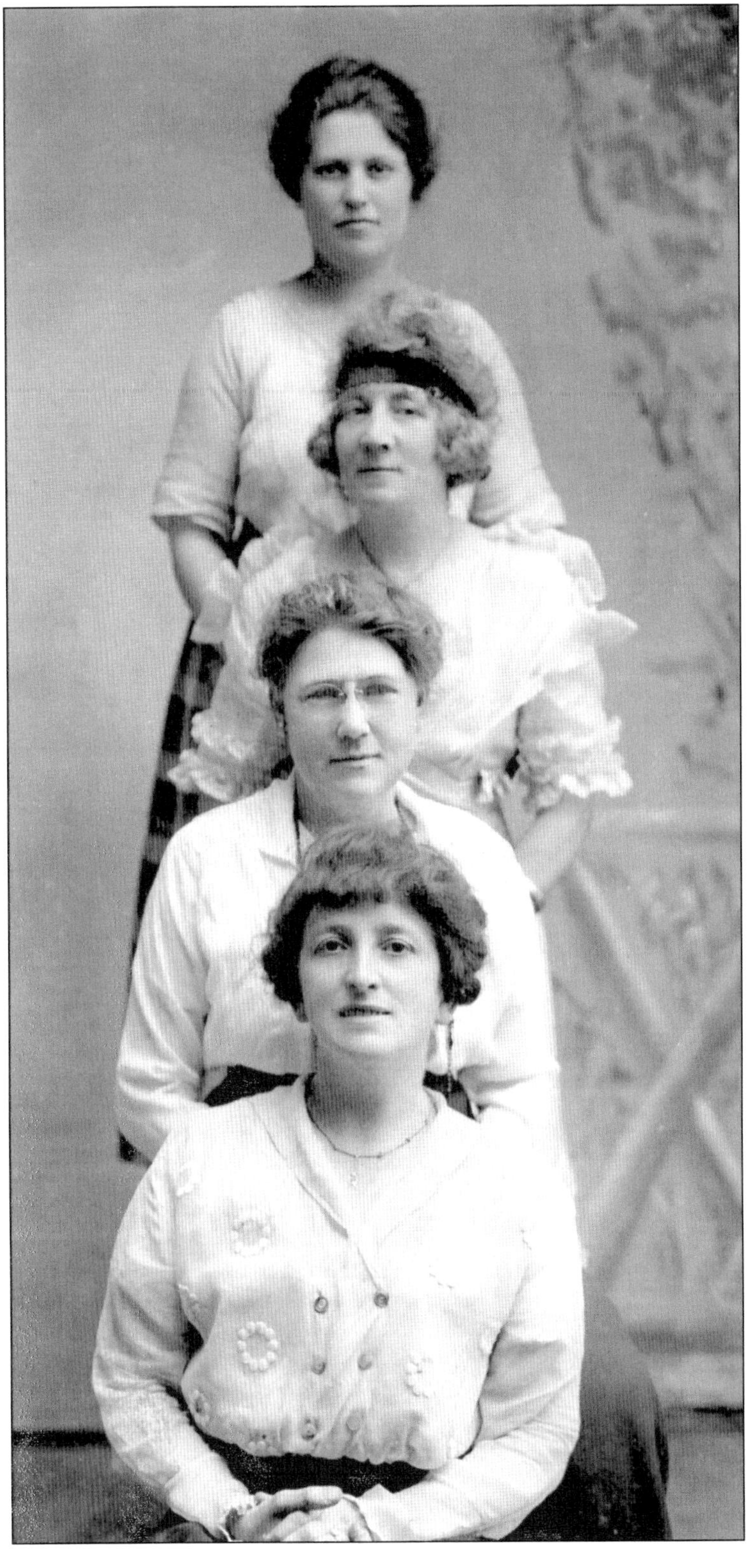

In 1920, Oregon's highway department chose a highway route through Sandy, rather than over the "Devil's Backbone" through Marmot. In celebration, a parody of "You'll Take the High Road and I'll Take the Low Road" was sung by the Sandy Women's Vocal Quartet. The members are, from top to bottom, Edna Esson, Bertha Purcell, Mrs. J.M.C. Miller, and Mrs. Samuel Allen. (Courtesy of SHS and Philip Jonsrud.)

Alice Scales is shown here in 1915. She and her husband, Jack, came to Sandy in 1912 and ran several businesses. They purchased the home of Percy and Blanche Shelley, which had been the Revenue Hotel before the Shelleys moved it to Proctor Boulevard. Jack and Edna remodeled it to form the Dew Drop Inn—later T-J's, and now the Sandy Family Restaurant.

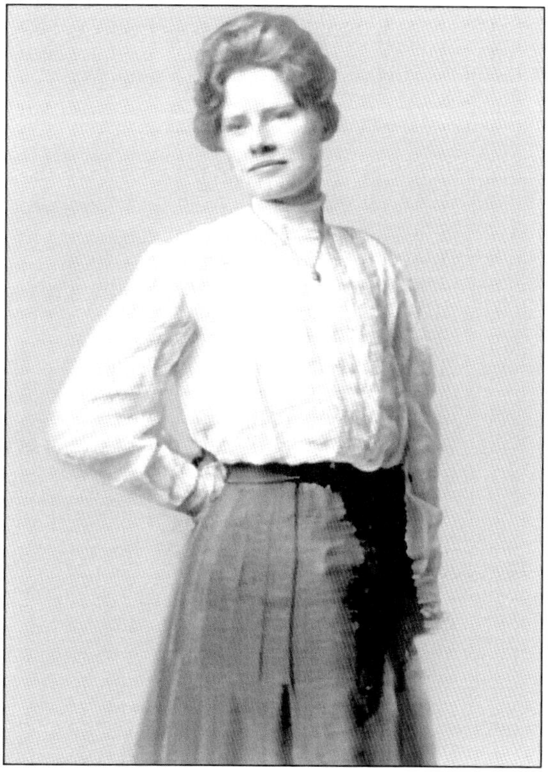

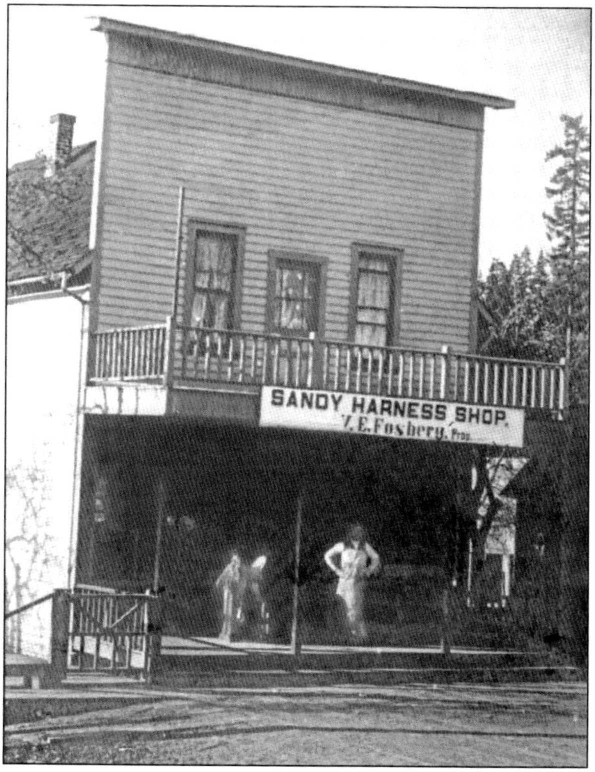

While her husband, Thomas, was in the service, Edna Scales bought Fosberg's Harness Shop and scrapped it for lumber to build Scales Clothing and Dry Goods. Later, it was Decker and Scales Clothing. When Thomas returned from the war, he added a menswear and shoe store. The building was sold in the 1960s and now houses the Sandy Community Action Center. (Courtesy of SHS and the Fosberg family.)

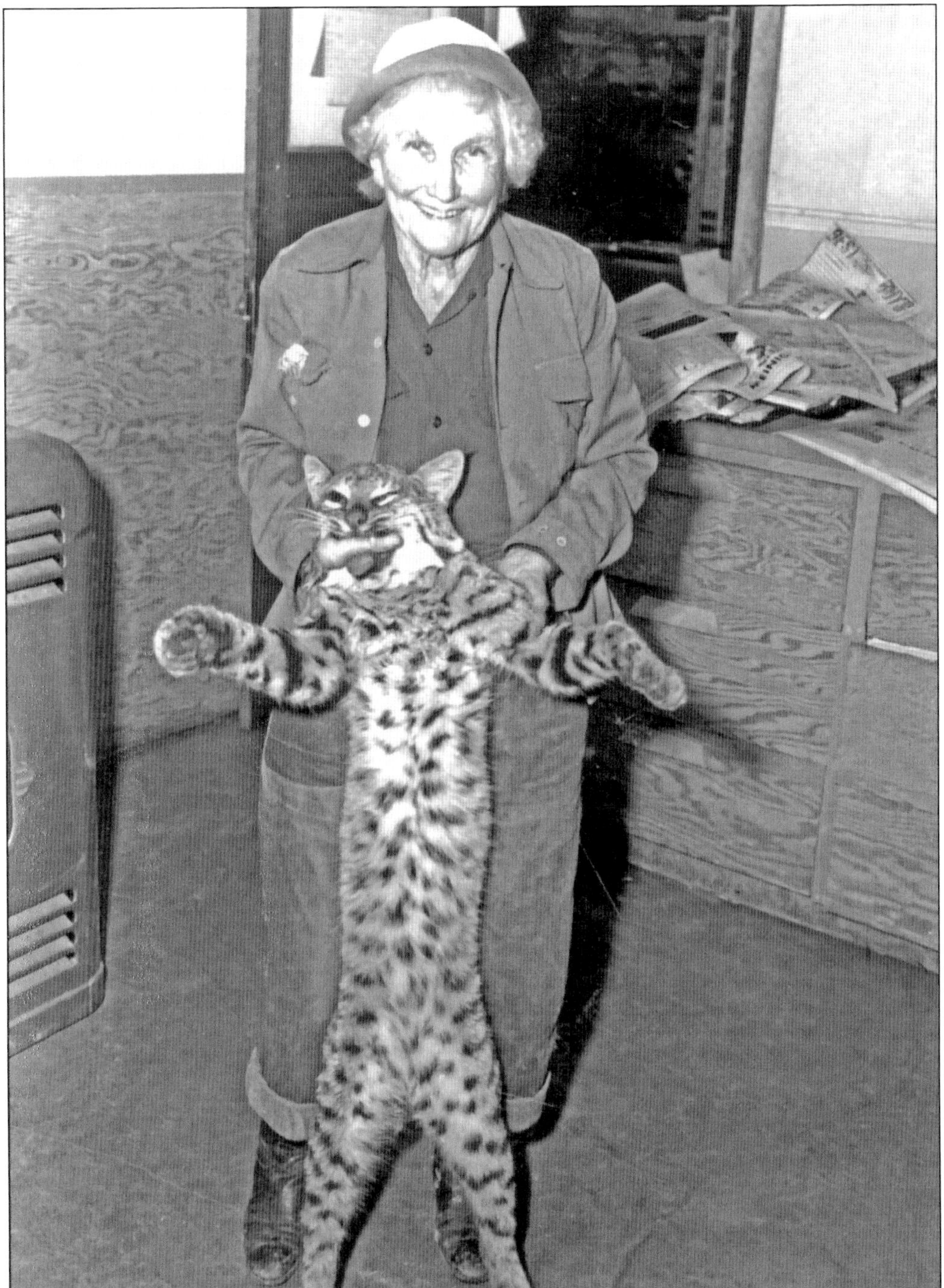

Sandy's most colorful personality was Nettie Connett, shown here in the photograph that appears in an issue of *Time* magazine. She bought and sold land and timber, hunted, and at least once was arrested for manufacturing and selling moonshine during Prohibition. She always said the Dew Drop Inn was her office, and she was known for standing on her head on a barstool. (Courtesy of SHS and Nettie Connett.)

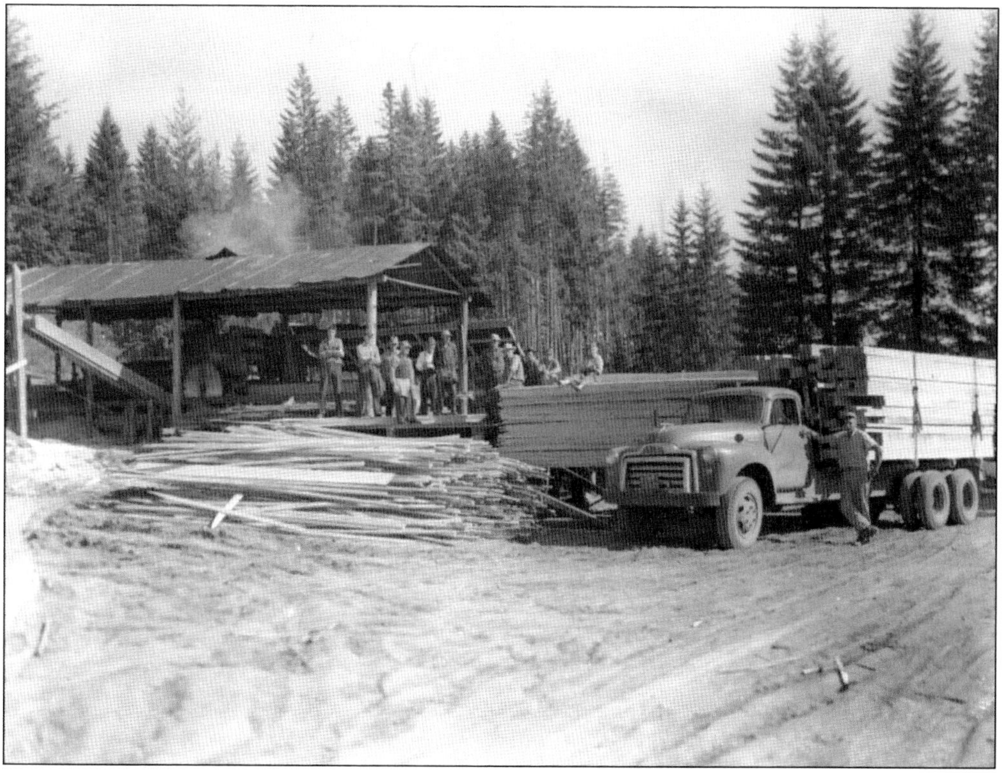

Nettie Connett is seen here sitting on a lumber pile at one of the many mills and businesses she had an interest in. Despite her cantankerous facade, Connett was reported by many to have a heart of gold. She would often show up at the home of a struggling family without notice and with a truckload of supplies, asking nothing in return. (Courtesy of SHS and the Yoerger family.)

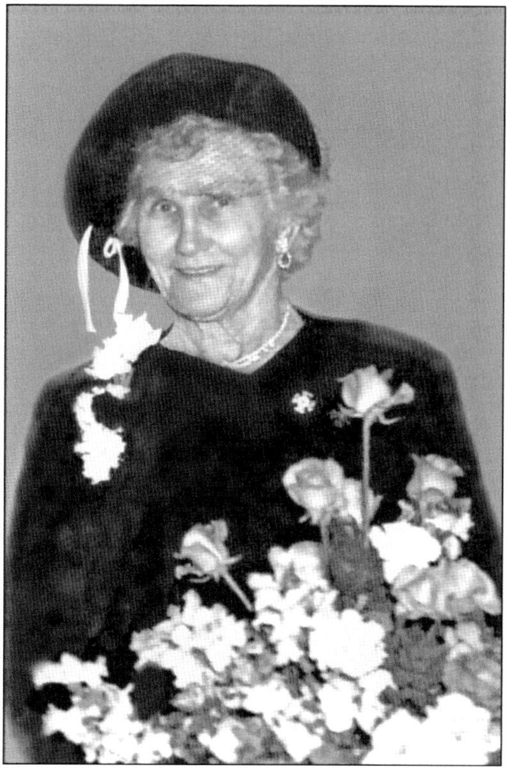

Hardly anyone ever saw Nettie Connett dressed in anything but old blue jeans and a logger's plaid shirt, but on Valentine's Day in 1953, she surprised everyone. Once, she wore a pretty flowered dress to a wedding, and someone asked where her jeans were. "Right here," she roared, pulling up the hem of her dress so her denims could be seen. (Courtesy of SHS and the Connett family.)

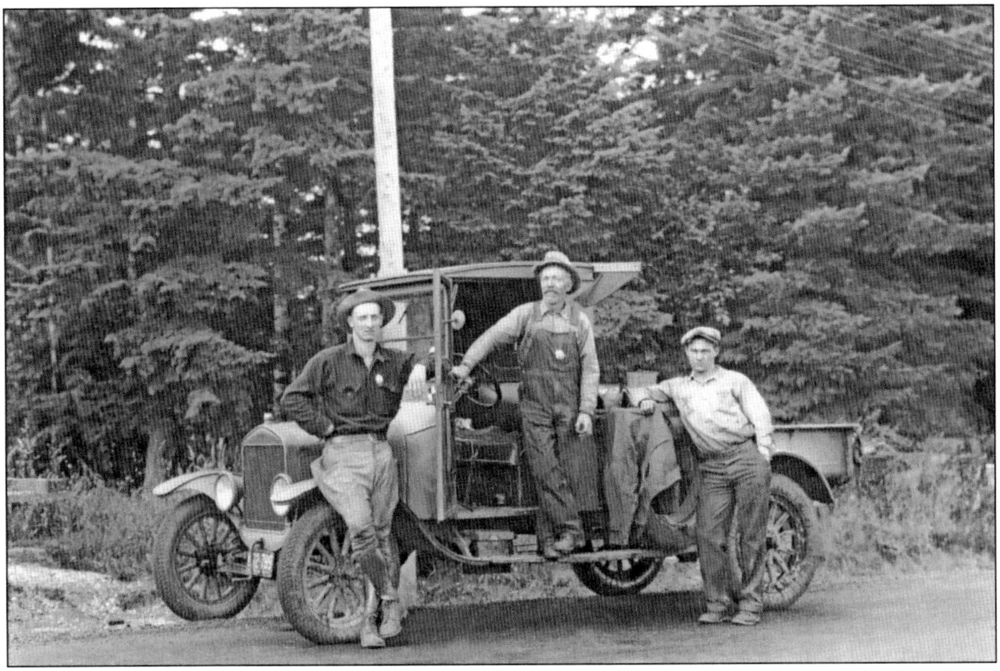

George Gernan (right) leans against a Ford Model T pickup with an Oregon license plate dated 1927. The two men on the left are wearing badges, but they are not wearing uniforms and do not look like regular law officers. They might be revenuers, looking for hidden stills, like the one (or more) that Nettie Connett is said to have operated. (Courtesy of SHS and Kate Schmitz.)

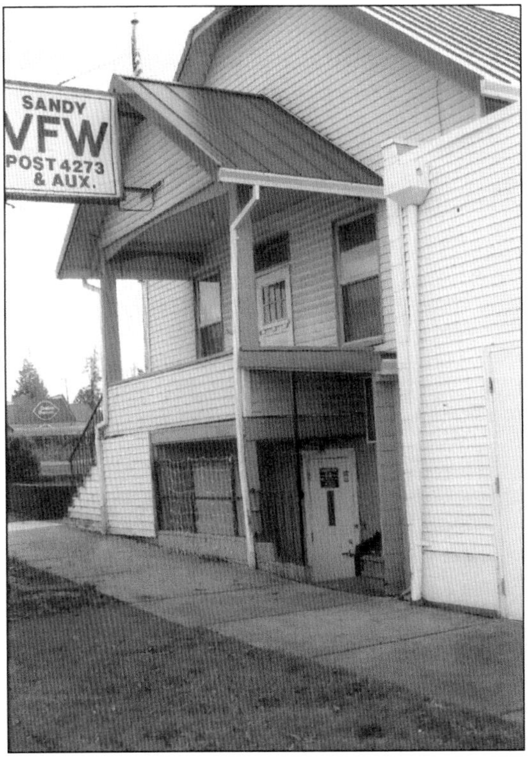

The building erected in 1936 by the Sandy Women's Club is now occupied by Post 4273 of the Veterans of Foreign Wars. The Sandy Library, which once occupied the tiny space behind the basement door, was moved to city hall, then to a disused clothing store on Proctor Boulevard, and finally to a building covering nearly a city block constructed especially for the library in 2012.

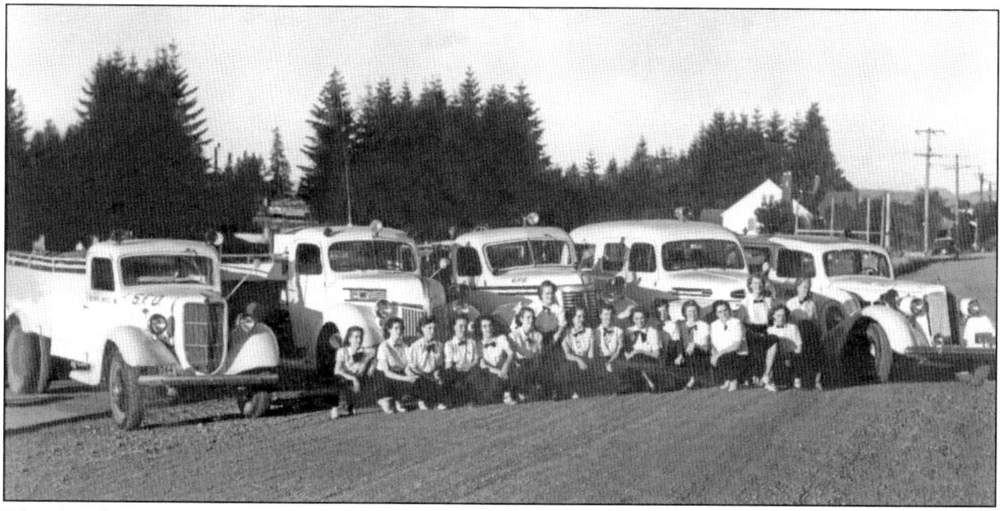

The Sandy Fire Department was formed in the 1930s, when the city purchased a Ford Model T chemical truck. However, records show that an organized fire department as early as 1912 had pulled chemical fire engines. In later years, with motorized fire apparatus, whenever the whistle blew, whoever happened to be around took the truck and went to the fire. These women volunteers certainly did their share.

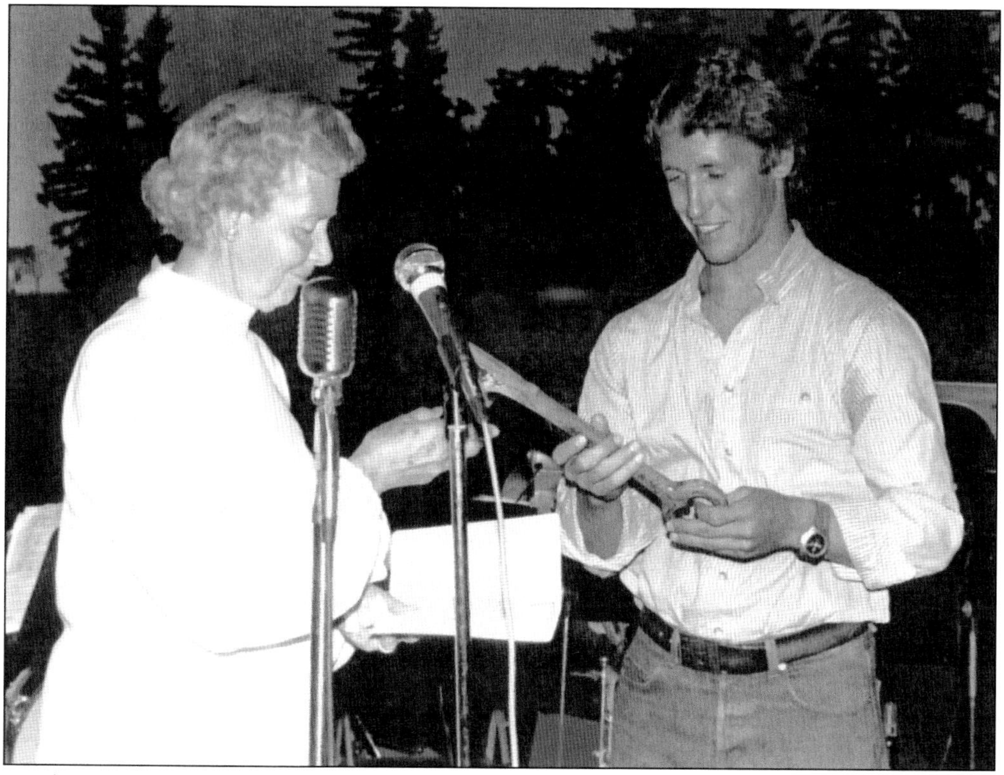

Sandy's second female mayor, Ruth Loundree, presents the key to the City of Sandy to William "Bill" Johnson, the gold medalist in downhill skiing at the 1984 Winter Olympics in Sarajevo, Yugoslavia. Bill had attended Sandy High School and got his early training in the downhill event while skiing in the Mount Hood area. (Courtesy of SHS and Nancy Gregson Spencer.)

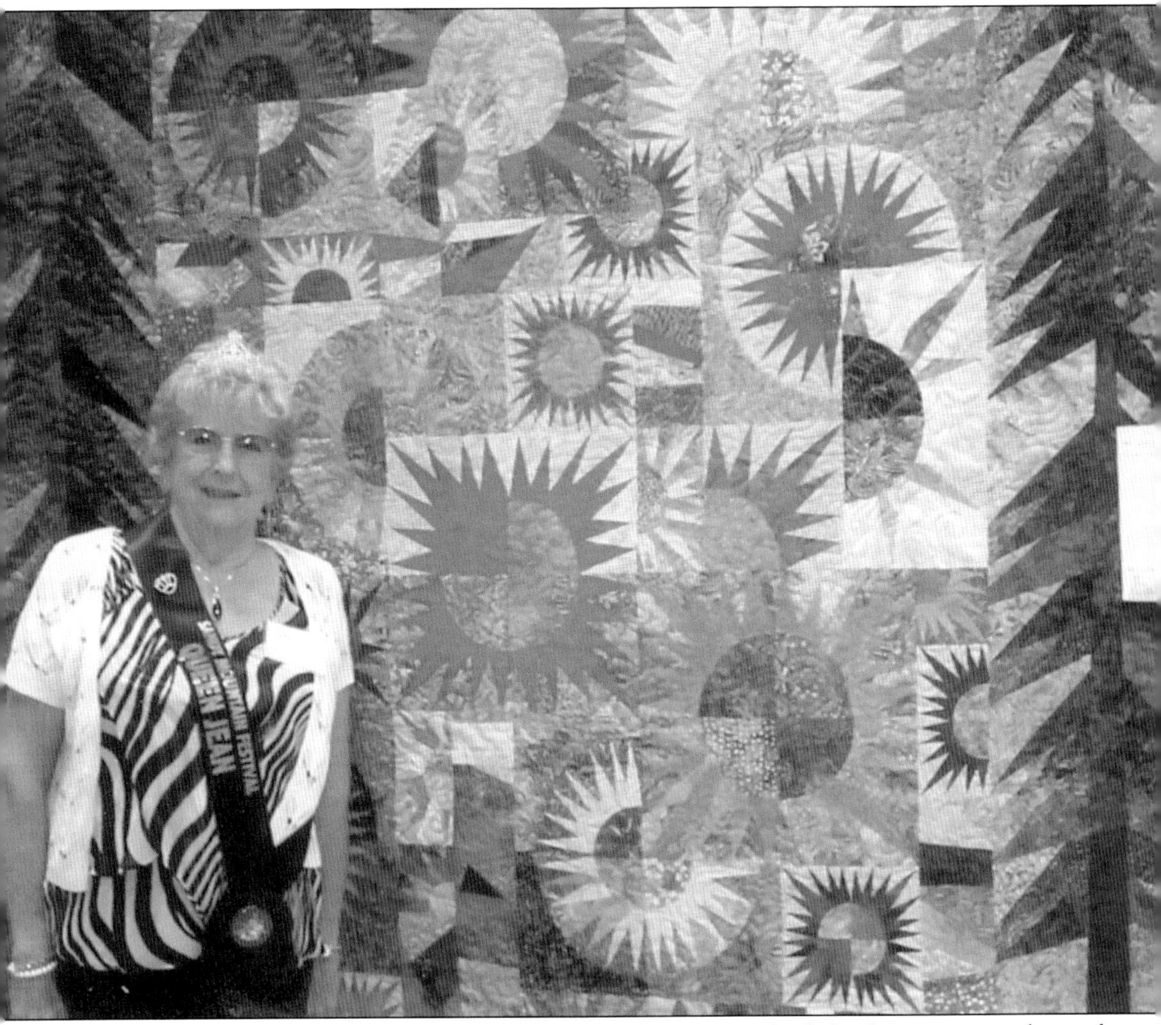

Every year, the Sandy Historical Society has a quilt show to raise funds for the museum, and one of the quilts is raffled off at the Sandy Mountain Festival. The Queen of the Festival, elected on the basis of a lifetime of community service, gets to pick her favorite. In 2013, Jean Rolli, descendant of the Bacon family of pioneers, was the queen. She poses here with her favorite quilt.

Seven

The Rise of Commerce

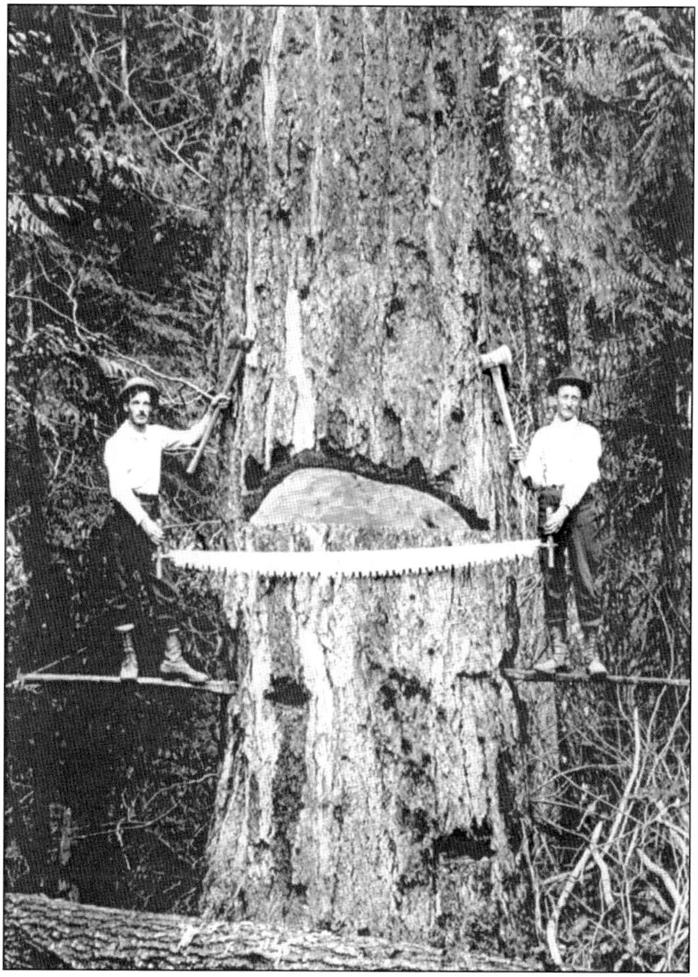

Gilbert Jonsrud (right) and his unidentified partner stand on springboards to fell this old-growth fir in the early 1900s. They have just chopped out the underscore, which determines the direction the tree will fall. A springboard set into a notch chopped into the tree served as a platform for the loggers.

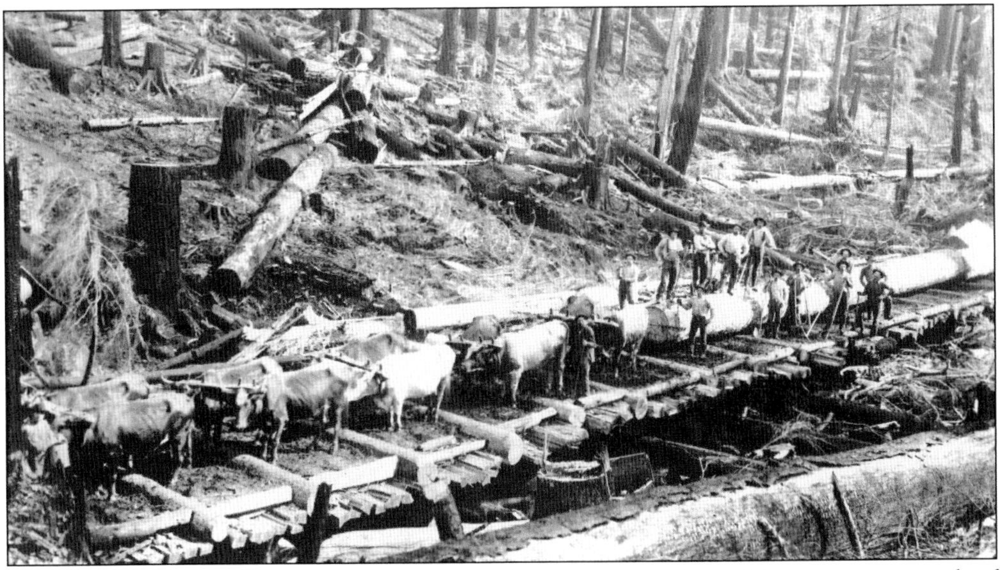

A five-yoke oxteam is shown yarding logs on a skid road in the Larch Mountain area north of Sandy in the 1890s for the Donahue Logging Company. Eliminating the friction from pulling them over rough ground allowed the logs to glide relatively smoothly over the skids on their way to the sawmill. (Courtesy of SHS and Philip Jonsrud.)

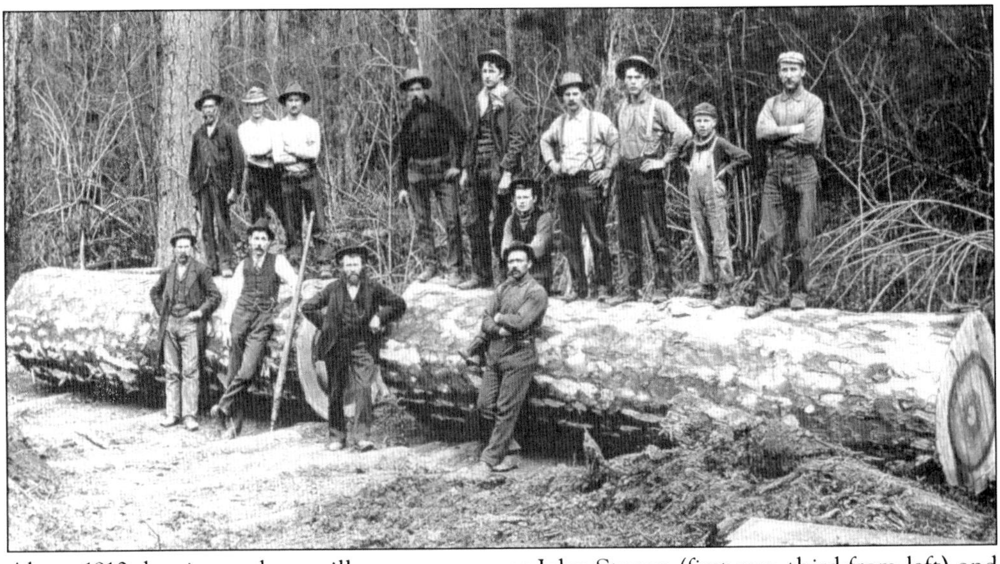

About 1910, logging and sawmill company owner John Strauss (first row, third from left) and part of his crew take a break to pose for the camera. Strauss came to America from Switzerland when he was 26 and homesteaded 80 acres in the Sandy Ridge area. He prospered and helped others, donating land for two schools and the Sandy Ridge Cemetery. (Courtesy of SHS and Brian Ten Eyck.)

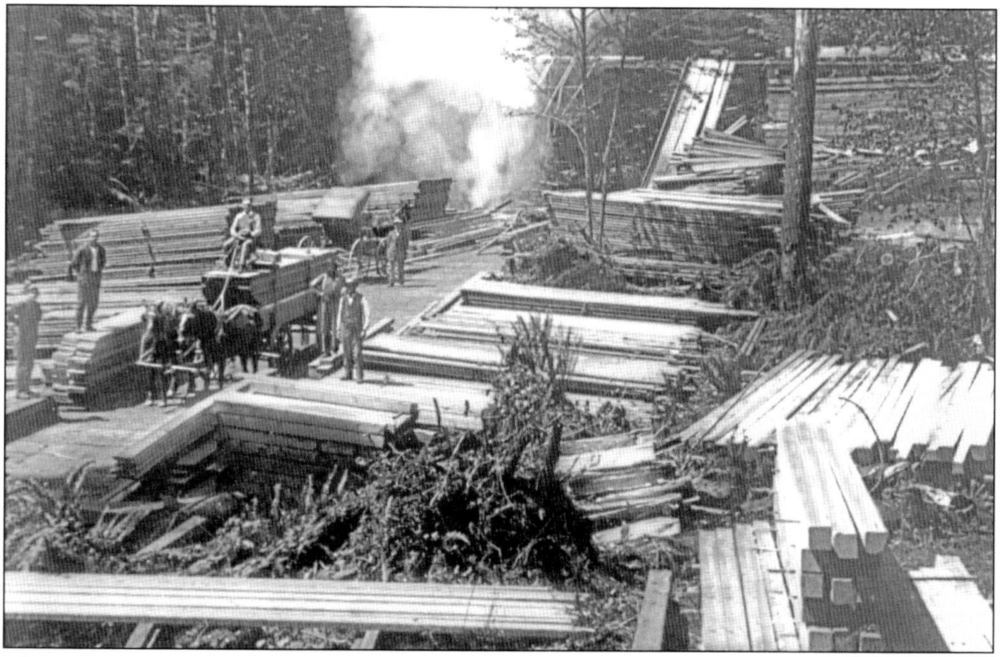

This is a typical sawmill lumber storage yard, thought to be Proctor and Strauss' Sandy Fir Lumber Company around 1906. By 1920, cars and trucks had displaced horses. In the background, lumber from the mill has been dumped from rollers into a tangled mess, from which the boards were sorted, moved to this yard, and piled with spacers for air-drying. (Courtesy of SHS and Phil Jonsrud.)

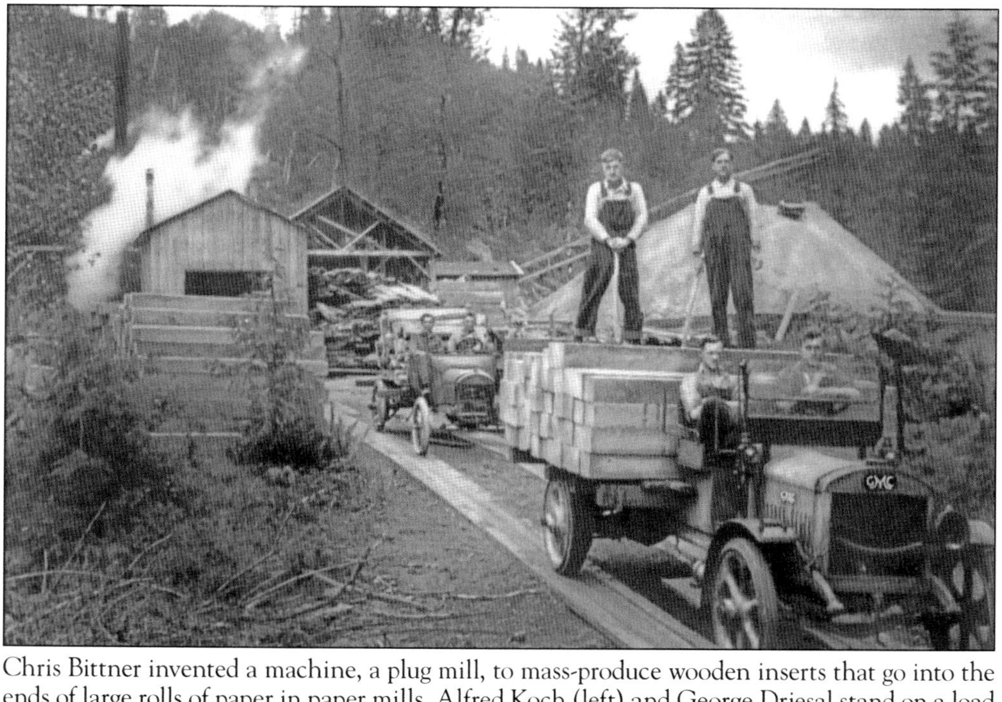

Chris Bittner invented a machine, a plug mill, to mass-produce wooden inserts that go into the ends of large rolls of paper in paper mills. Alfred Koch (left) and George Driesal stand on a load of ties. Albert Schwartz is driving, and his passenger is unidentified. In the Ford truck in the rear are Henry Schwartz (left) and Ed Hein.

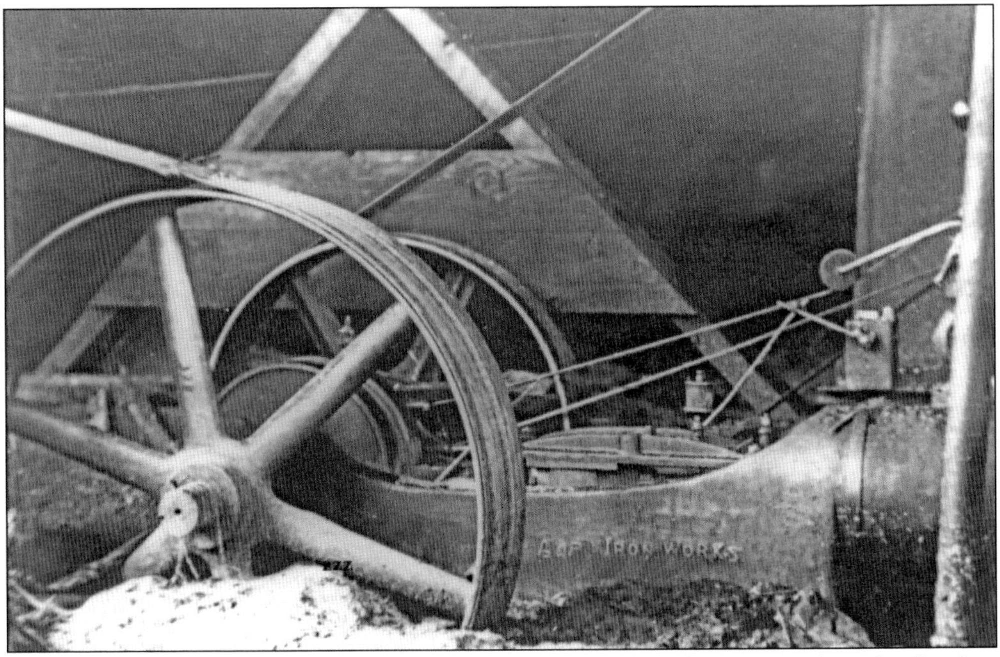

The Bittner plug mill near Dodge Park came to a grinding halt about 1910, when the flooding Sandy River washed sand into the machinery. Note the flat belts and pulleys in use at the time. Such belts running over cylindrical pulleys quickly wander off the pulleys. To prevent this, at least one pulley is usually "crowned," machined to a slightly "spindle-shaped" profile.

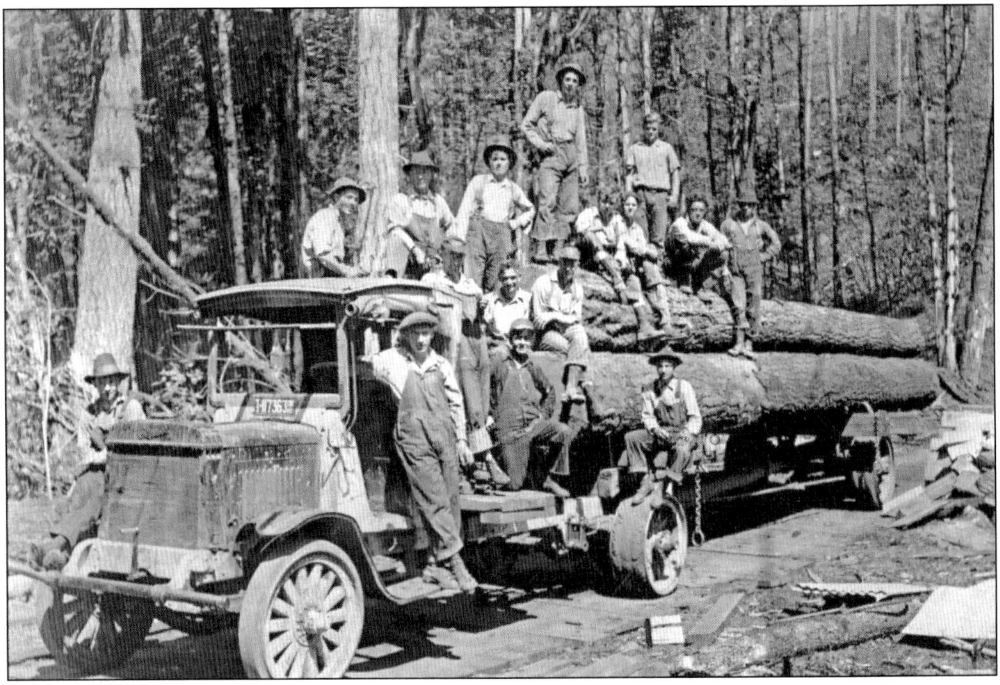

By 1920, it was no longer necessary to rely on horsepower. As primitive as it looks, this service-model, hard-rubber-tired logging truck was a vast improvement. Theodore Gray is the driver, and Arthur Jonsrud is third from the right on the top log. (Courtesy of SHS and Dennis Gray.)

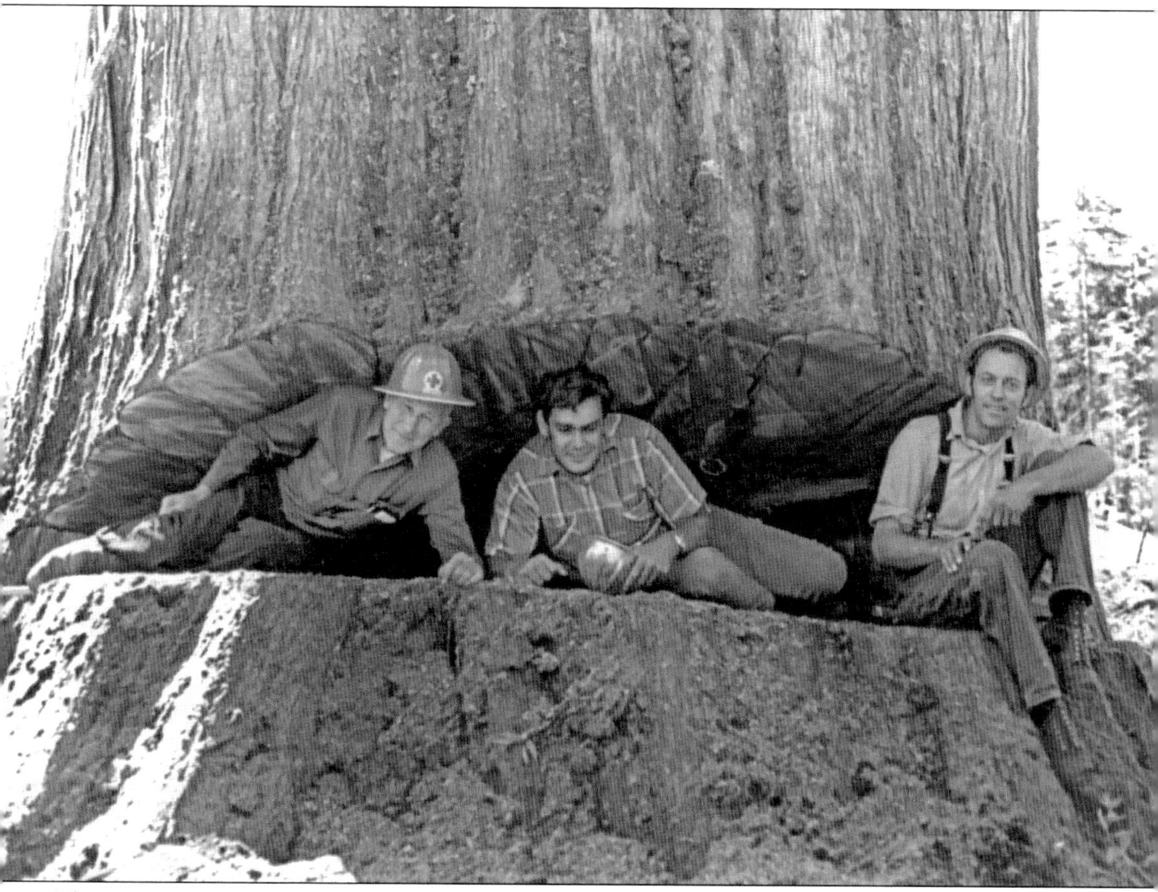

This giant western red cedar, over 12 feet in diameter at the cut, provided a perfect opportunity for some hardworking loggers to take a break and show off their handiwork in 1973. Shown here are William Barnes (left), Earl Cooper (center), and Kenneth Valentine. (Courtesy of SHS and William Harsey.)

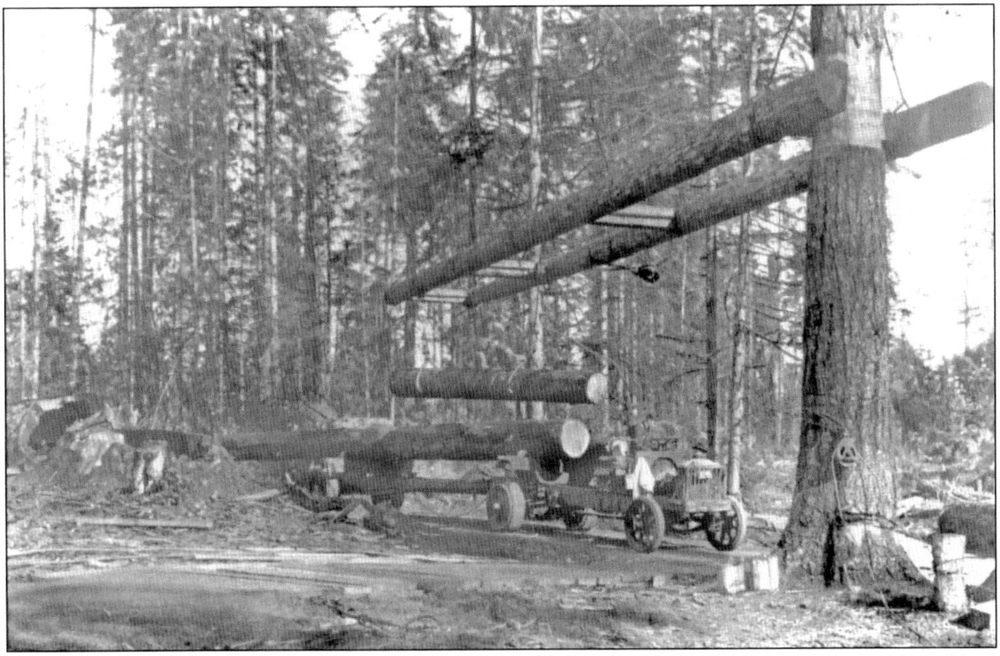

Trucking logs was so much more efficient than yarding them with oxen or horses, but there still remained the problem of loading them. Eventually, high-lead logging became the standard, especially on steep hillsides, but until that technology took hold, several ingenious methods were tried, like this one at the Bruns-McIntyre Logging Company in 1929.

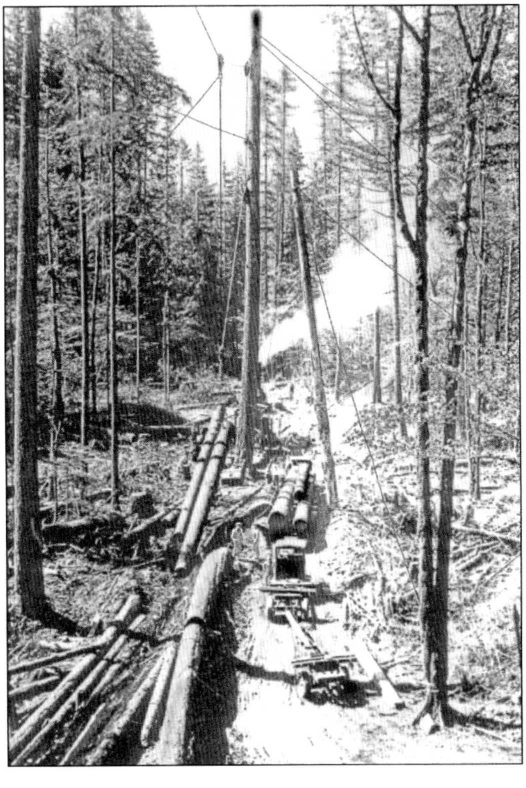

This high-lead logging operation at Marmot, near Sandy, illustrates the technique developed by Oscar Wirkkala in 1904. The method uses two cables and two winches. Winding up the main line pulls the logs in; winding up the haulback pulls out the butt rigging for more logs or another "turn." Elevating the cables assists in pulling the logs free of obstructions on the ground.

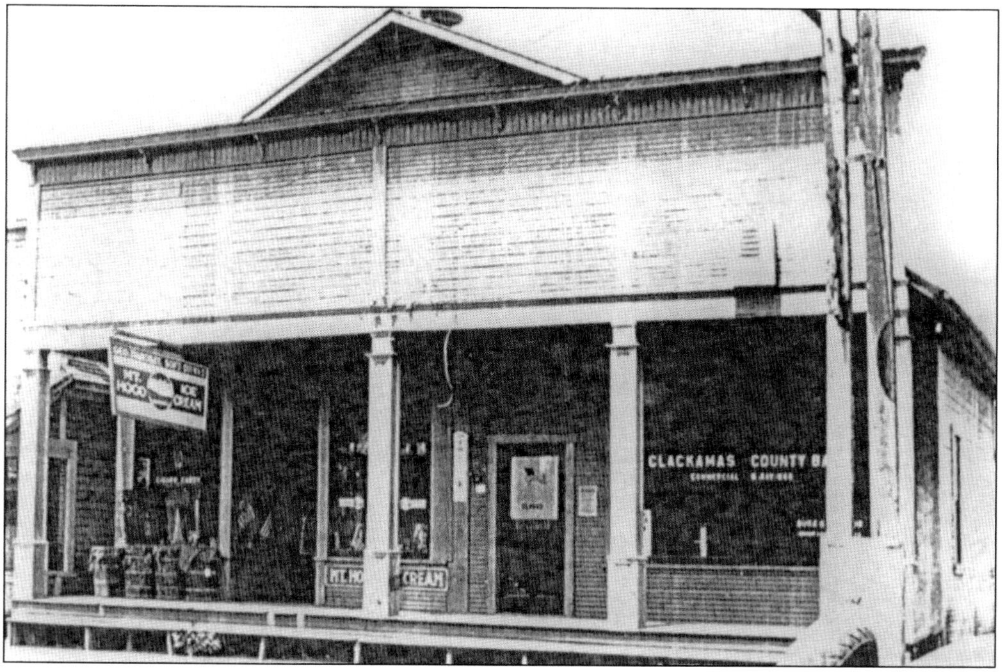

Clackamas County Bank began in a tiny real estate office in 1911. In 1918, Walker A. Proctor bought a controlling interest for $10,000 and erected this building on Main Street, where the Cejka Building now stands. The right half served the bank, and the left half was a rental, housing George Maronay's confectionery and, later, Dr. Walter Noehrens's medical office. (Courtesy of SHS and Phil Jonsrud.)

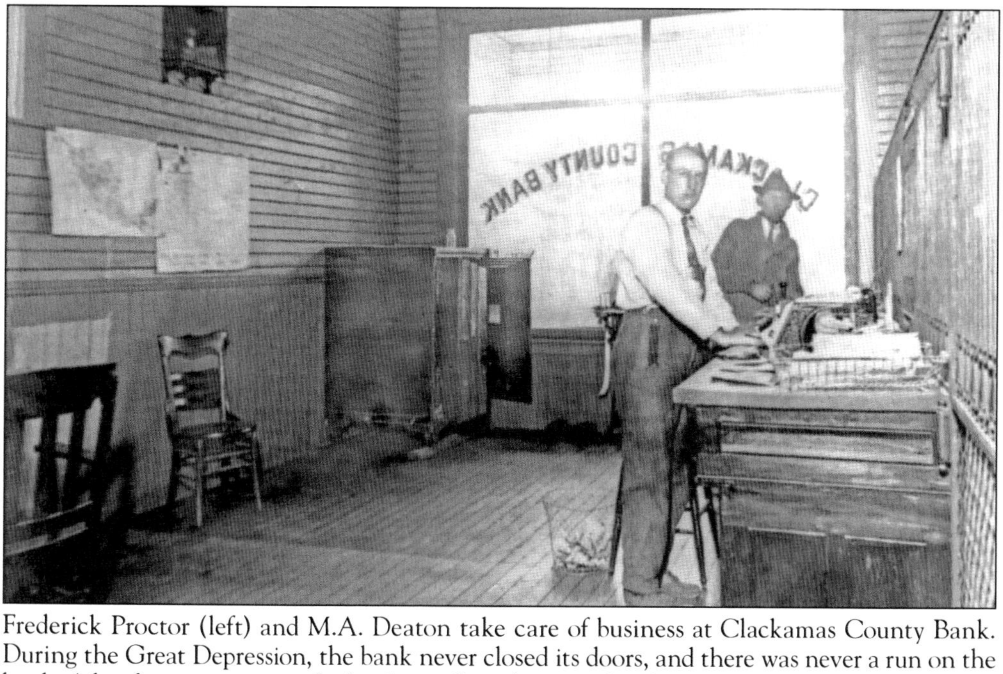

Frederick Proctor (left) and M.A. Deaton take care of business at Clackamas County Bank. During the Great Depression, the bank never closed its doors, and there was never a run on the bank. After five generations, the bank is still in the same family. Proctor's sister Eugenia Proctor Alt was the first woman to be president of any bank in Oregon.

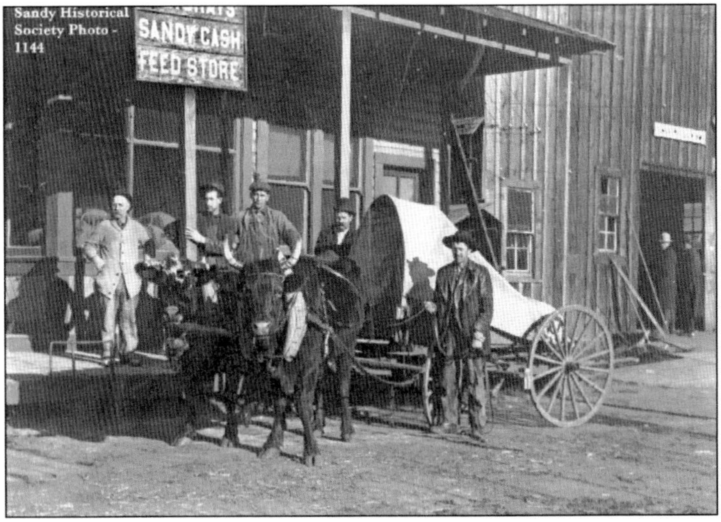

Patrick Gray (far left) stands in front of his feed store, and Frank Zastra (right) holds the reins of his oxen in 1912. The three men in the center are unidentified. Henry Perret's Sandy Carriage Shop is on the right. Gray and his sons were very active in civic affairs, especially the Sandy Booster Band. Gray was one of the first councilmen in the new city of Sandy.

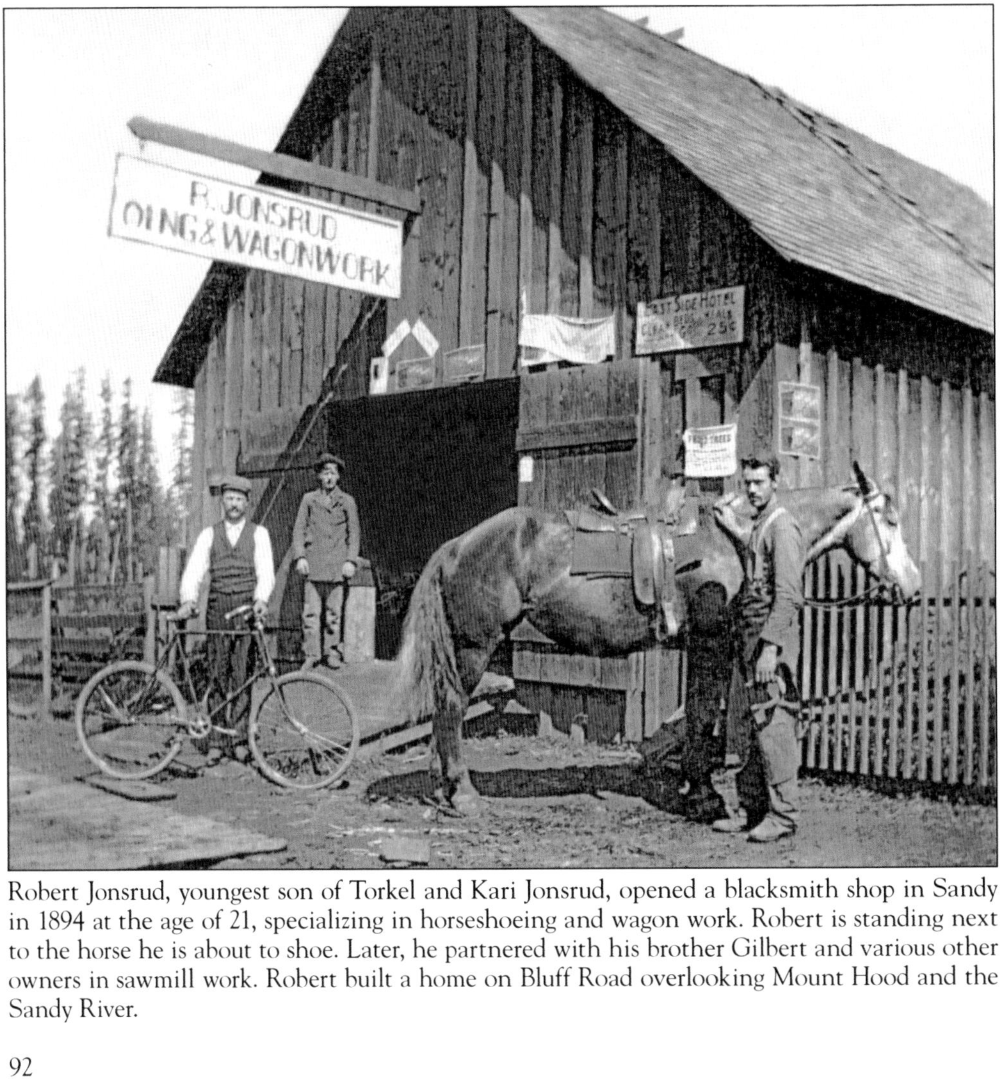

Robert Jonsrud, youngest son of Torkel and Kari Jonsrud, opened a blacksmith shop in Sandy in 1894 at the age of 21, specializing in horseshoeing and wagon work. Robert is standing next to the horse he is about to shoe. Later, he partnered with his brother Gilbert and various other owners in sawmill work. Robert built a home on Bluff Road overlooking Mount Hood and the Sandy River.

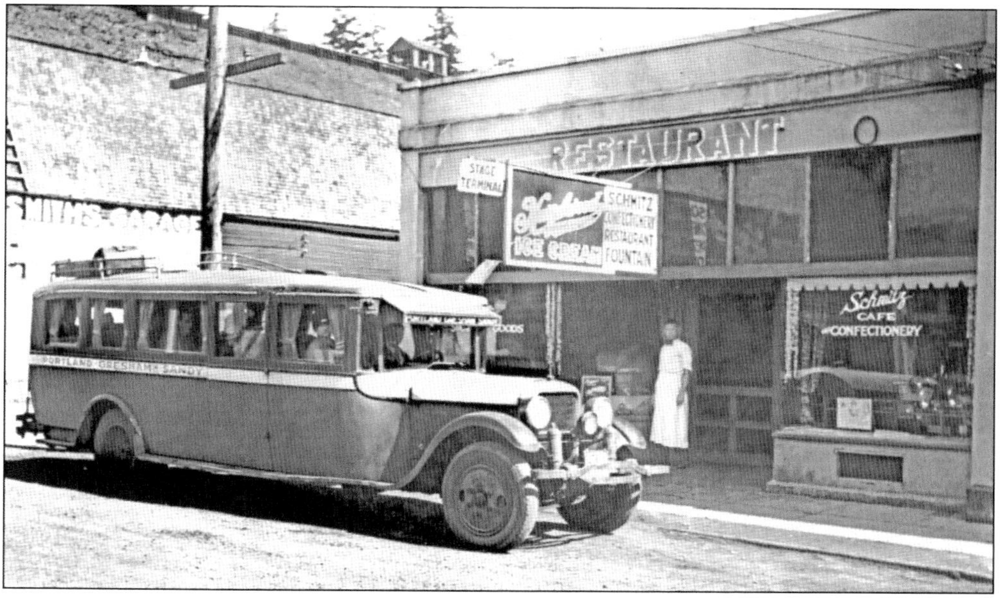

In 1923, Franklin Schmitz stands in front of the café he and his wife, Kate, operated in the Junker Building on Main Street in the 1920s and 1930s. Many who attended local dances would crowd into the Schmitz Café during the midnight intermissions. Parked at the curb is Otto Aschoff's bus, called a stage in those days. (Courtesy of SHS and Kate Schmitz.)

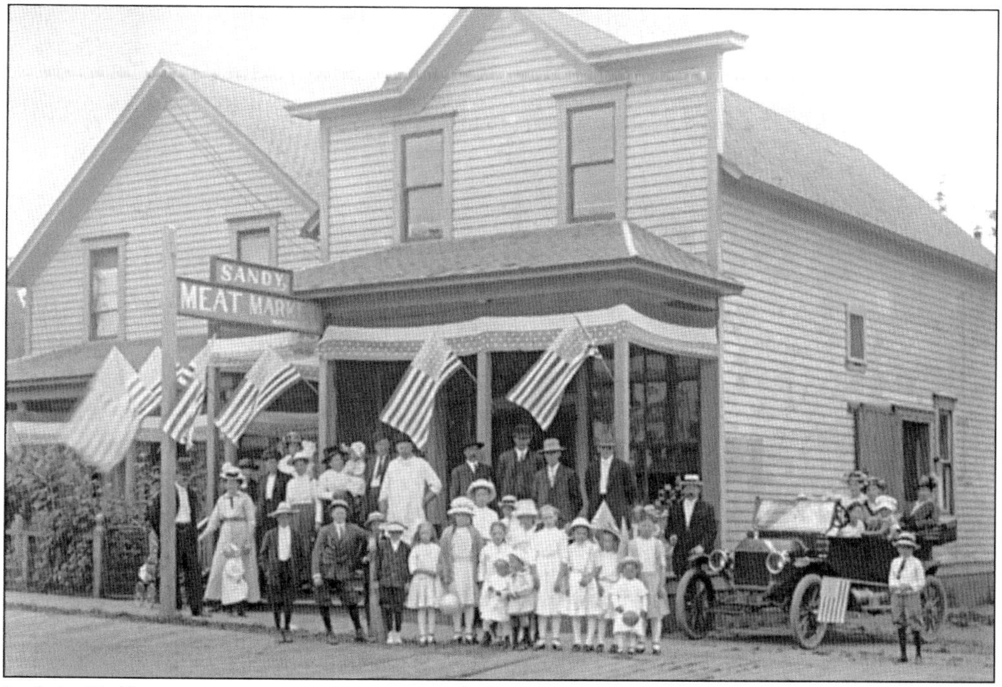

Ludwig Hoffman, a carpenter, came to Sandy from Germany by way of Minnesota in 1907 and built several schools and homes before buying the Sandy Meat Market and erecting an adjoining house, which still stands. His Sandy Market delivered supplies to sawmills, the US Forest Service, and other government projects. He poses here, his left hand on the fender of his automobile, with his family and employees during an Independence Day celebration in 1912.

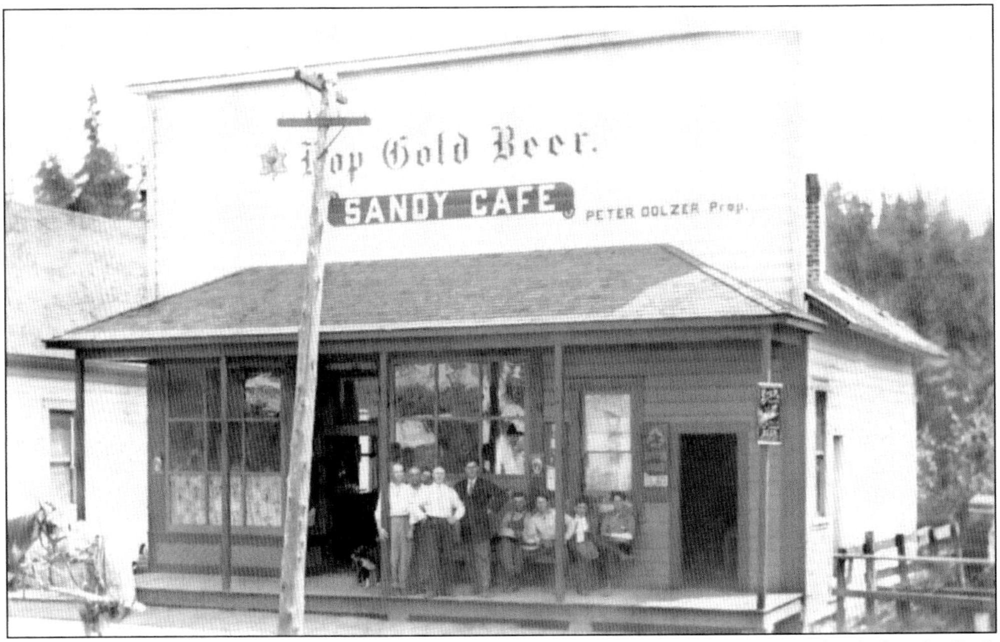

Located where the Junker Building now stands on Pioneer Boulevard, Peter Dolzer's Sandy Cafe was built just after the turn of the century. It burned down in October 1913. Several other buildings on what was then Main Street burned down in one of three devastating fires in the central part of Sandy. (Courtesy of SHS and the Dolzer family.)

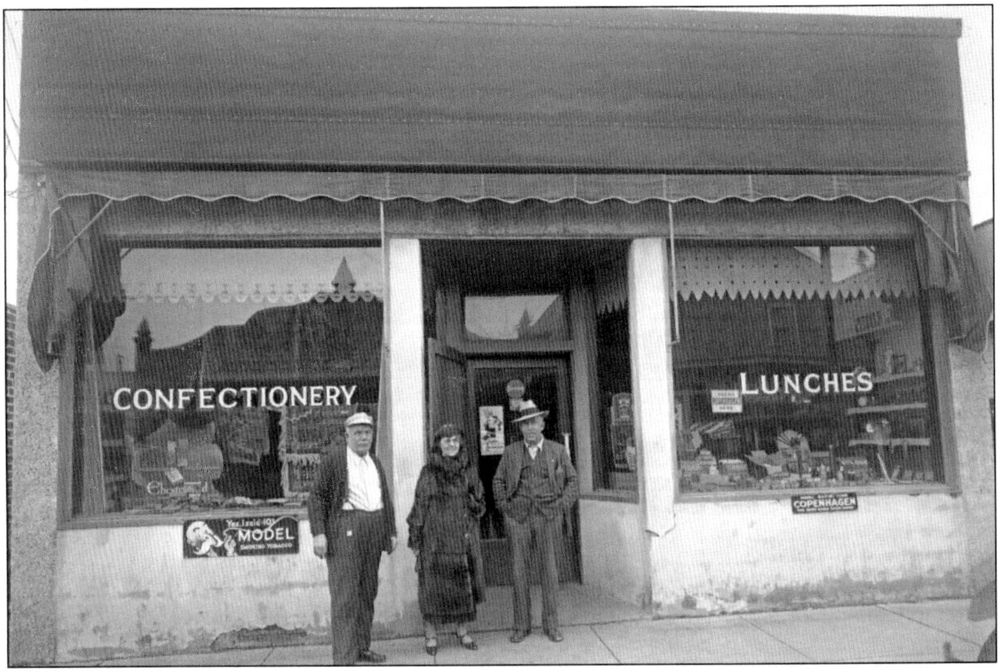

George Maronay (left) stands with his sister Catherine Stewart and an unidentified customer in front of the Sandy Confectionery and Lunch Room, which Maronay operated in the 1920s and 1930s. He had joined the gold rush to the Klondike, but returned in 1898 and helped Elijah Coalman construct the first lookout tower on top of Mount Hood. (Courtesy of SHS and Dennis Gray.)

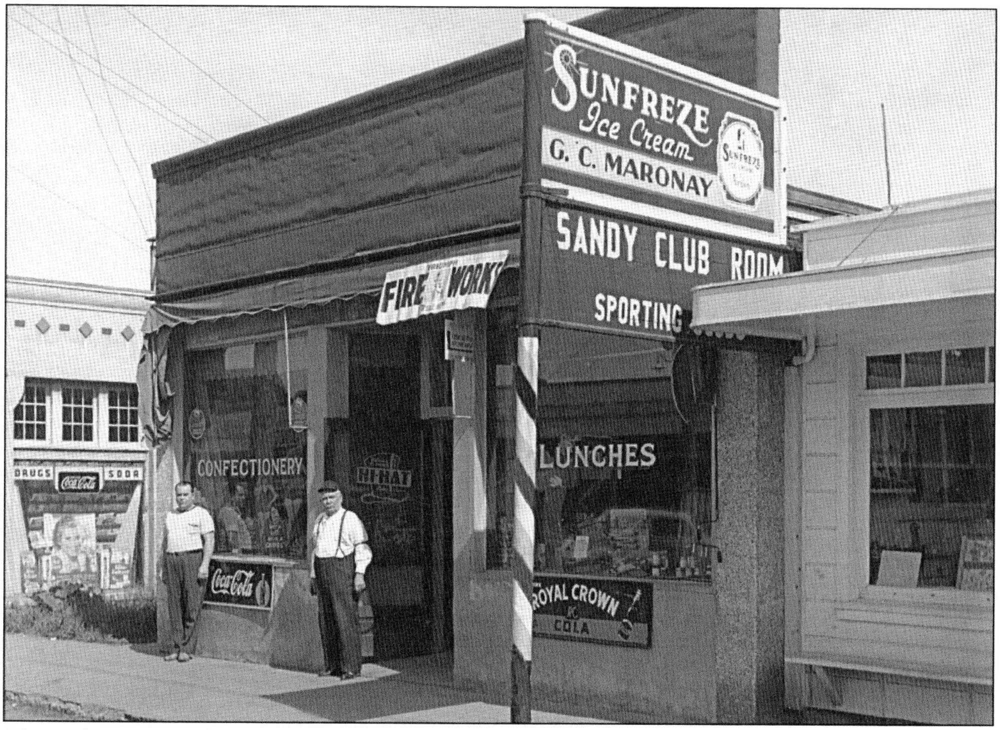

Cleaned up, painted, and refinished, Maronay's confectionery had also become the Sandy Club Room. Ronald Esson's Sandy Drug Store is on the left. A barbershop is on the right in the Frank Christensen home, which also housed a telephone office, and later the Walrad Insurance office. The parking lot between the Double Dragon Restaurant and Ace Hardware has taken the place of the confectionery and the barbershop.

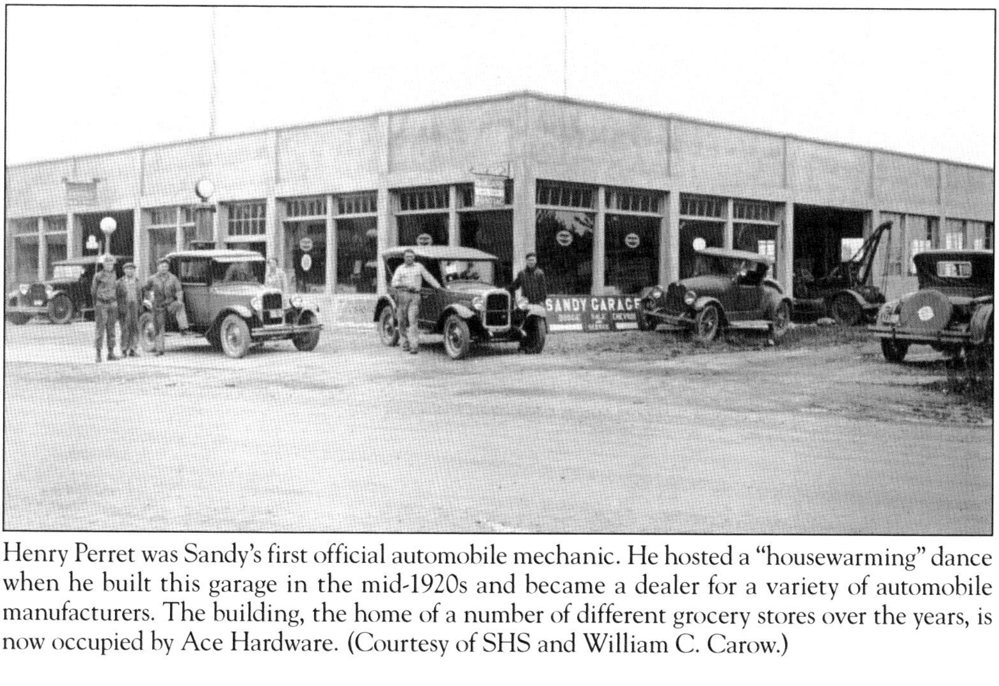

Henry Perret was Sandy's first official automobile mechanic. He hosted a "housewarming" dance when he built this garage in the mid-1920s and became a dealer for a variety of automobile manufacturers. The building, the home of a number of different grocery stores over the years, is now occupied by Ace Hardware. (Courtesy of SHS and William C. Carow.)

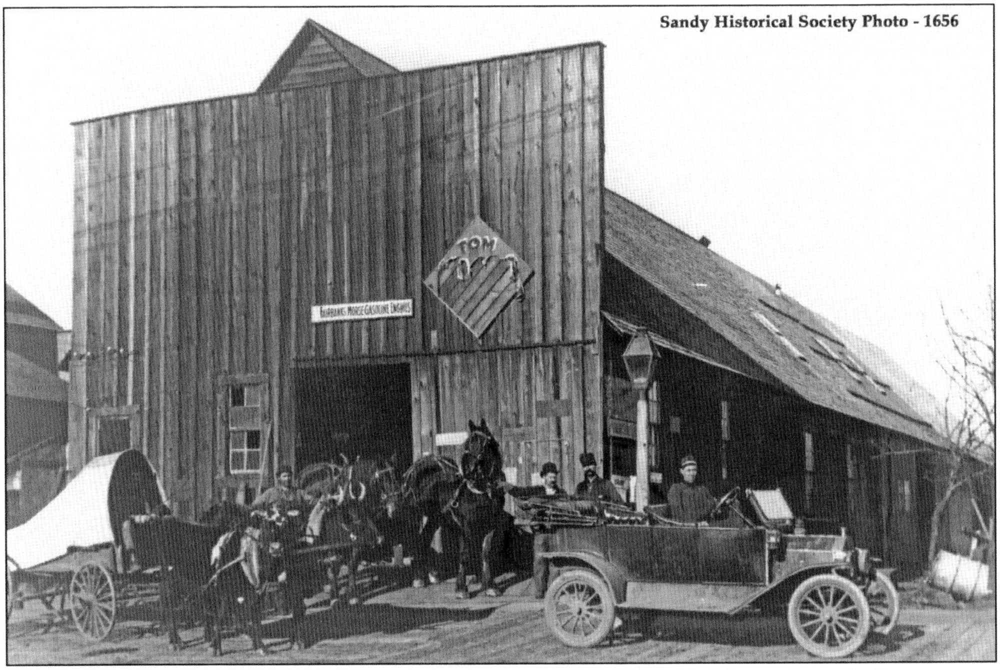

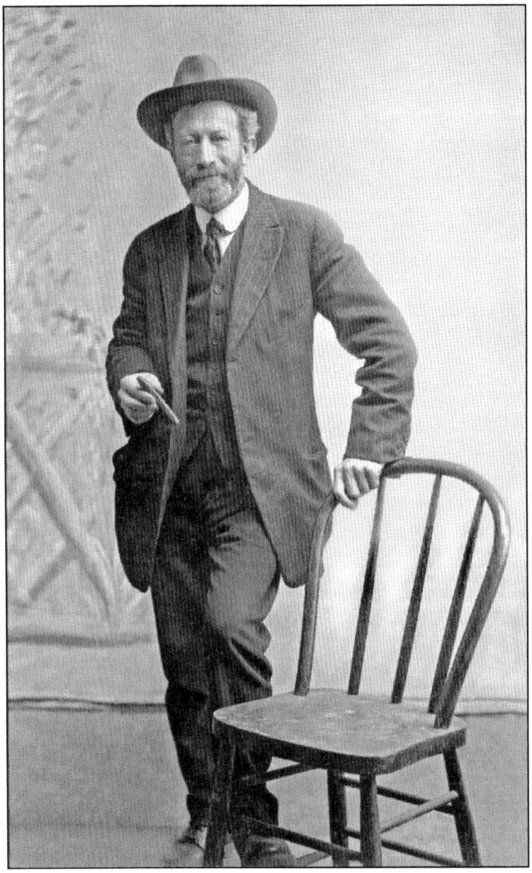

Shown here is Henry Perret's Carriage Shop in 1913; it was later a garage and, still later, an automobile dealership. Perret stands between the oxteam and the horse. His partner, John Bickford, is in the driver's seat of the car, and the two men between them are unidentified. The man in the wagon is Frank Zaster. (Courtesy of SHS and Philip Jonsrud.)

Dr. Alfred Williams, affectionately called "Doc Yak" after a cartoon character of the time, for his love of conversation, was a pharmacist who tried several times to pass the state medical examination. The medical board in 1918 finally granted him a license because of the shortage of doctors. He was known for his success in "curing" influenza symptoms with his white, pink, and black pills.

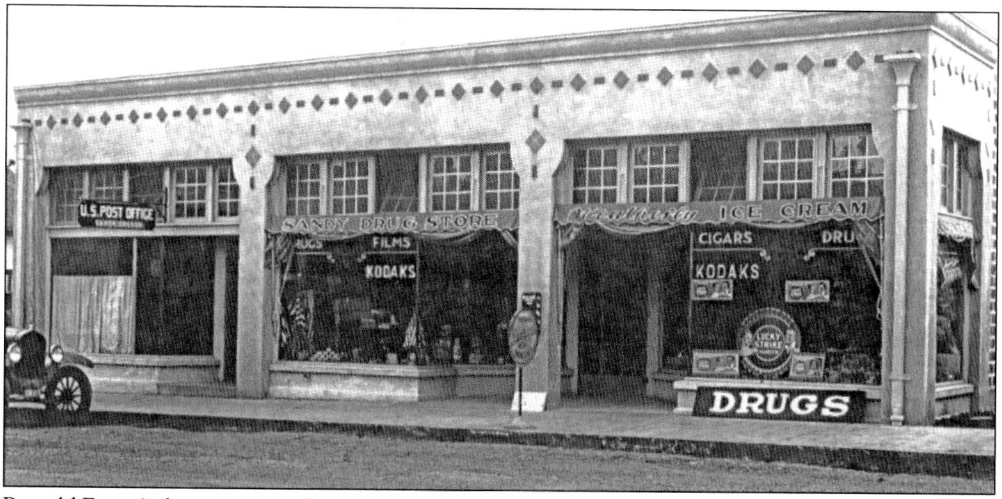

Ronald Esson's drugstore, on the site of Junker's Sandy Hotel, which burned down in 1923, was the center of town in 1924 and continued so when Ivan and Agnes Barker took it over in 1933. The Barkers moved their operation to Proctor Boulevard in the mid-1950s, and this building became Opal's Café for a time. Since 2002, it has been the Double Dragon Chinese Restaurant.

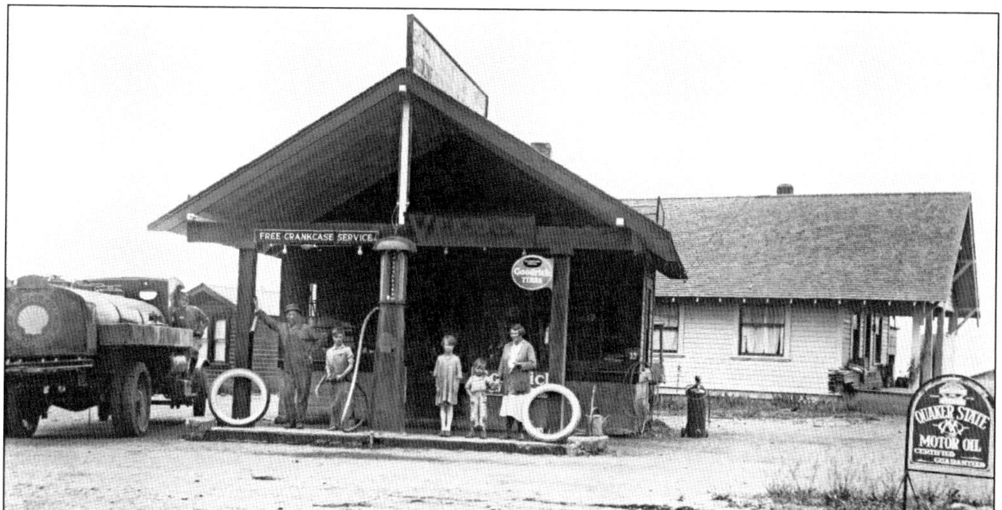

Emil Bittner stands with his family at his service station in 1924. Shown are, from left to right, Emil, Franklin, Myrtle, August, and Myrtle Bittner. Emil was a brother of Franklin and Bill Bittner, who operated the Bittner Plug Mill. Bittner's home is in the background. The service station faced Main Street and is the site of the Arco station at the east end of town.

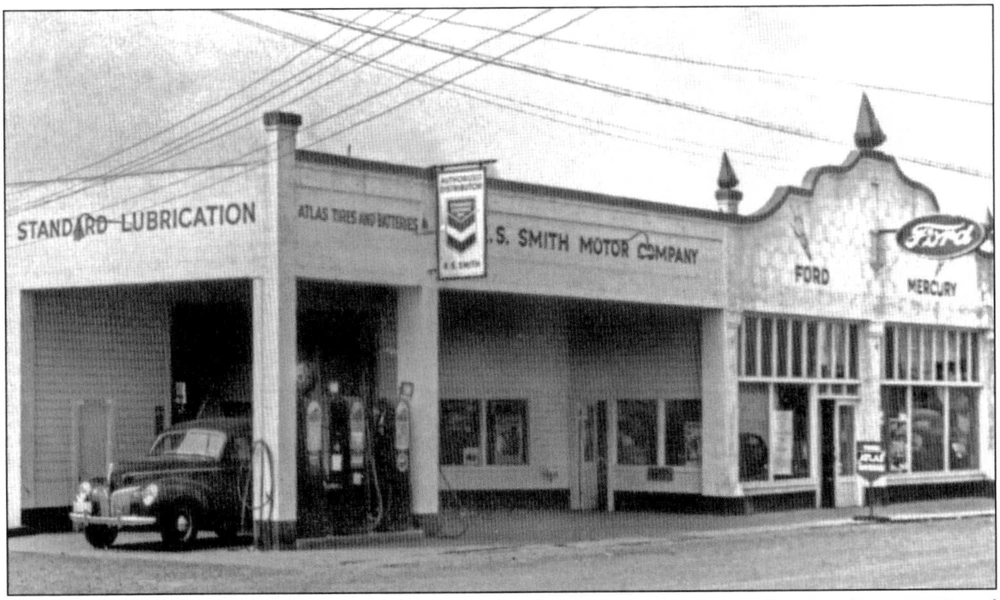

Robert Smith first owned a blacksmith shop in nearby Boring, then moved to Sandy in 1909 and graduated to automobile repair and sales. He erected this concrete building on the site of his old garage in 1935, at the corner of Main Street and Highway 211. It has seen use as an antiques store, a bicycle shop, and a secondhand store. (Courtesy of SHS and the Smith family.)

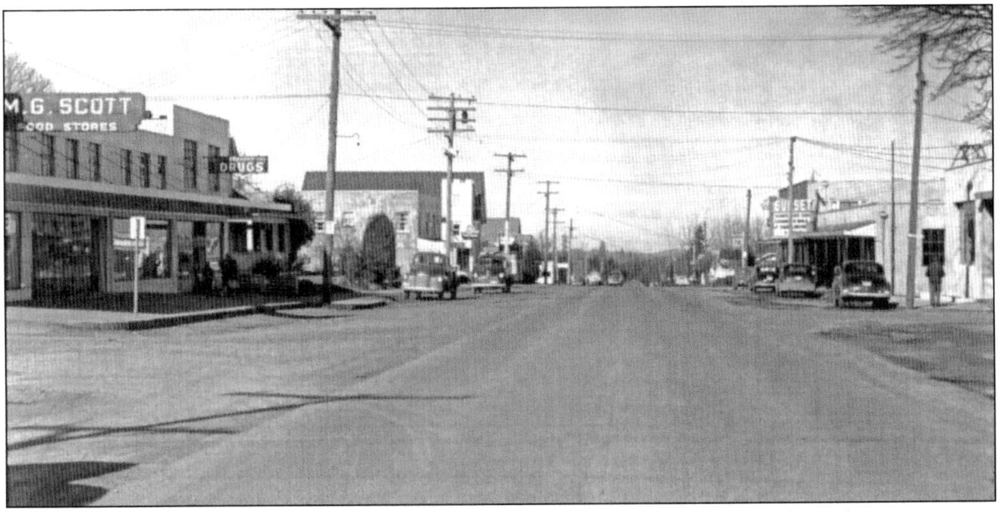

The west-facing view in this photograph of Sandy in the mid-1950s was taken from the intersection of Proctor Boulevard and Shelley Avenue. In the left foreground is M.G. Scott's Food Store, now the site of the new Sandy City Library. Ivan Barker had Economy Drugs in a portion of Scott's store. In the right foreground is a portion of the new Clackamas County Bank Building, and beyond it is the Sunset Theater.

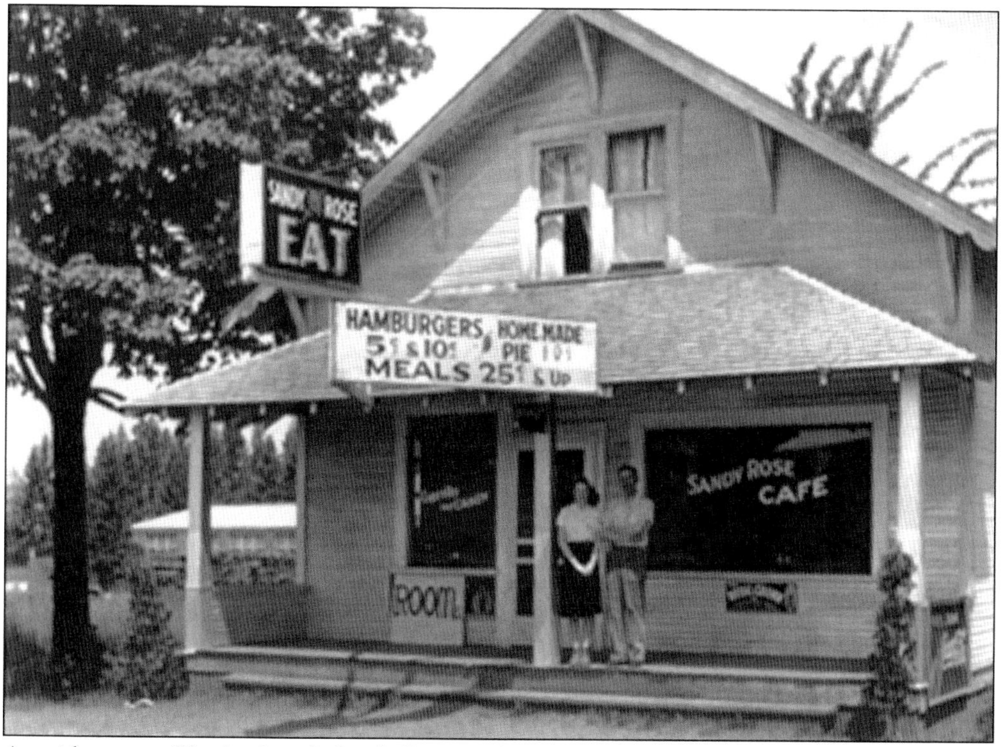

At midcentury, Charles Lane's Sandy Rose Café, on Pleasant Street, one block off the Mount Hood Highway, was a homey place to get wholesome food. In the background is Sandy Grade School, built in 1931 on land donated by John Strauss. The café building has been moved around the corner and down the street and converted into a private home. (Courtesy of SHS and Dennis Gray.)

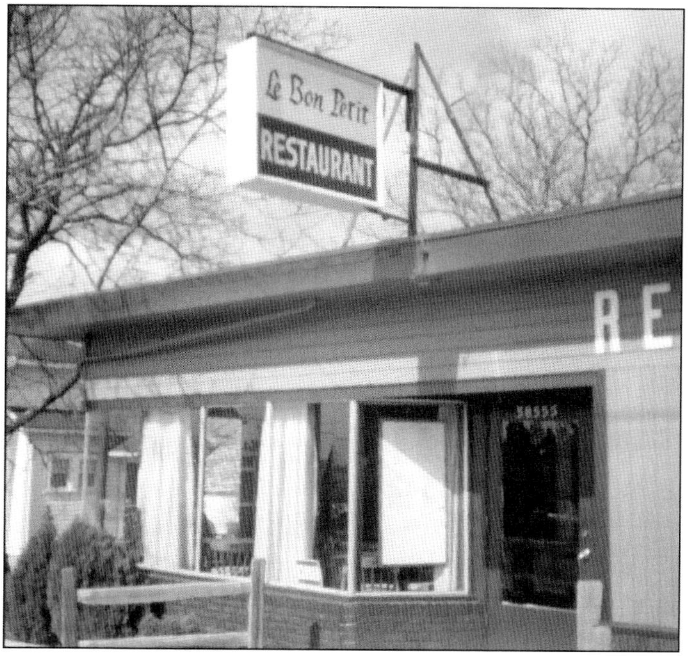

Le Bon Petit restaurant on Proctor Boulevard had been the office of the Sandy Truck Line, then Mount Hood Delicatessen, then the Elusive Trout Pub. Today, it is simply the Trout. It has always been a popular, distinctive, and somewhat eccentric place to dine. When it was the Elusive Trout, the owners regularly posted an exotic "word of the week" for patrons to try to define.

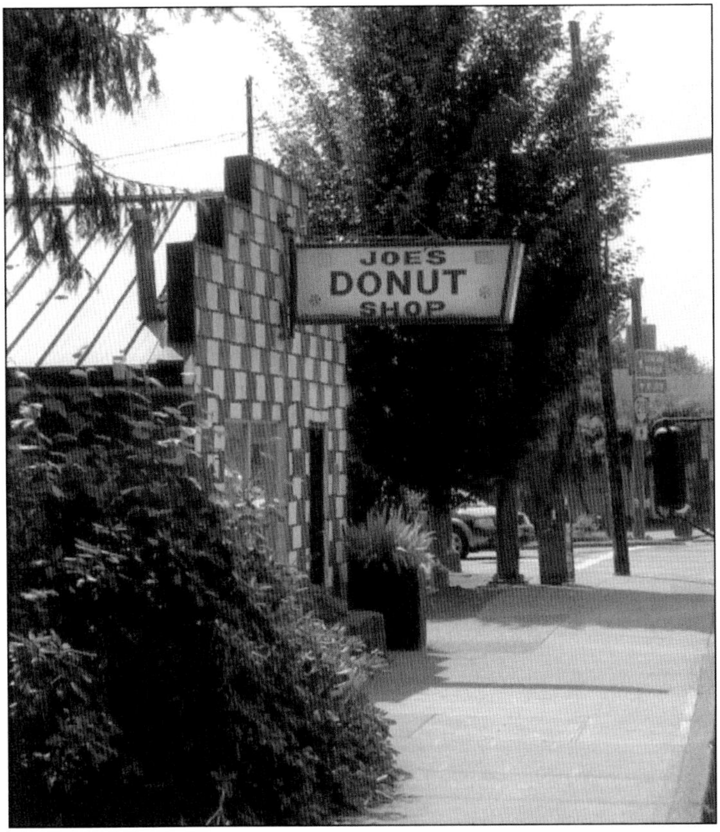

"Nationally acclaimed" Joe's Donuts has only been at the corner of Pioneer Boulevard and Highway 211, next to Sandy City Hall, since 1974, but it has quickly become a Sandy landmark and sensation, popular all the way from Portland to Mount Hood. An extra attraction is the knowledge that thousands of pioneer wagons rolled over this very spot on the Barlow Road portion of the Oregon Trail.

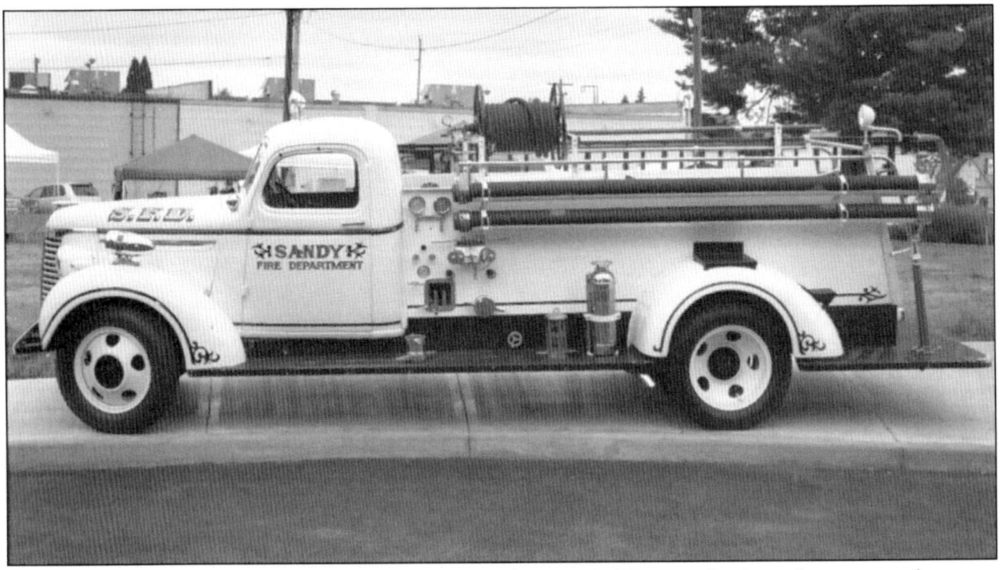

The Sandy Rural Fire Commission was organized in 1940. The city budgeted money to buy one fire truck, but restricted its use to fires within the city limits. Volunteers raised $500 at fundraising events and bought a 1941 Ford chassis and built the body themselves to specifications. This fire truck is kept in pristine condition and is used to show how far the Sandy Fire Department has come.

Eight

Sandy Pioneer Association

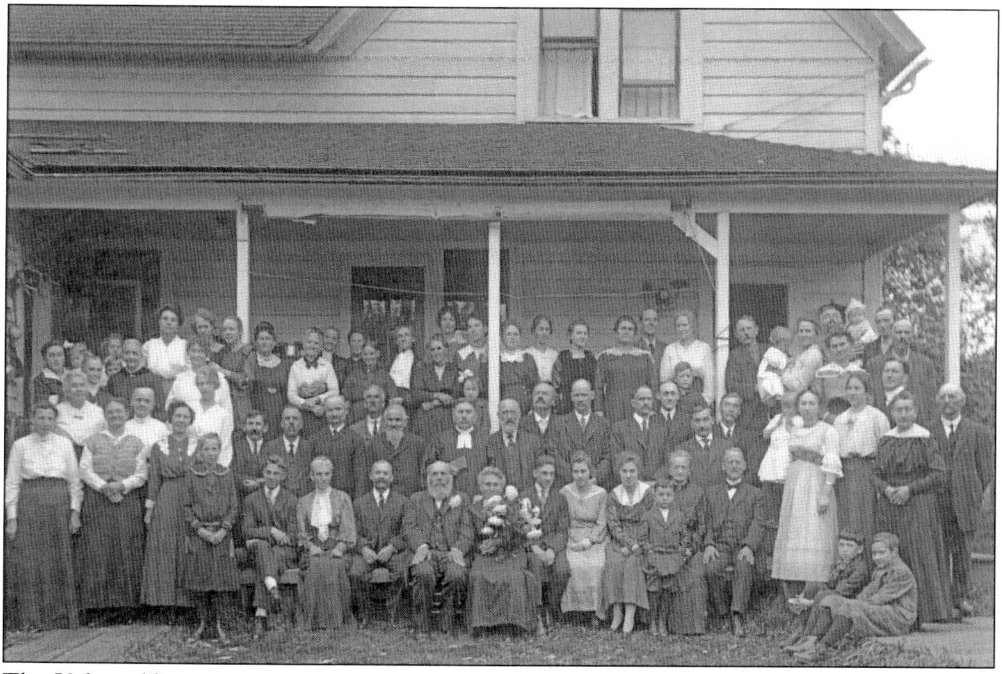

The 50th wedding anniversary of Mr. and Mrs. Henry Koch was celebrated in 1916 at the Caspar Junker home in Sandy. Represented are many time-honored families of Sandy: Revenue, Meinig, Aschoff, Krebs, Lundeen, Gray, Sharnke, Wewer, Fischer, Beers, Perret, Scales, Schmitz, Dittert, Lohrman, and Kubitz. Nearly everyone in this photograph has a street or section of town named for them.

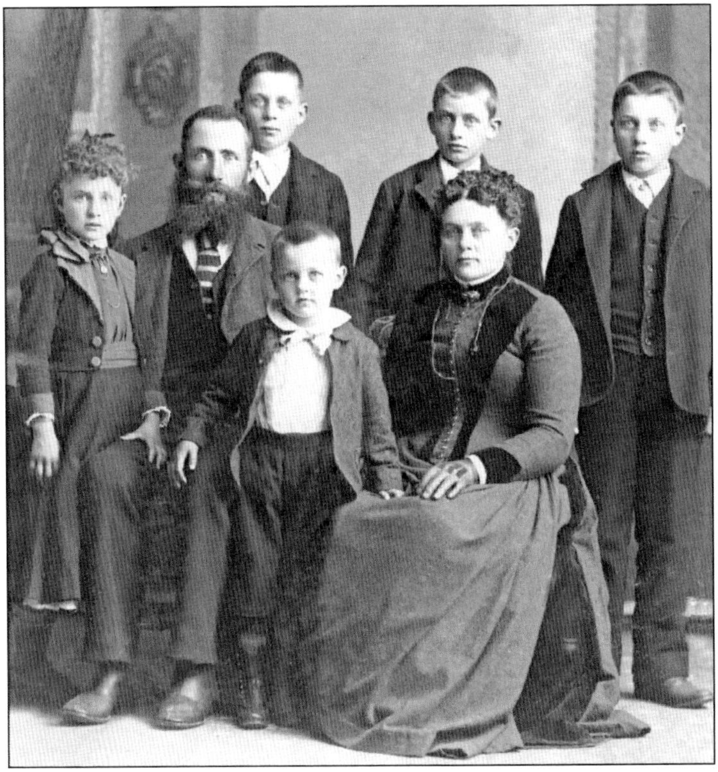

Nels and Hannah Johanson Nelson came from Sweden, met and married in Portland, and settled between Sandy and Kelso. Posing here are, from left to right, (first row) Anne, Nels, Milton, and Hannah; (second row) John, Be, and Ned. Nels was instrumental in building schools and roads. Be grew up and donated the land for the Sandy Pioneer Park, a prime factor in creating the Sandy Historical Museum. (Courtesy of Dennis Gray.)

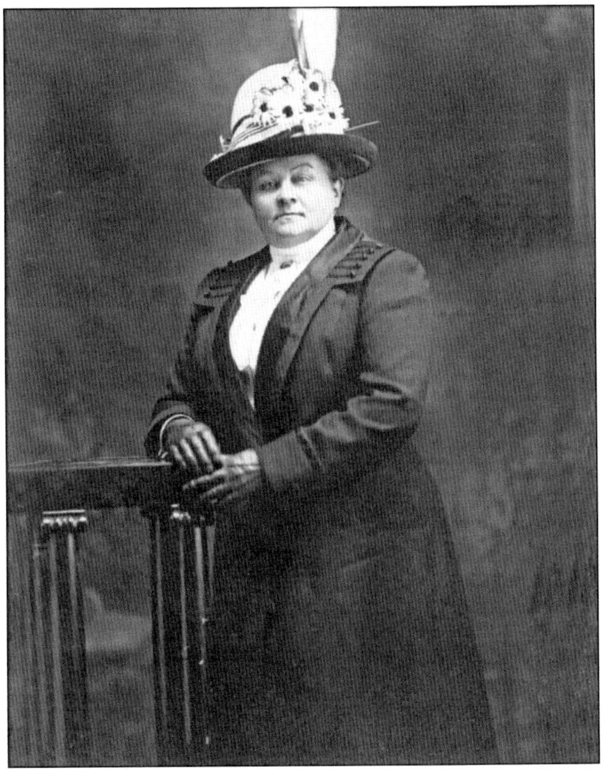

Hannah Nelson and her husband, Nels, settled in Kelso in 1876. She was said to have pulled a saw like her husband and often had to feel her way to the barn in the dark to milk, when the cows returned late. One of her sons was Be Nelson, who lived on the farm for 80 years and was a founder of the Sandy Pioneer Association.

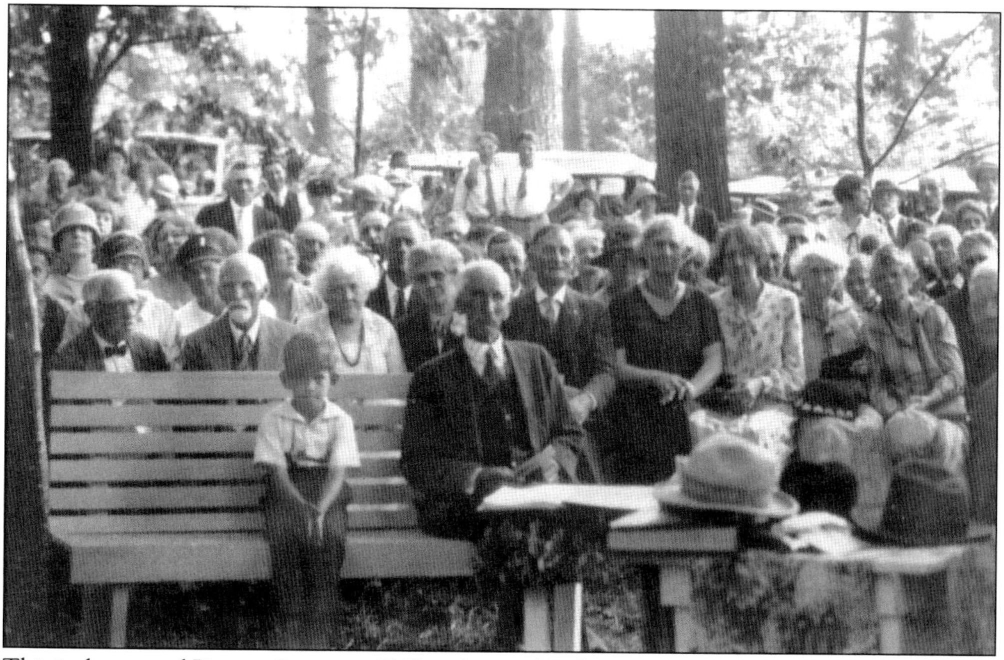

This is the second Pioneer Picnic, in 1927, in Jonsrud Park. Seated in front is seven-year-old Joseph Shelley, who would become president of the Sandy Historical Society in 2001 and a major donor to the building fund. Next to him is John Revenue, eldest son of Francis Revenue and the first president of the forerunner of the present historical society. (Courtesy of SHS and Joe Shelley.)

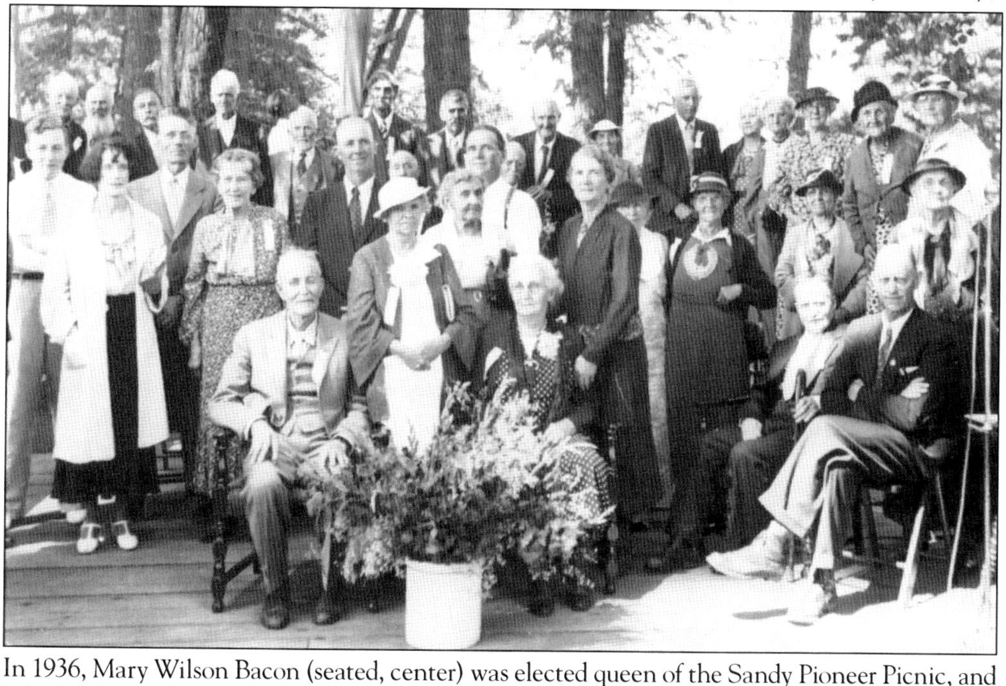

In 1936, Mary Wilson Bacon (seated, center) was elected queen of the Sandy Pioneer Picnic, and John McIntyre (seated, left) was named king. Mary Wilson was born in 1863 to pioneer parents and married Samuel Bacon in 1876. McIntyre and his wife, Winifred, ran a store, a post office, and a hotel east of Sandy for many years. (Courtesy of Jean Rolli.)

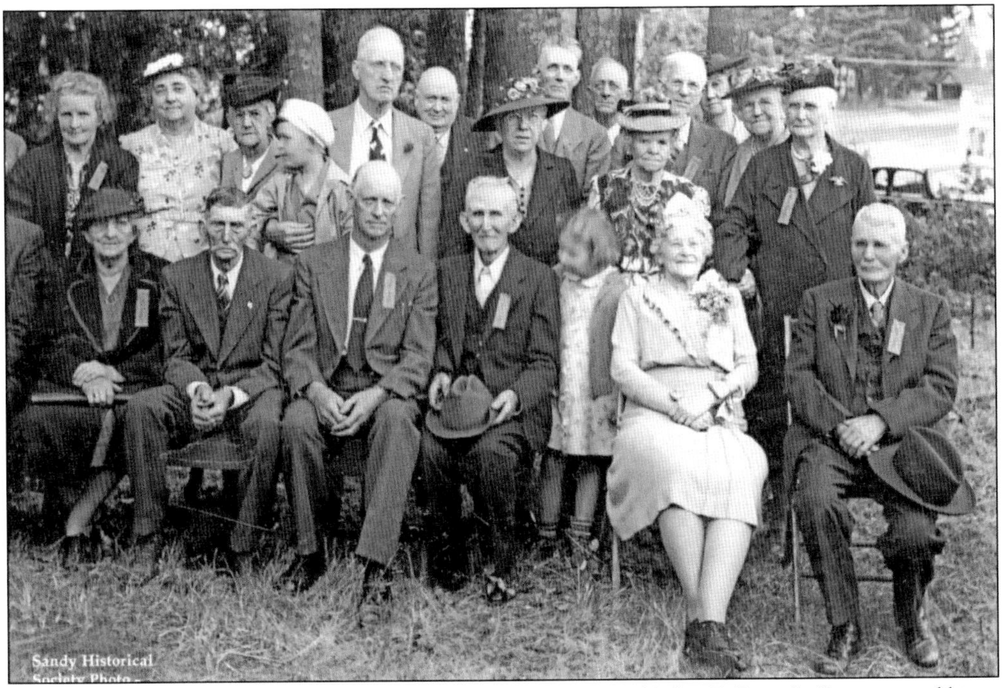

The Sandy Pioneer Association elected Eva Sleret Idleman and John E. Bramhall queen and king, respectively, of the 1944 Pioneer Picnic. They are shown seated at the right in this photograph. Charles and Eva Idleman came to Sandy in 1901 and bought the old Revenue store and later operated a secondhand store. Bramhall homesteaded at Aims, north of Sandy, and was postmaster there for a while.

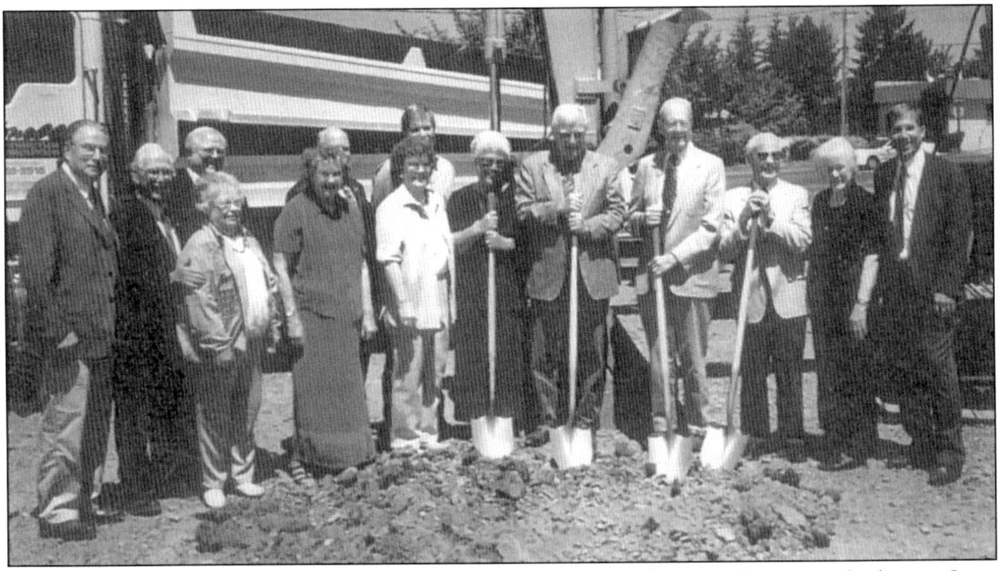

Ground breaking for the Sandy Historical Society Museum and Visitor Center took place in June 2004, after an arduous fundraising effort and generous donations from Joseph Shelley and Victor Bacon, among others. Holding the shovels are, from left to right, Dorothy Douglas, Jerry Lawson, Philip Jonsrud, and Joseph Shelley. Both Douglas and Lawson have held the office of president of the board of directors of the society.

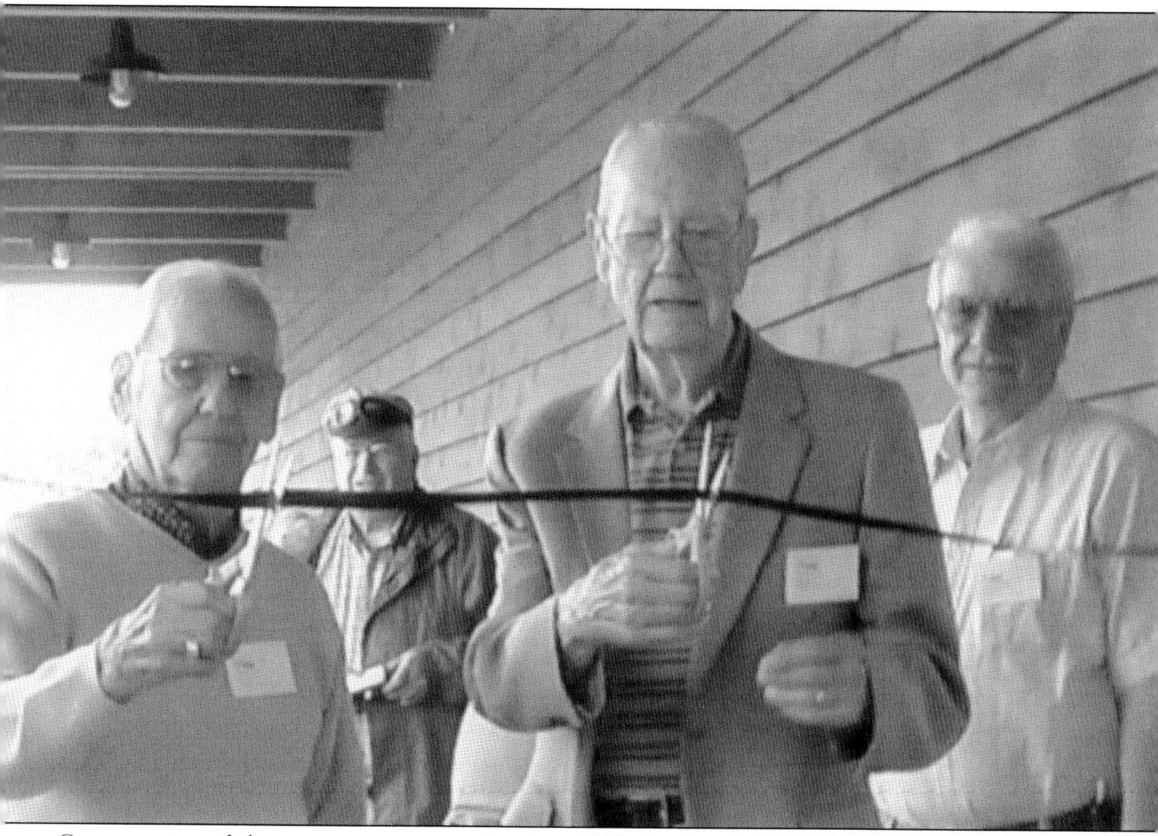

Construction of the museum was completed in 2007. On hand to cut the ribbon are Joseph Shelley (left) and Philip Jonsrud. Looking on are Jerry Lawson (far right) and local postal historian William White (rear). The museum is conveniently located between the two one-way routes through town, almost exactly where the pioneers would have reached the top of Meinig Hill on the Barlow Road.

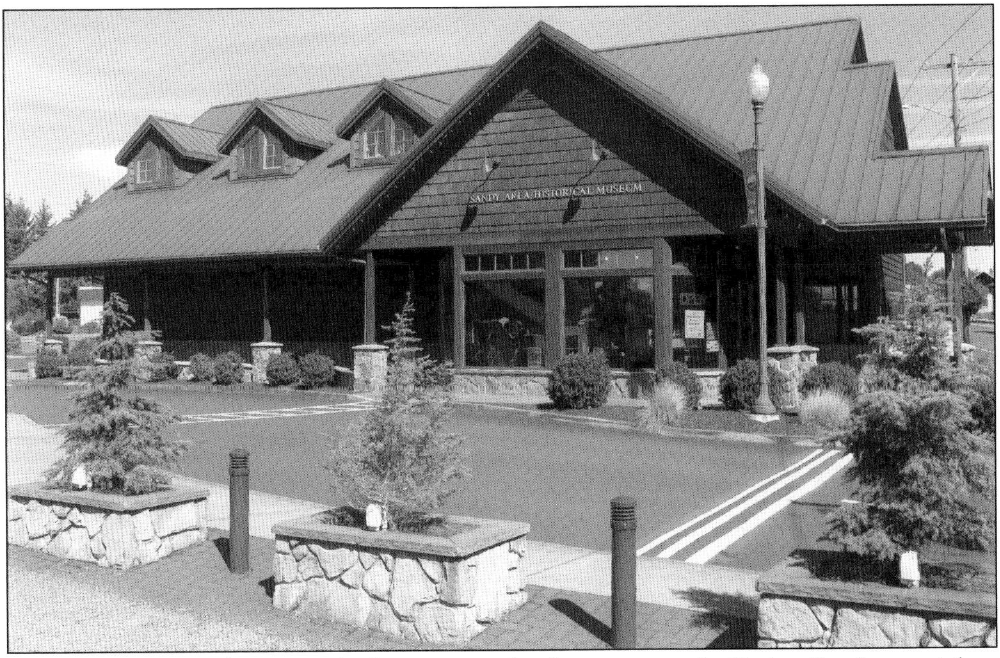

The Sandy Historical Museum displays maps and information on the Barlow Road, material on the founding Revenue family and others, and a historical display of the logging industry from the 1800s. Volunteers have created life-sized dioramas of pioneer homes, a blacksmith shop, and an early community bank. A historical library is available for research or enjoyment, and artifacts are on display. (Courtesy of Kenneth Funk.)

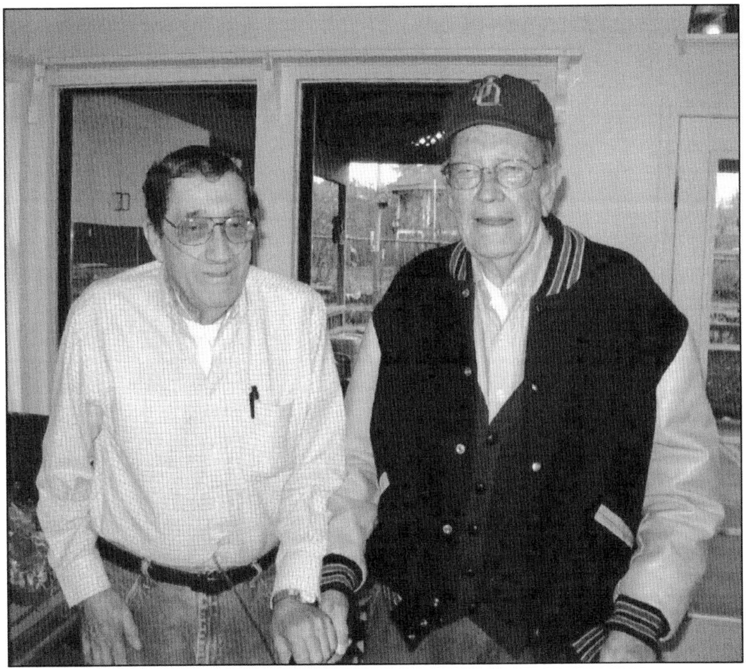

Without the tireless volunteer efforts of Dennis Gray (left) and Philip Jonsrud, who devoted their retirement years to preserving Sandy's history in literature, artifacts, and digitized photographs, this publication—and indeed the Sandy Historical Society—would not have been possible. Their recent passing is deeply regretted by the community. (Courtesy of Kenneth Funk.)

Nine

Celebrations, Parades, and Festivals

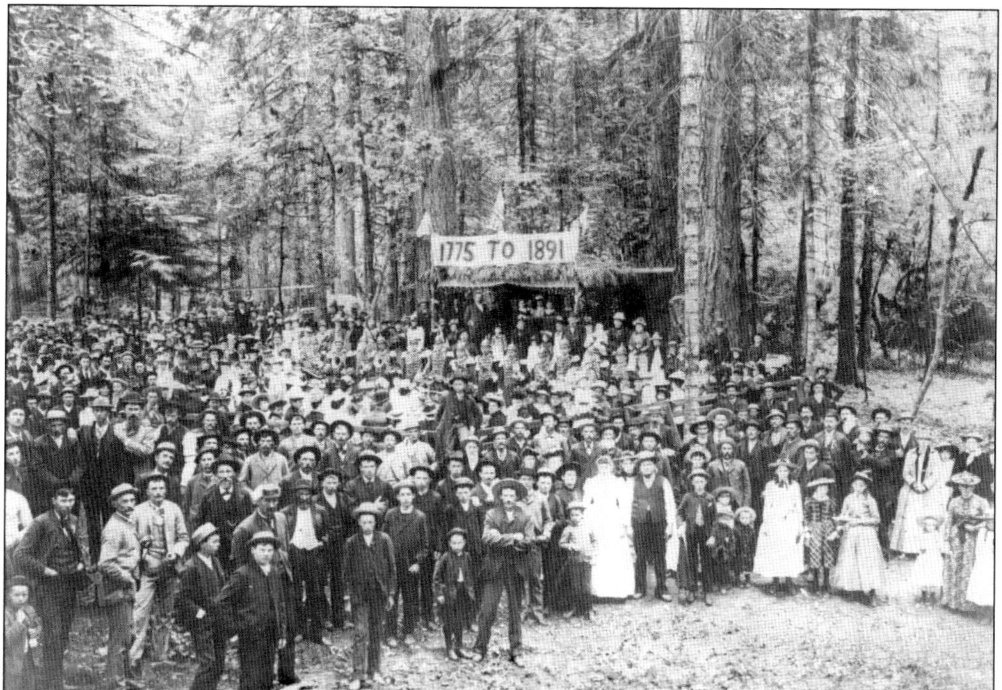

Pioneer life was hard, even as the 20th century dawned, and opportunities to gather and celebrate were welcomed by all. Rarely did this many citizens get together for one clear purpose. But what better occasion than the anniversary of the nation's birth? Sandy citizens in Meinig Park in 1907 went all-out to commemorate the signing of the Declaration of Independence.

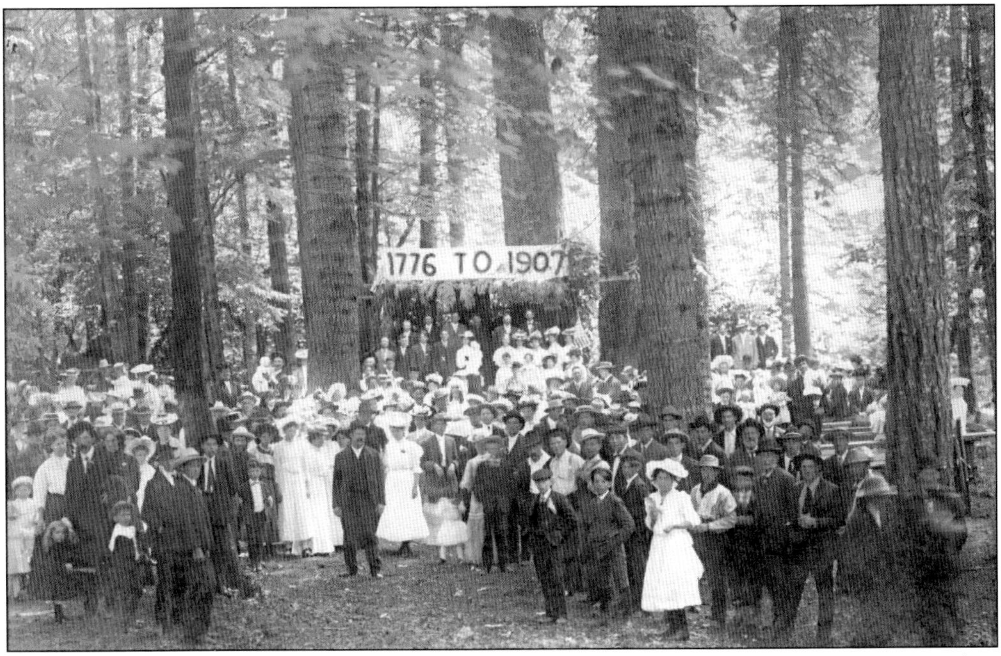

Perhaps this sort of gathering took place every year on Independence Day in Sandy. Few attendees can be identified, but Philip Jonsrud states that, in the next-to-last row on the platform, fourth from left, are his father, Robert Jonsrud, and then Philip's wife, Mathilde, holding their daughter Dorothy. Daughter Eunice stands in front of them. (Courtesy of Kate Schmitz.)

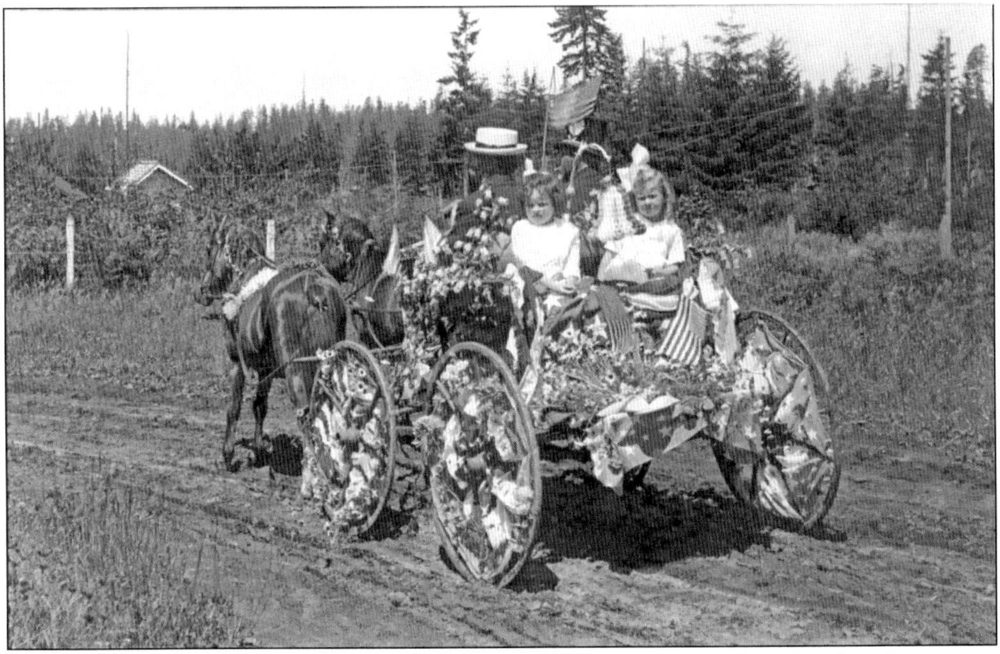

These two delightful little girls are headed to a parade. They are not identified, but they are on their way to Sandy on Independence Day. Traditions add rhythm and texture to people's lives, bind people together, give them something to look forward to, and simply provide a good deal of joy and satisfaction. (Courtesy of Kate Schmitz.)

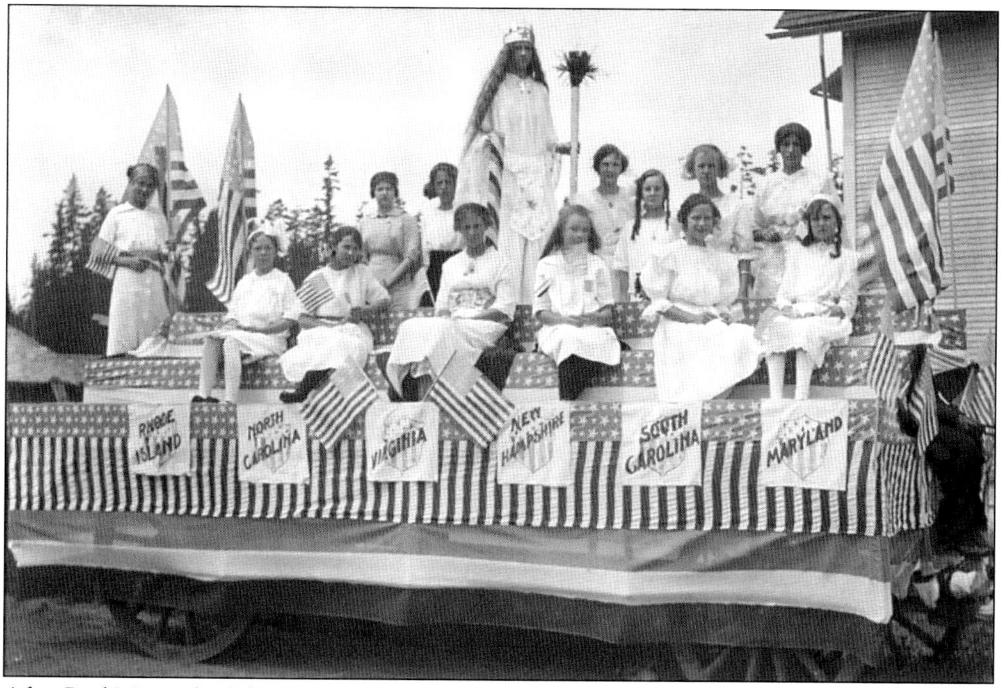

After Paul Meinig built his new store on Main Street and became the largest merchant in Sandy, he took the lead in organizing the parade every year, and there was a contest to see who could mount the most spectacular float. Here, Phyllis Matz is the reigning queen of the Independence Day Court. (Courtesy of Phyllis Matz.)

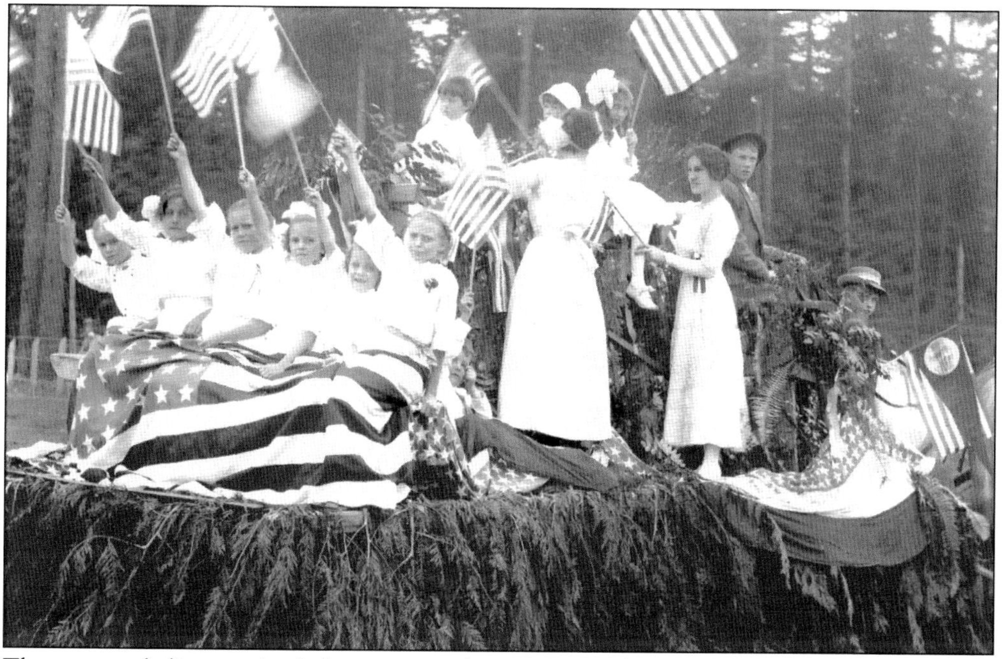

These young ladies are clearly having a good time waving their American flags for the camera. Patriotism ran high in these heady days just before the United States entered World War I. Kate (Junker) Schmitz is the lady standing at right. (Courtesy of Kate Junker Schmitz.)

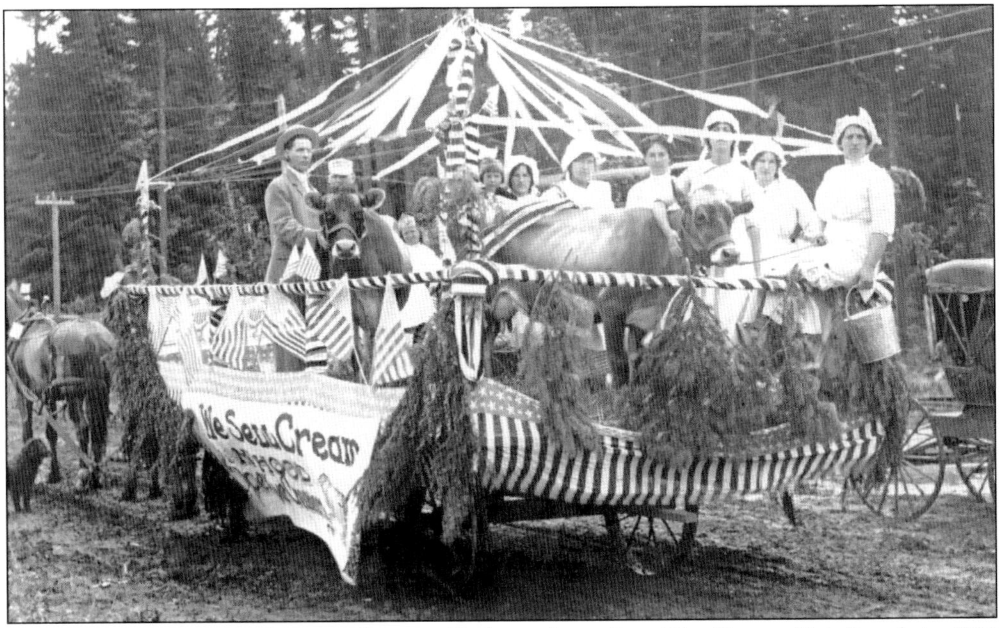

Not every parade in Sandy was in honor of Independence Day. The Grange Fair Parade in 1916 featured Willard Bosholm's Jersey cows. Willard's wife, Sadie, holds the milk pail, while other Grange members steady the cows. Jerseys, a small breed, are known for the high butterfat content of their milk and the lower maintenance costs attending their lower bodyweight. (Courtesy of Dean Gray.)

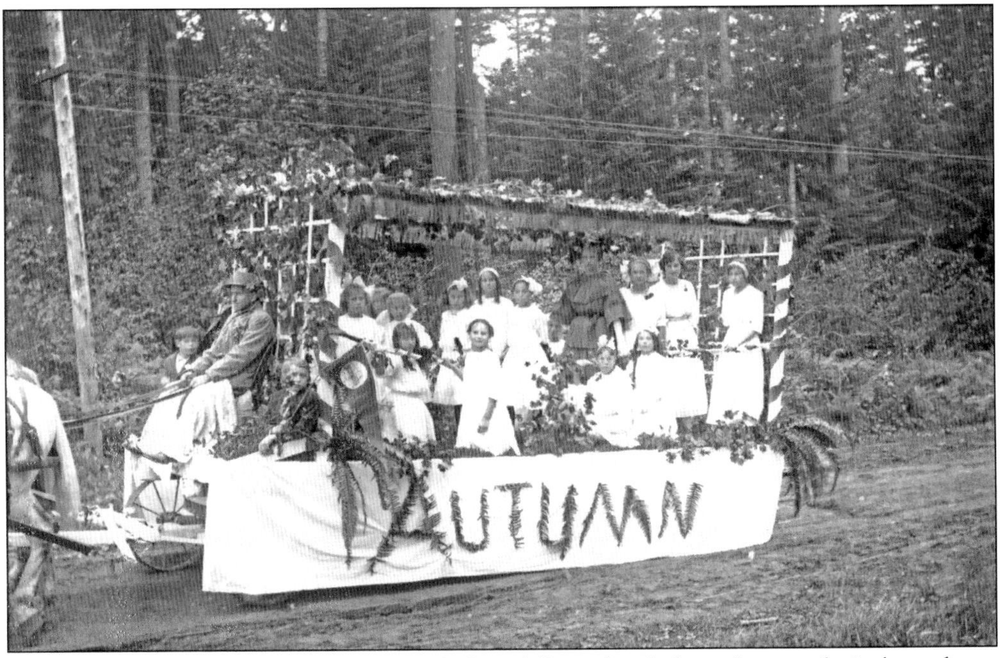

These young ladies are on their way to Sandy for a different kind of parade—not for Independence Day or the Grange, but simply to celebrate the season. Even today, Sandy has a massive Oktoberfest celebration in the first week of September. Just down the freeway, Boring has its Celebration in Boring on the same day in September. (Courtesy of Kate Junker Schmitz.)

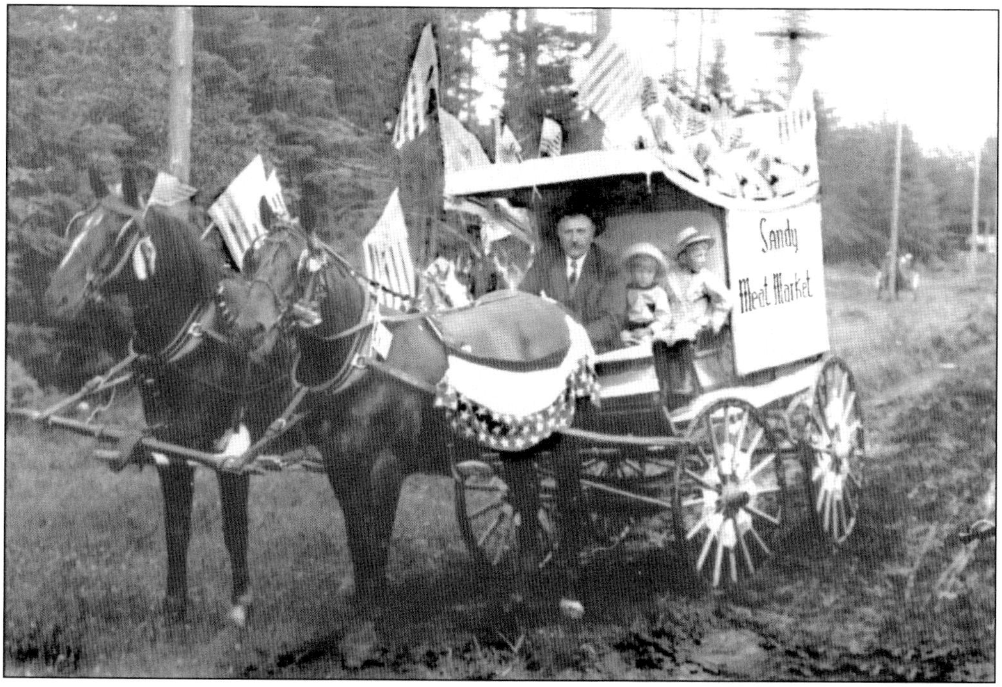

Not quite as flamboyant as the Meinig brothers, Ludwig Hoffman nevertheless made his mark in the 1912 Independence Day parade. Like the Meinigs, members of the Hoffman family have figured prominently in Sandy's civic affairs, serving often as mayors and city councilmen. Ludwig was a trustee in 1907 at the formal organization of Immanuel Lutheran Church. (Courtesy of Phil Jonsrud.)

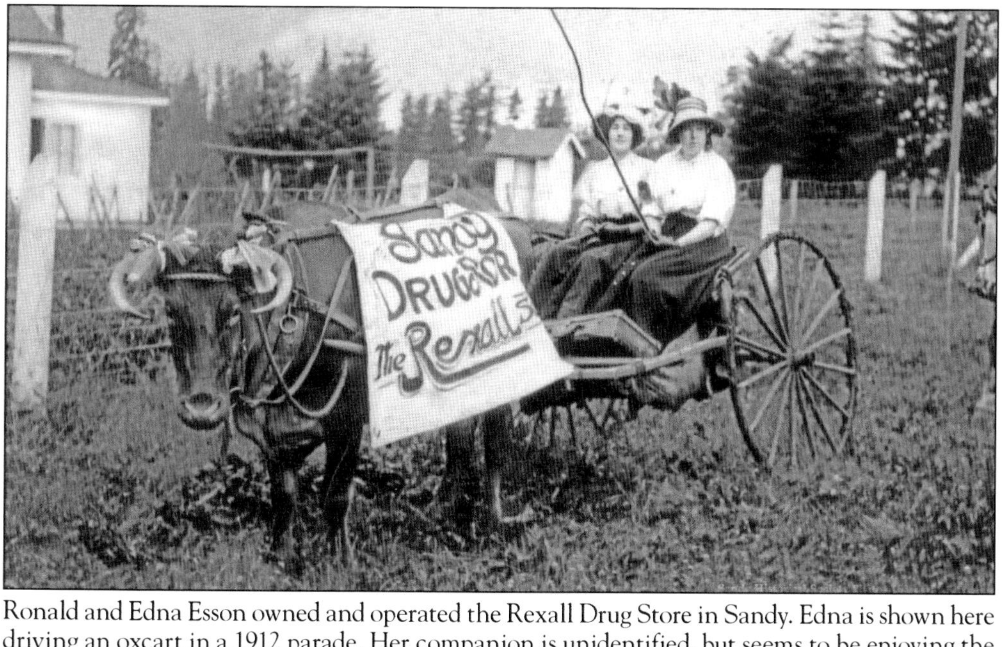

Ronald and Edna Esson owned and operated the Rexall Drug Store in Sandy. Edna is shown here driving an oxcart in a 1912 parade. Her companion is unidentified, but seems to be enjoying the ride. Esson's drugstore was on Main Street (now Pioneer Boulevard). By mid-century, they owned another one on Proctor Boulevard, two blocks away.

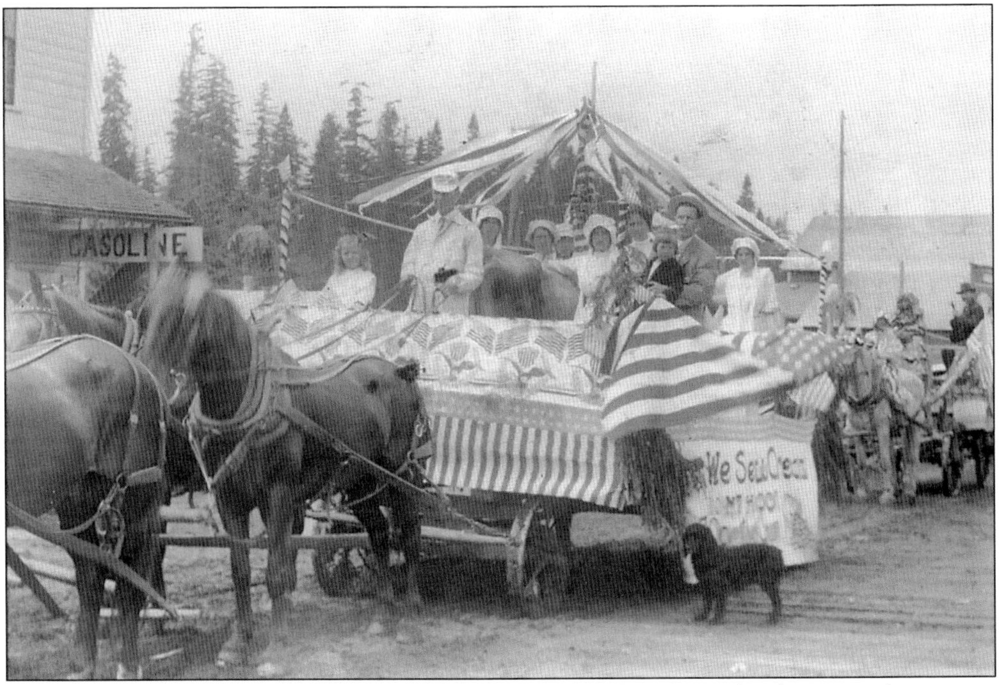

This is yet another view of Willard Bosholm's Jersey cows. This was evidently a time of transition in the field of transportation. Gasoline is for sale, so automobiles must be in use, but all the floats seem to be drawn by horses. (Courtesy of SHS and Richard Meinig.)

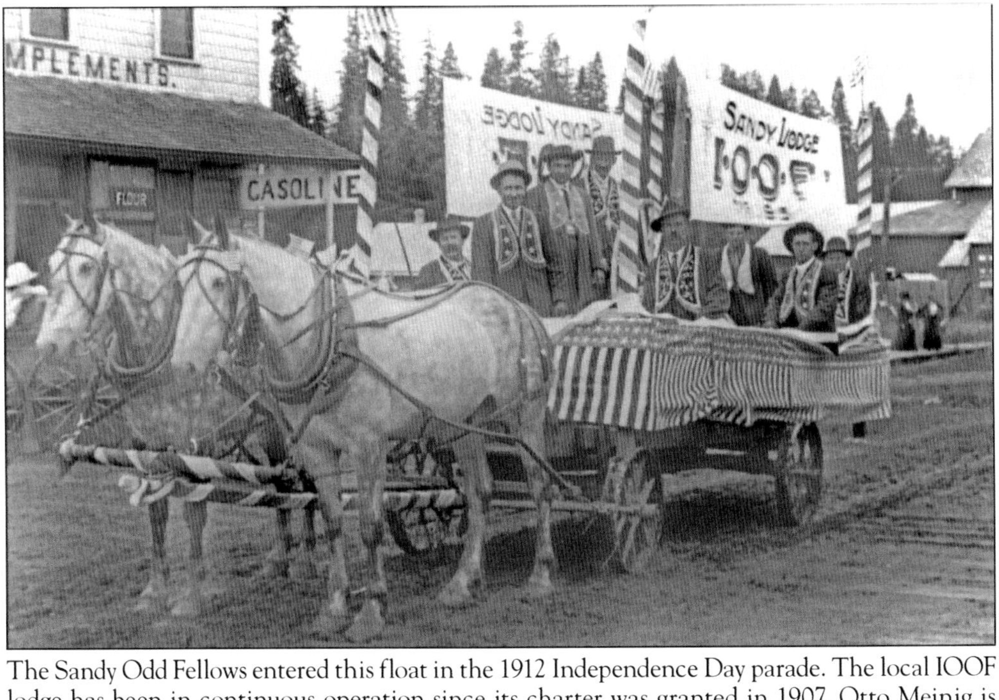

The Sandy Odd Fellows entered this float in the 1912 Independence Day parade. The local IOOF lodge has been in continuous operation since its charter was granted in 1907. Otto Meinig is standing at the left front on the float; seated to the left of Meinig is Arthur Baumback. (Courtesy of Philip Jonsrud.)

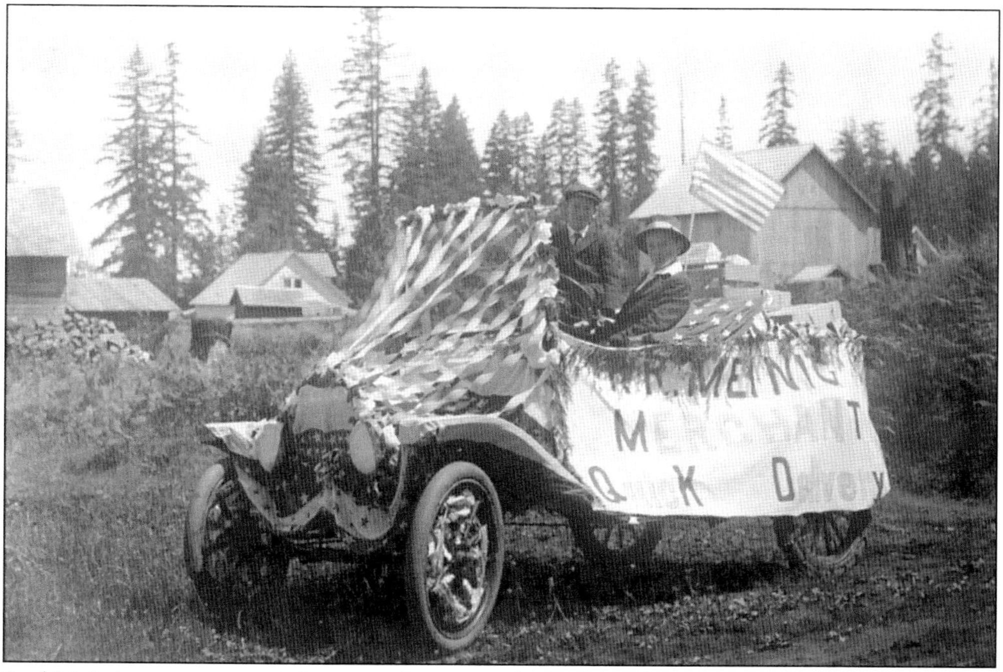

Paul Meinig commissioned this second entry in the Independence Day parade to emphasize an added benefit to his dry goods, grocery, and hardware business: quick delivery. No doubt, he wanted to compete with Ludwig Hoffman, whose meat wagons were delivering not only meat, but other supplies to customers as far away as Maupin, on the other side of Mount Hood.

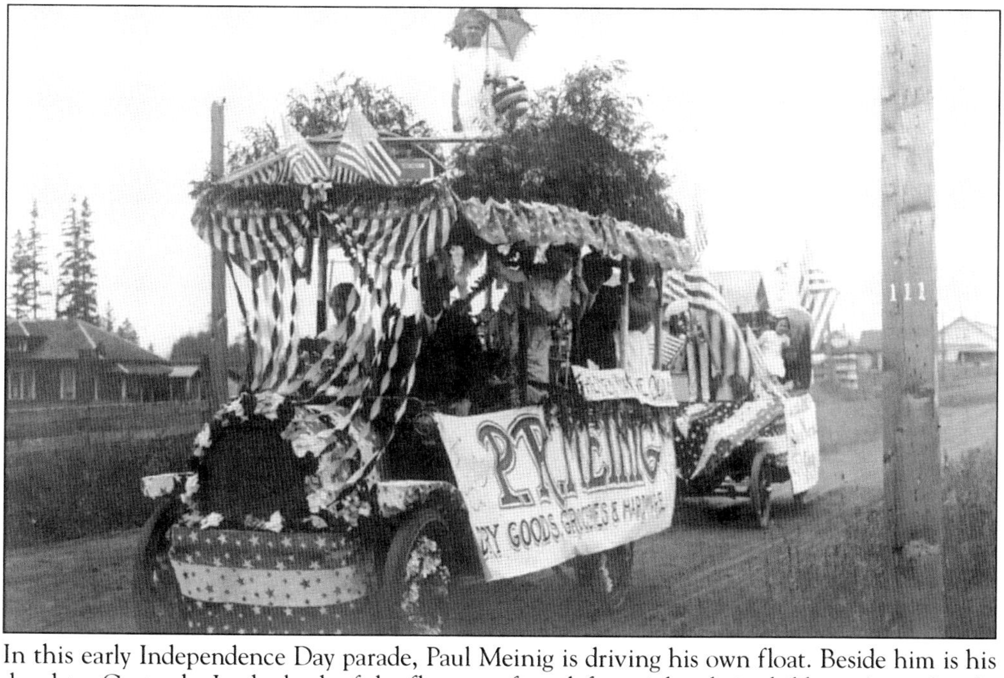

In this early Independence Day parade, Paul Meinig is driving his own float. Beside him is his daughter Gertrude. In the back of the float are, from left to right, their children: Anna Smith, Alfred Meinig, and Frances Meinig. Paul Meinig was born in Saxony in 1869 and came to America with his parents when he was two. (Courtesy of Phyllis Matz.)

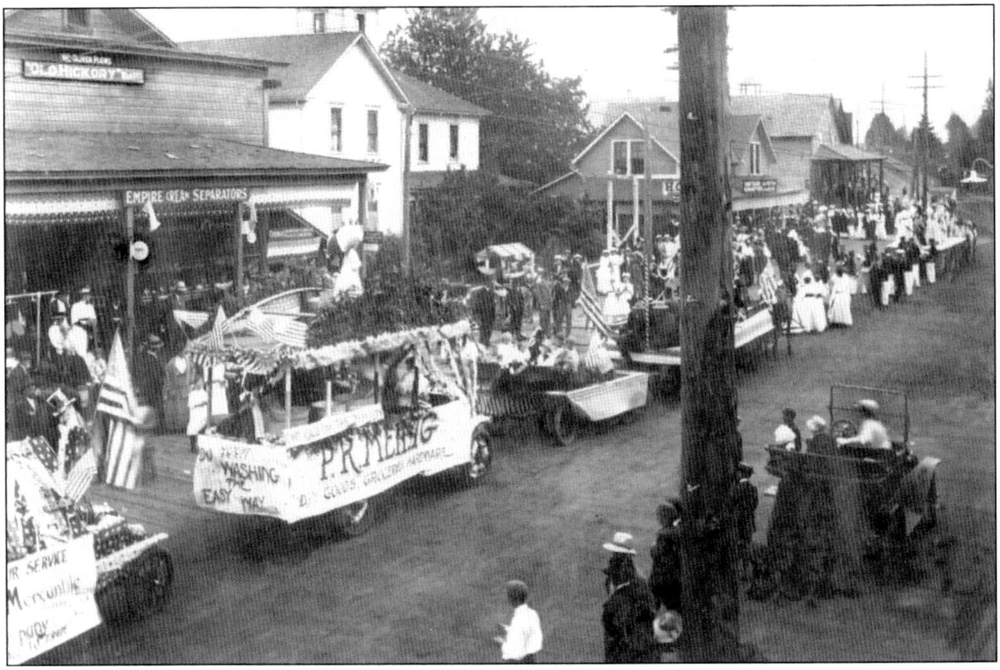

In 1915, the P.R. Meinig Mercantile float passes the old Revenue store. Wolf's Sandy Hotel, built by Baron Otto von Scholley and once owned by Caspar Junker, is the white building. The banner on the back of the float reads, "Do your washing the easy way." The washtubs inside the float seem to be illustrating the hard way. (Courtesy of Edward Wolf.)

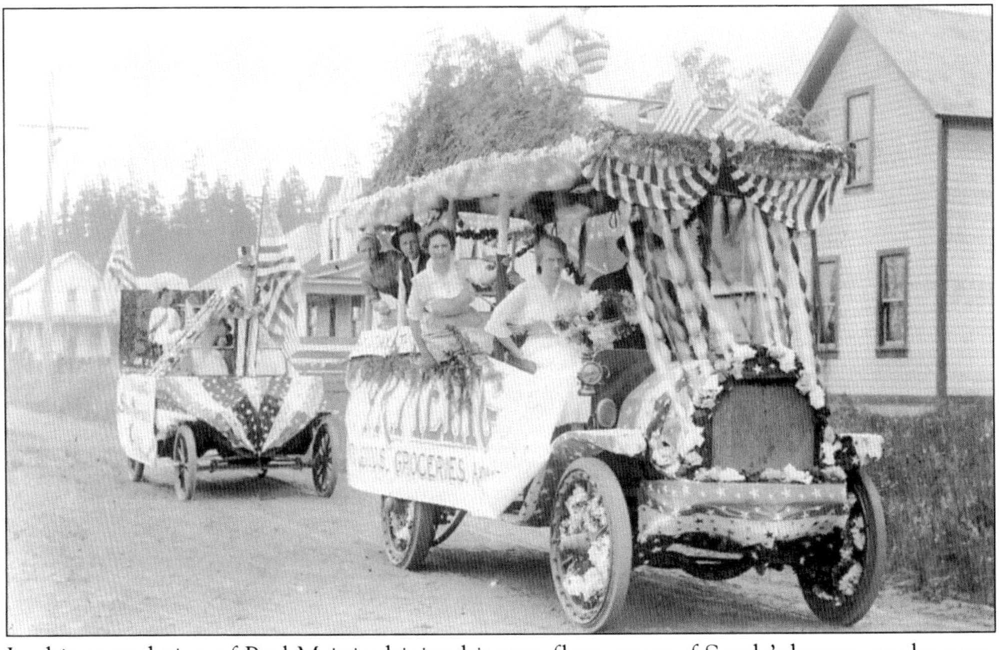

In this second view of Paul Meinig driving his own float, some of Sandy's homes can be seen. Paul's daughter Gertrude is on the passenger side in front, Frances Meinig and Alfred Meinig are in the back, and Anna Smith is in the center. The little girl standing on top, without a seat belt, is unidentified. (Courtesy of Phyllis Matz.)

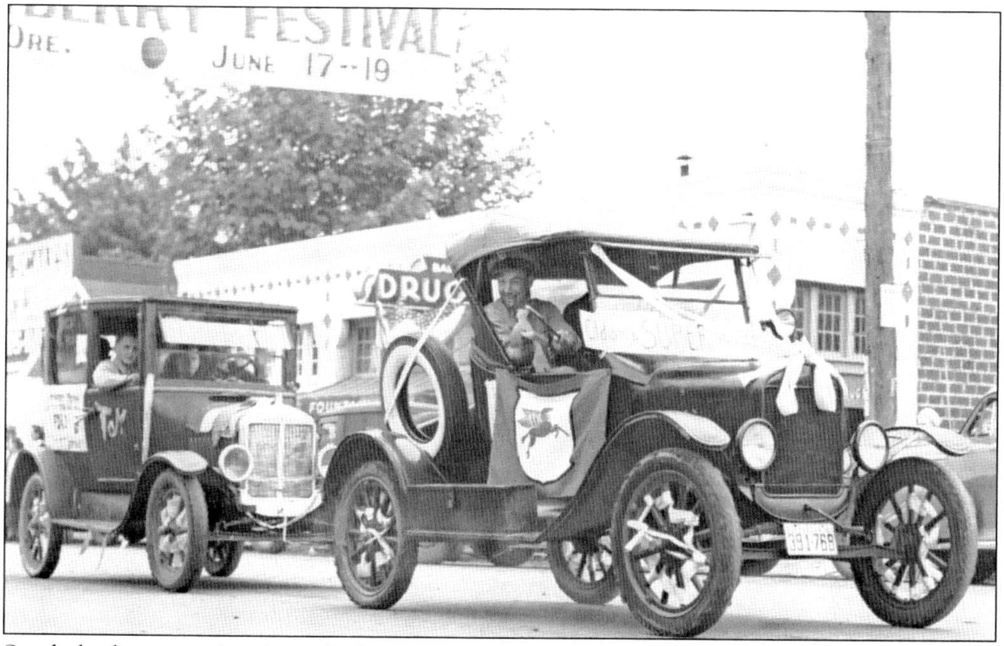

Sandy had no parades through the Great Depression and the war years, so the Strawberry Festival Parade in 1950 was planned, with barbecue, strawberries, and ice cream. The *Sandy Post* reported that the event drew 8,000 visitors to town. The last float in the parade was a pickup truck hauling an outhouse with no door. Who sat in the outhouse, smiling and waving? It was Nettie Connett, of course!

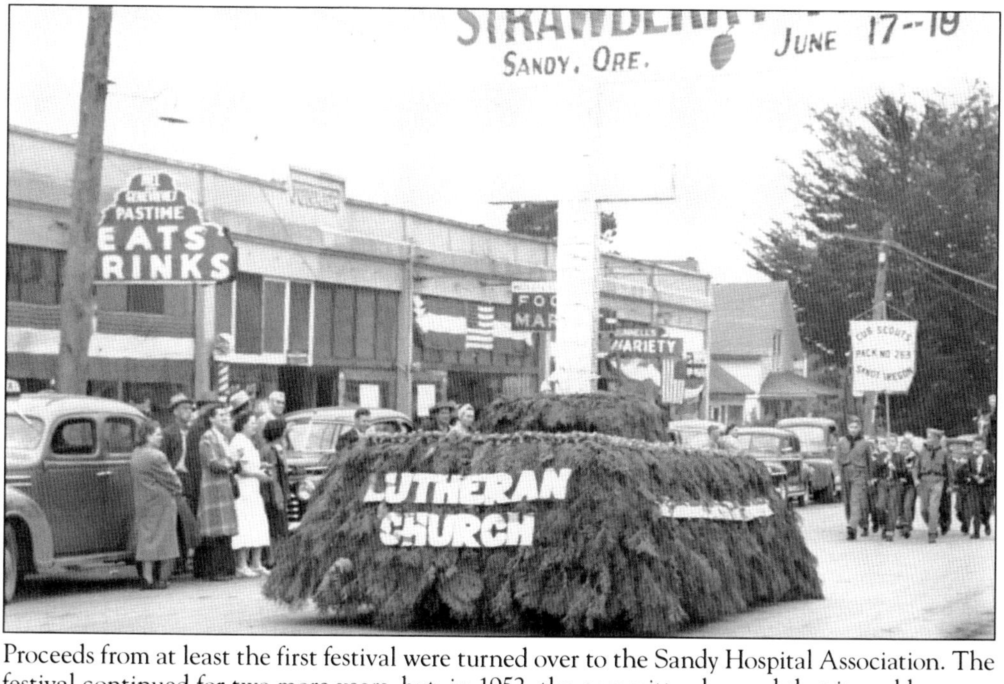

Proceeds from at least the first festival were turned over to the Sandy Hospital Association. The festival continued for two more years, but, in 1952, the committee learned that it could not use the high school fields for some of the events, because of a conflict with the school's need for the space. So that was the end of the Strawberry Festival.

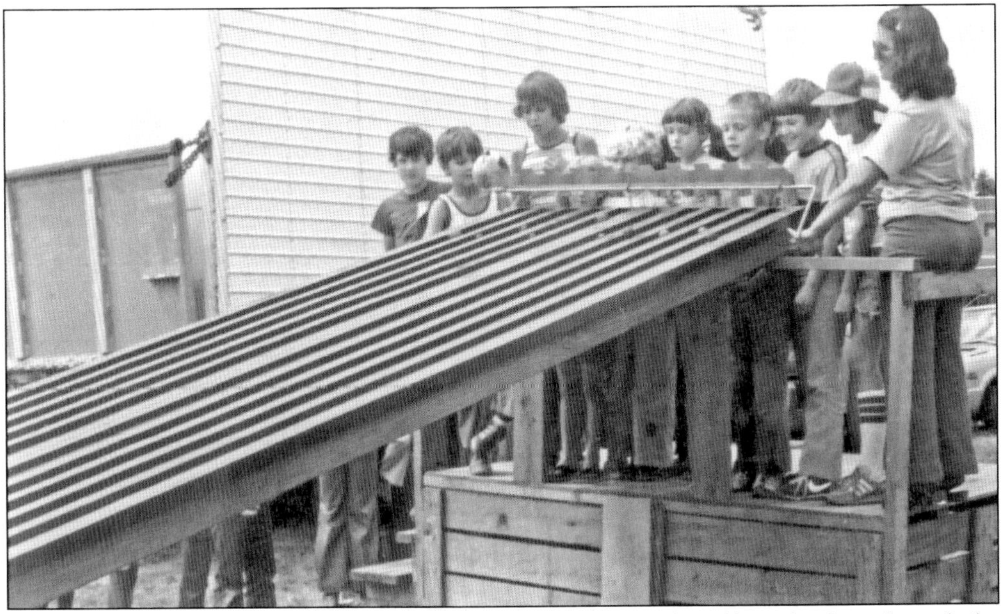

In 1973, the first Sandy Mountain Festival was presented, conceived, and brought about through the efforts of John Armstrong, Lynn Ellis, and Ann Fenwick. Since then, the festival has grown to be the largest event in Clackamas and East Multnomah Counties. In 1976, the festival committee took advantage of the short-lived pet rock fad to stage pet rock races. (Courtesy of Dennis Gray.)

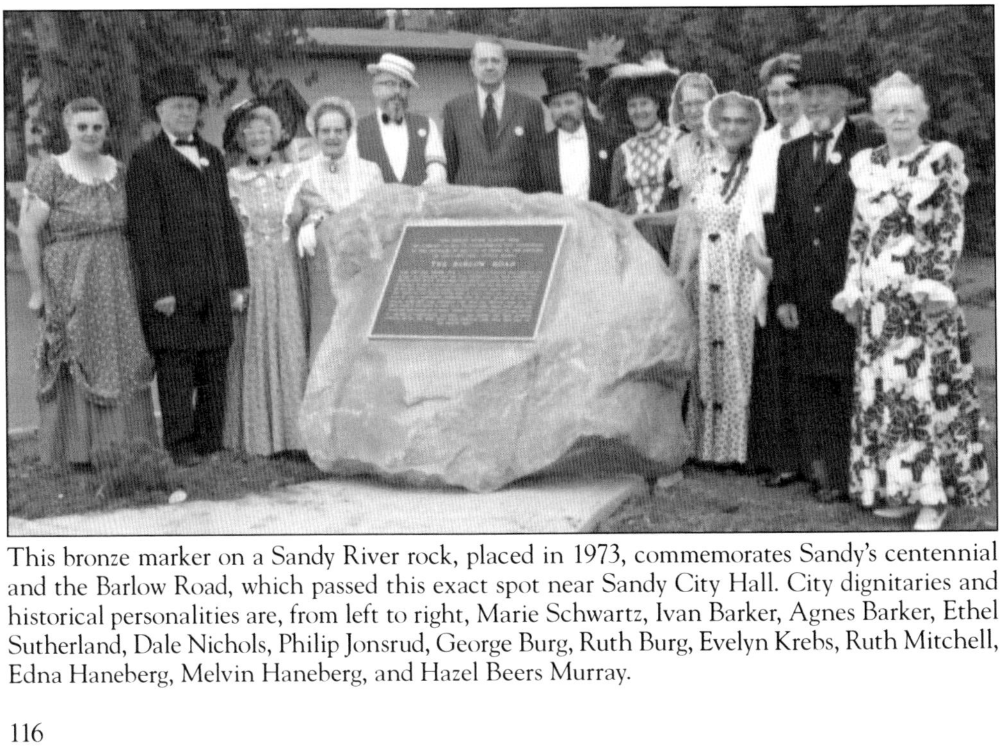

This bronze marker on a Sandy River rock, placed in 1973, commemorates Sandy's centennial and the Barlow Road, which passed this exact spot near Sandy City Hall. City dignitaries and historical personalities are, from left to right, Marie Schwartz, Ivan Barker, Agnes Barker, Ethel Sutherland, Dale Nichols, Philip Jonsrud, George Burg, Ruth Burg, Evelyn Krebs, Ruth Mitchell, Edna Haneberg, Melvin Haneberg, and Hazel Beers Murray.

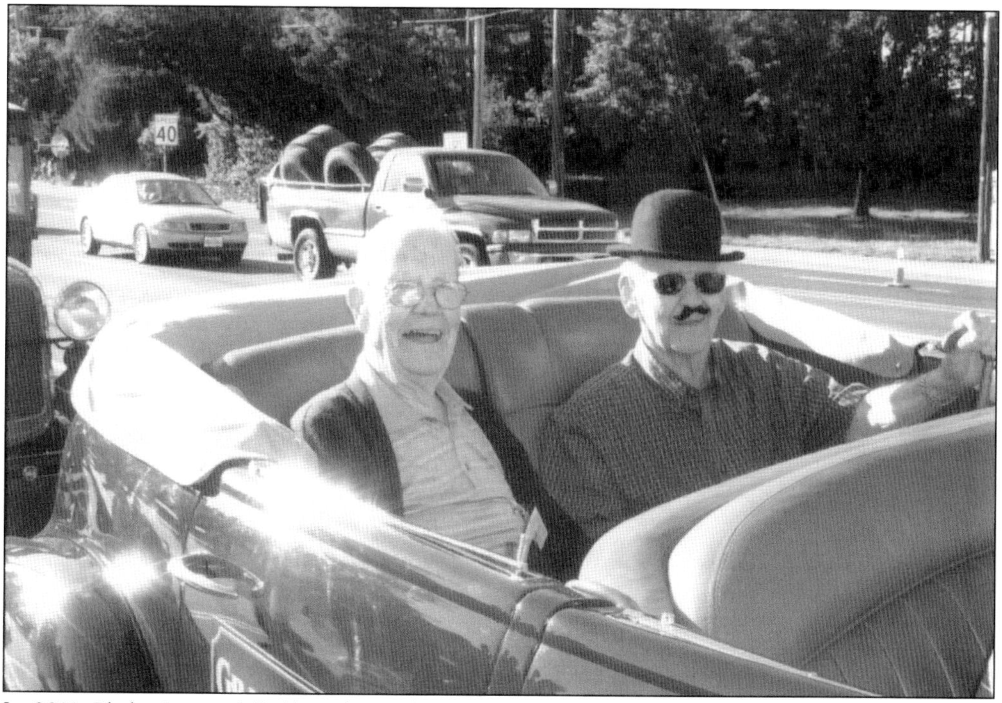

In 2011, Philip Jonsrud (left) and Joseph Shelley enjoy their ride in the parade that begins the Sandy Mountain Festival. Typically, over 10,000 spectators line Pioneer Boulevard to watch the parade and over 50,000 visit the little town each year. The festival was initiated to give artisans from throughout the Northwest an opportunity to display their wares on the paths of Meinig Memorial Park. Usually, over 150 artisans participate.

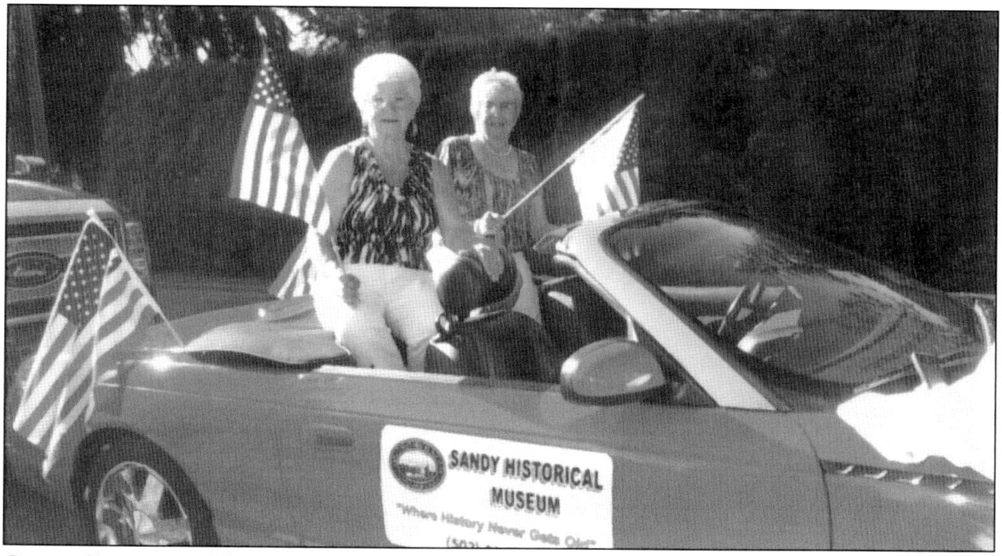

Connie Revenue Selzler (left) and Jean Rolli represent the Sandy Historical Museum in the 2013 Sandy Mountain Days parade in a bright red Thunderbird driven by museum volunteer Nancy Spencer. Revenue was queen of the festival in 2009, and Rolli was queen in 2012. For some, the high point of the festival would be the many food booths strategically placed throughout Meinig Park to raise funds for nonprofit organizations. (Courtesy of Jean Rolli.)

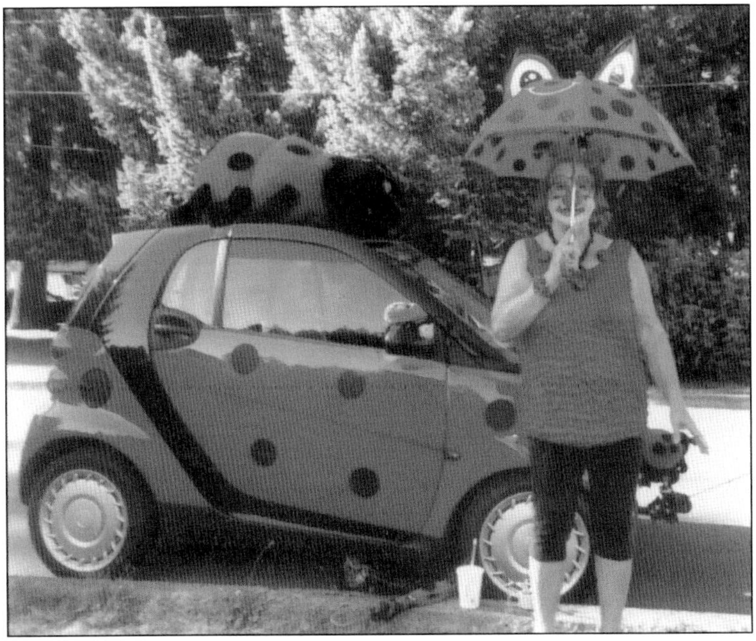

In 2014, Connie Revenue Selzler went all out and decorated her smart car and herself as ladybugs, in a long-standing tradition of participants dressing and bedecking themselves as peculiarly as possible. Some characters in the past have been Smokey the Bear, Sasquatch, and a juggling pioneer on an eight-foot unicycle.

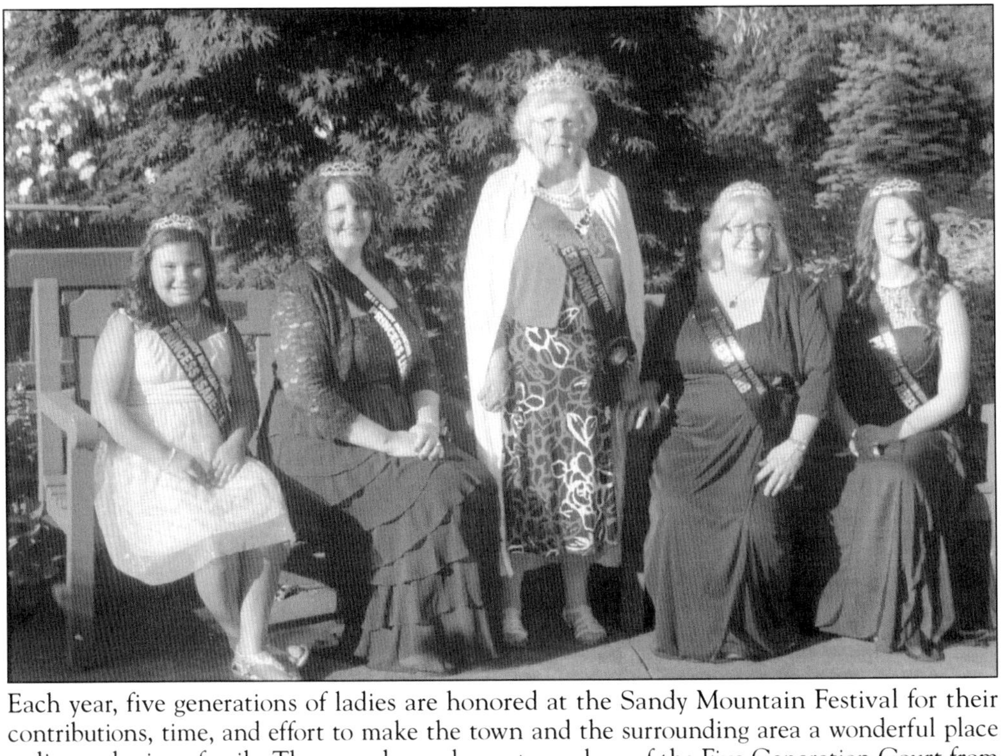

Each year, five generations of ladies are honored at the Sandy Mountain Festival for their contributions, time, and effort to make the town and the surrounding area a wonderful place to live and raise a family. They are chosen by past members of the Five Generation Court from community nominations. The 2014 members are, from left to right, Isabella Manzano, Lisa Martinez, Queen Donna Vedder, Barbara Clare, and Rebecca Rutledge.

Ten

MAIN STREET—SANDY RENAISSANCE

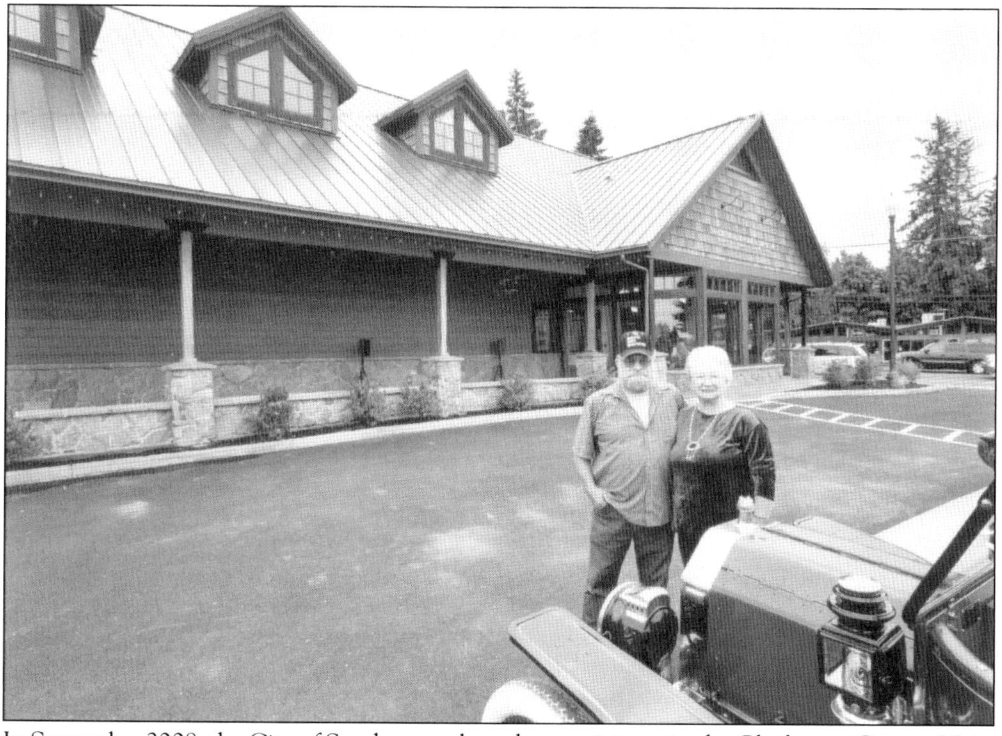

In September 2008, the City of Sandy was selected to participate in the Clackamas County Main Street Program. Sandy is committed to downtown revitalization using the Main Street Four-Point Approach. Sandy Historical Museum, emblematic of both the old and the new, is a center of this effort. Connie Revenue Selzler, representing Sandy's founding family, also illustrates this endeavor. She is shown here with her husband, Leroy Selzler.

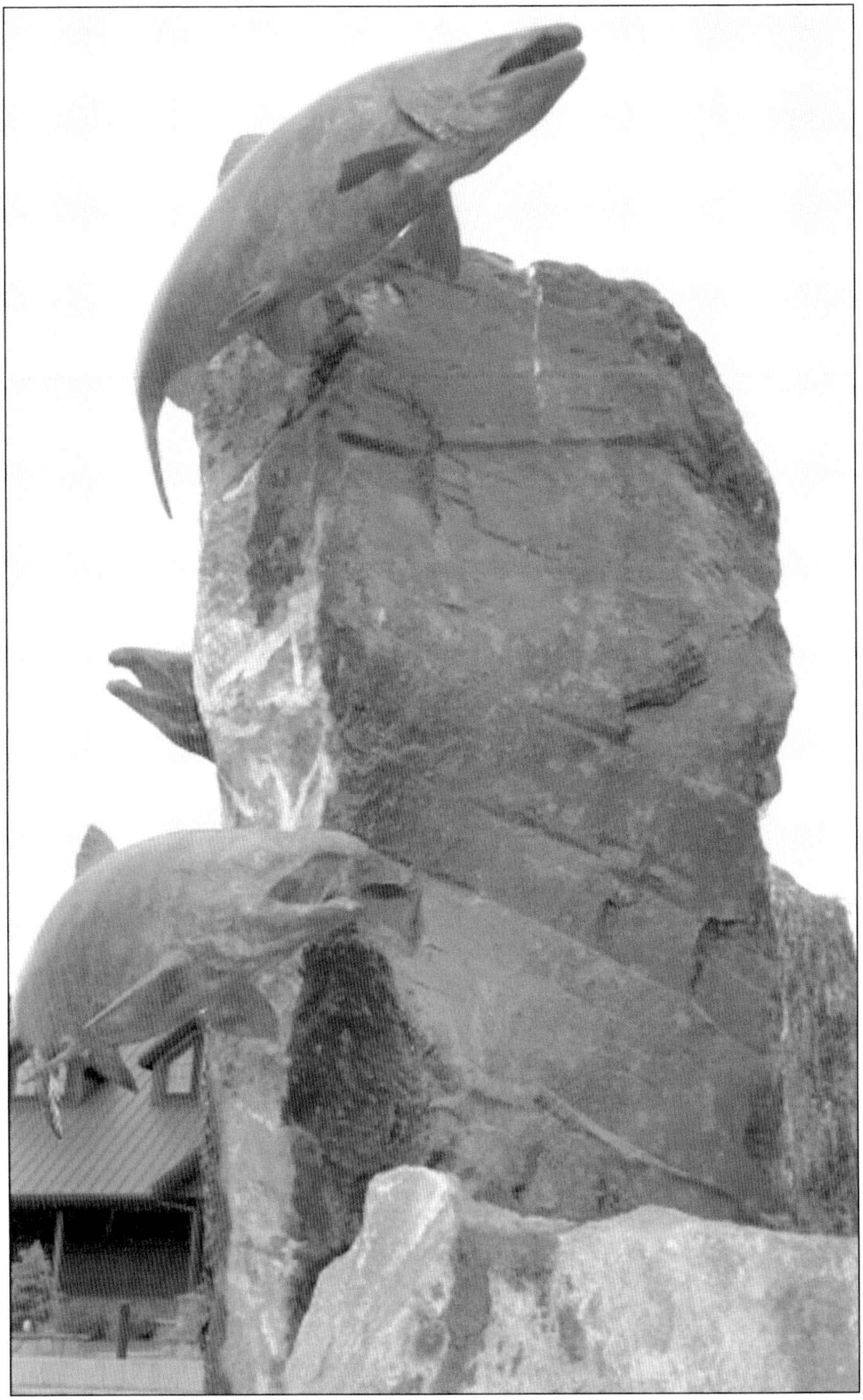

This sculpture, depicting the countless salmon that used to fill the streams in western Oregon, is in Hoffman Square, in front of the Sandy Historical Museum (background) and directly across the street from Sandy City Hall. Over this very spot rolled covered wagons transporting some 50,000 pioneers, starting in 1845, when Samuel Barlow built the Mount Hood Road.

This view of the salmon sculpture indicates clearly why the pioneers were so determined to reach their destination before the bad weather hit. Even in the summer, there are snow hazards in the passes over Mount Hood, and winter traveling in the Cascades can be hazardous even with modern means of transportation.

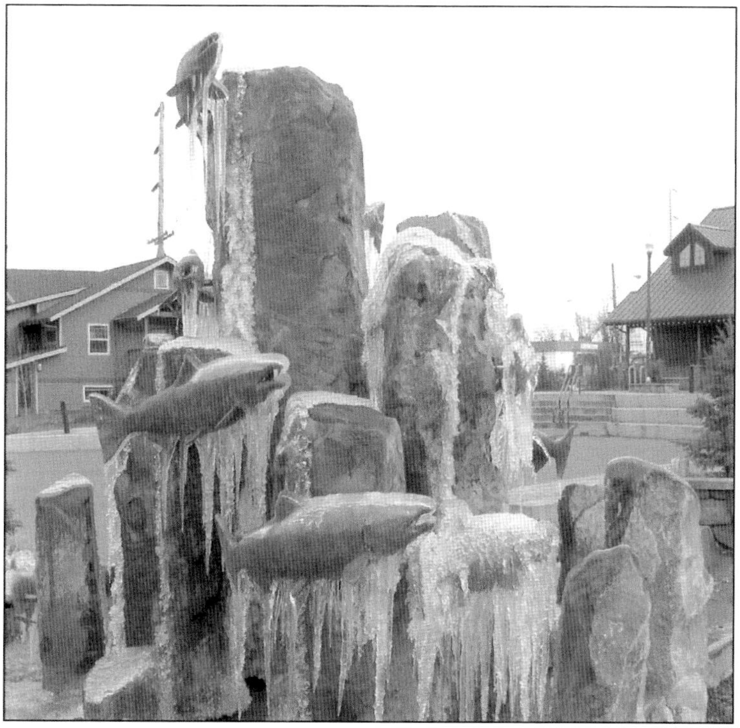

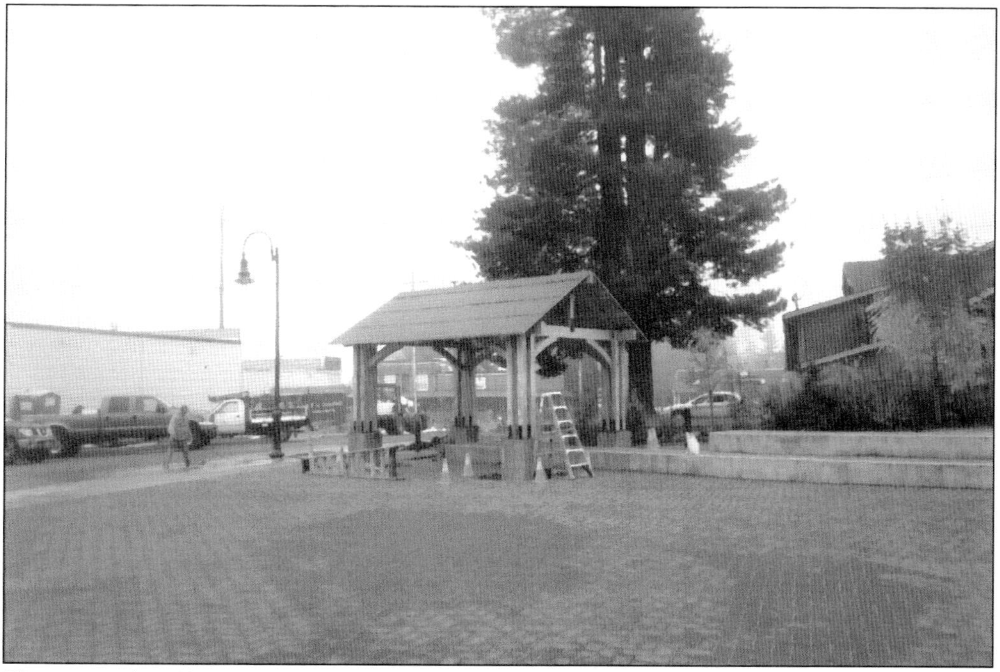

This view of Hoffman Square, once a weed-filled lot where the Sandy Chamber of Commerce hosted a Beer Garden and Music Fair during Sandy Mountain Days, is a stone's throw from several historic Sandy sites. To the left is the Goodwill Industries building, where Paul Meinig's Mercantile once stood. To the right is the building made of upright cedar logs where Dr. Alfred "Yak" Williams had his office.

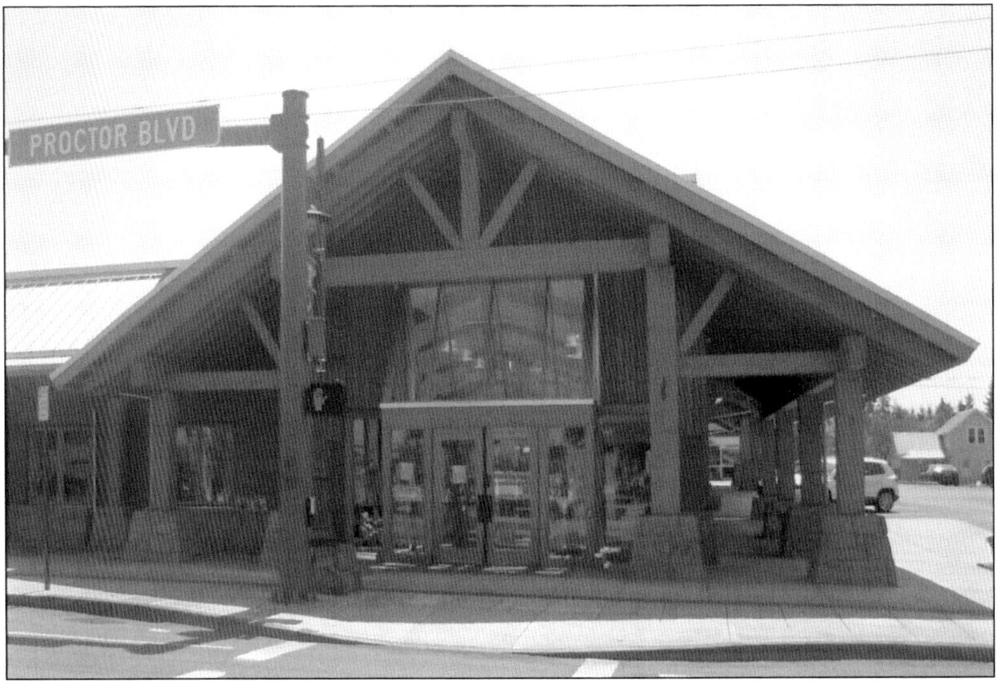

On March 12, 2012, the "new" Sandy City Library was dedicated. It had received such an extensive face-lift that most residents thought of it as a completely different building, a far cry from the tiny basement area it once had in what is now the Veterans of Foreign Wars hall. Its distinctive architecture reflects the "Sandy Style," initiated by the city council in 2007.

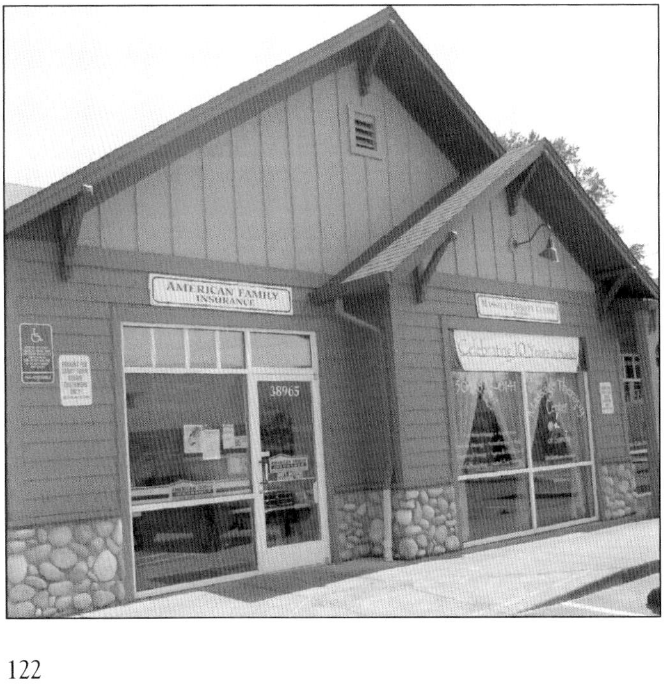

Believing that the city of Sandy needed a distinctive look, instead of the haphazard appearance it had accumulated over 150 years, Mayor Linda Malone and City Planner Tracy Brown spearheaded a movement to adopt the "Sandy Style," also called the "Cascadia Style," for all buildings that would be constructed or remodeled in downtown Sandy. Here is where the original St. Michael's Catholic Church used to stand before it burned in 1917.

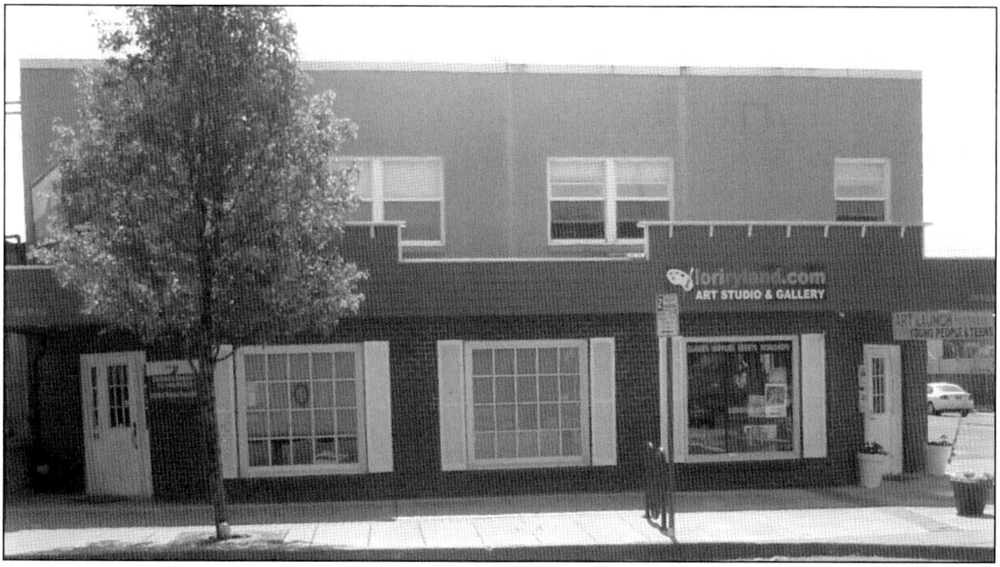

Promotion of the arts is considered to be crucial to most downtown revitalization programs. In Sandy, Lori Ryland's art studio and gallery is a major improvement over the saloons and livery stables that used to line the town's major streets. Her extensive body of work has been shown in many venues, and she has received grants for art classes, offered to young people and teens, in her studio and gallery.

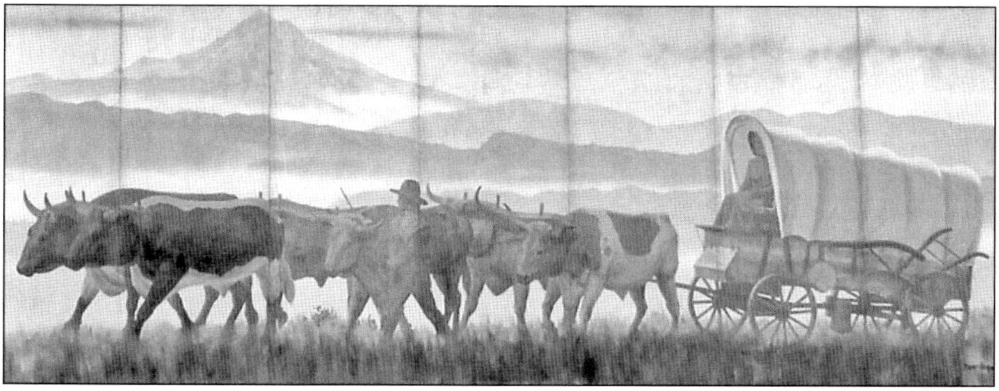

Brightwood artist Roger Cooke painted this mural, *Peaceful Vistas*, in 1993 to mark the sesquicentennial of the beginning of covered-wagon migration over the Oregon Trail. It is on the east side of the Ace Hardware building on Meinig Avenue and Pioneer Boulevard, almost exactly where the original Gerdes store and post office stood.

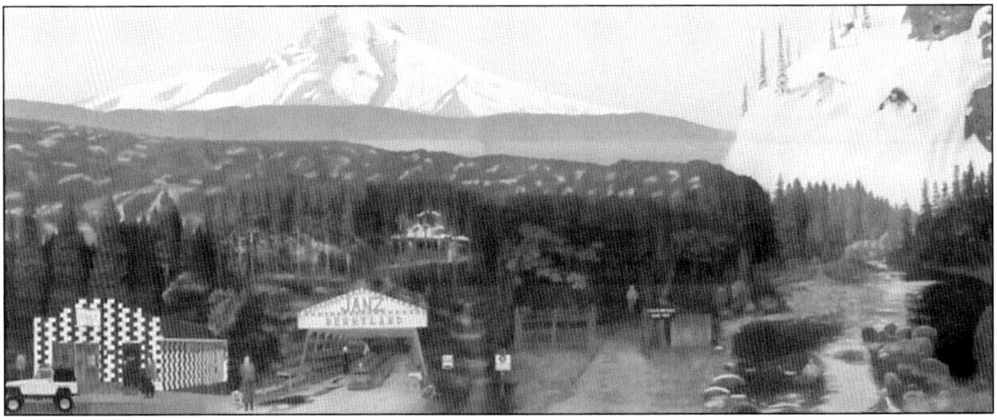

This is half of a two-part mural, *A Sense of Community*, painted in 1994 by William Garnette. It is a montage of well-known Sandy-area highlights and graces the Melvin Haneberg Community Center building on the south side of Pioneer Boulevard, near the west end of Sandy's one-way couplet. It features Joe's Donuts, Janz Berryland, the Barlow Tollgate, the Sandy River, and Mount Hood.

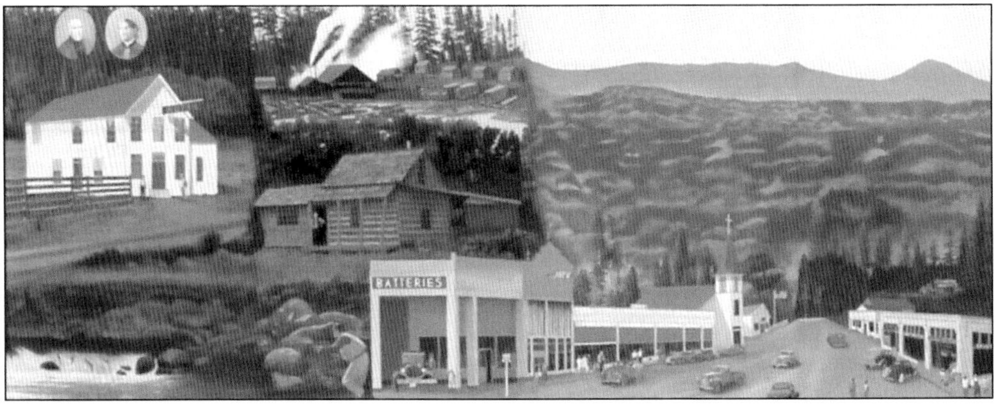

This is the other half of William Garnette's mural, showing Francis and Lydia Revenue, the old Revenue Hotel, a typical lumber mill, Robert S. Smith's automobile service building, the Junker Building, Immanuel Lutheran Church, the Ronald Esson drugstore building, and a representative log cabin. Of course, not all of these buildings were standing at the same time.

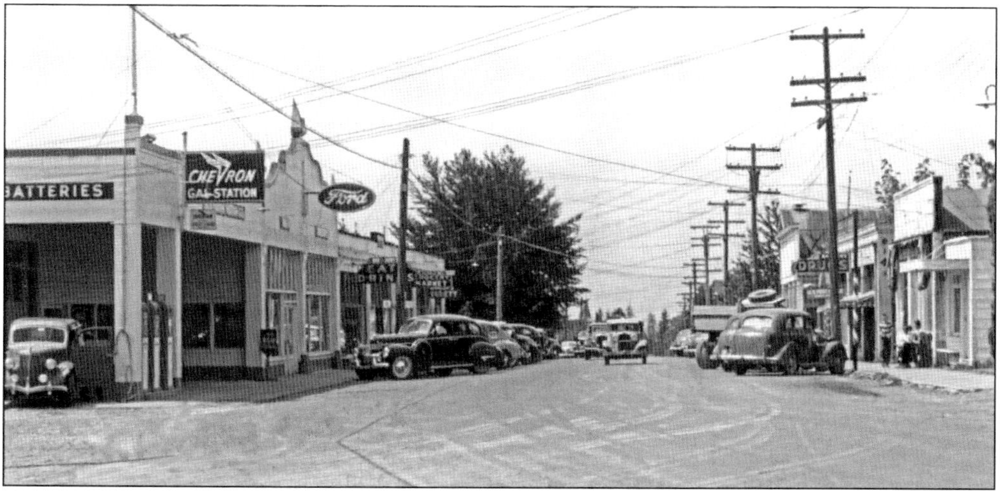

When the Sandy City Council passed resolutions calling for adherence to the "Sandy" or "Cascadia" style of architecture, it deliberately made allowances for preserving several traditional and historic white buildings, essential to a sense of Sandy's past. These included the Robert Smith Building (left), the Junker Building beyond it, and the Ronald Esson drugstore building (right).

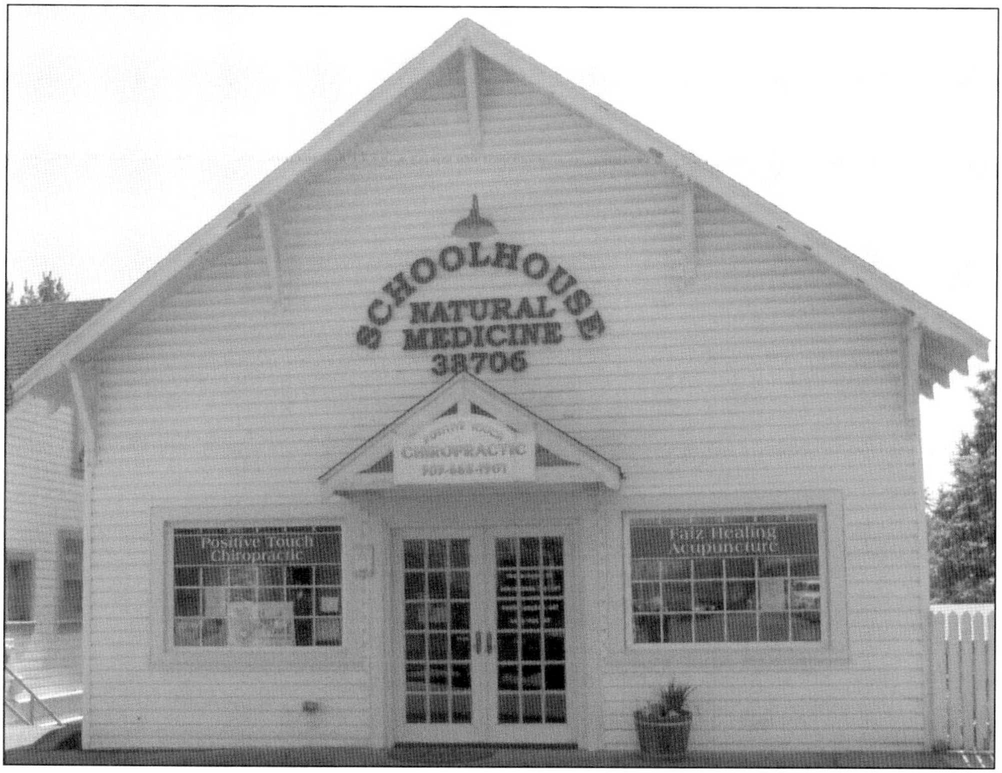

One of the buildings that has never been a candidate for razing or substantial remodeling is the former Lutheran parochial school. The building has come a long way, from being home to catechisms and religious instruction to its present use as a store selling natural medicine and chiropractic and acupuncture treatments. On the other hand, some might not find these practices so contradictory, after all.

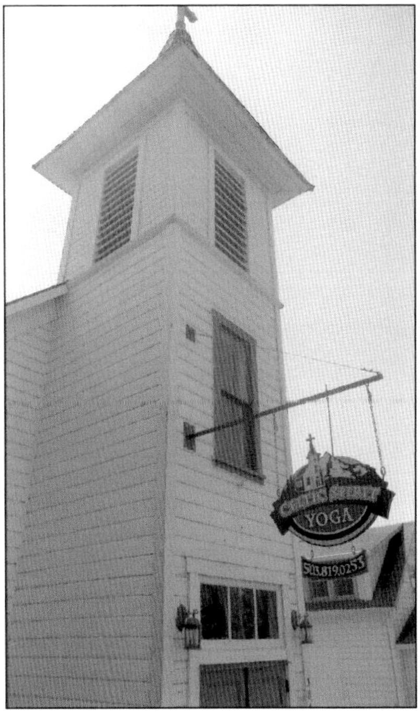

A central landmark for well over a century, this is one of the so-called white buildings, not likely to be torn down or extensively remodeled, although its use has changed several times over the years, and will probably change several more times. Some have suggested that if it ever stops being used commercially, the structure might be made into a small, specialized museum.

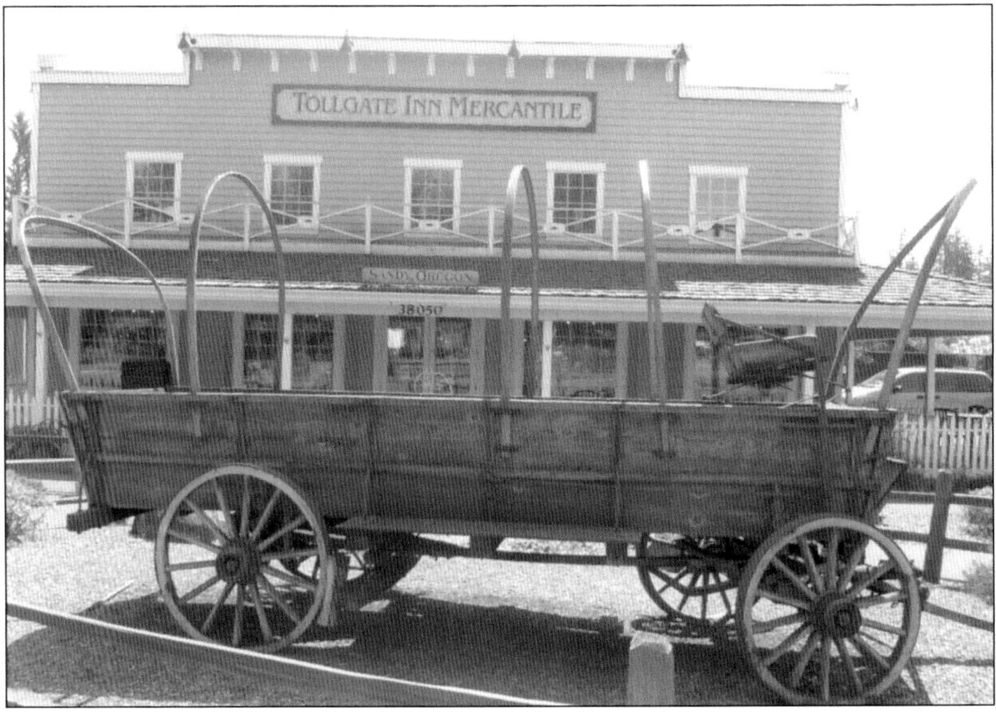

The Mount Hood Fruit Market became the Tollgate Inn, at Pioneer Boulevard and Bluff Road, in 1980. There was no need to induce the owners to adopt the "Sandy Style" of architecture, as they had embraced it and made it a part of the atmosphere from the very beginning, including this restored "uncovered" covered wagon. Portlanders traditionally stop here on the way to or from Mount Hood.

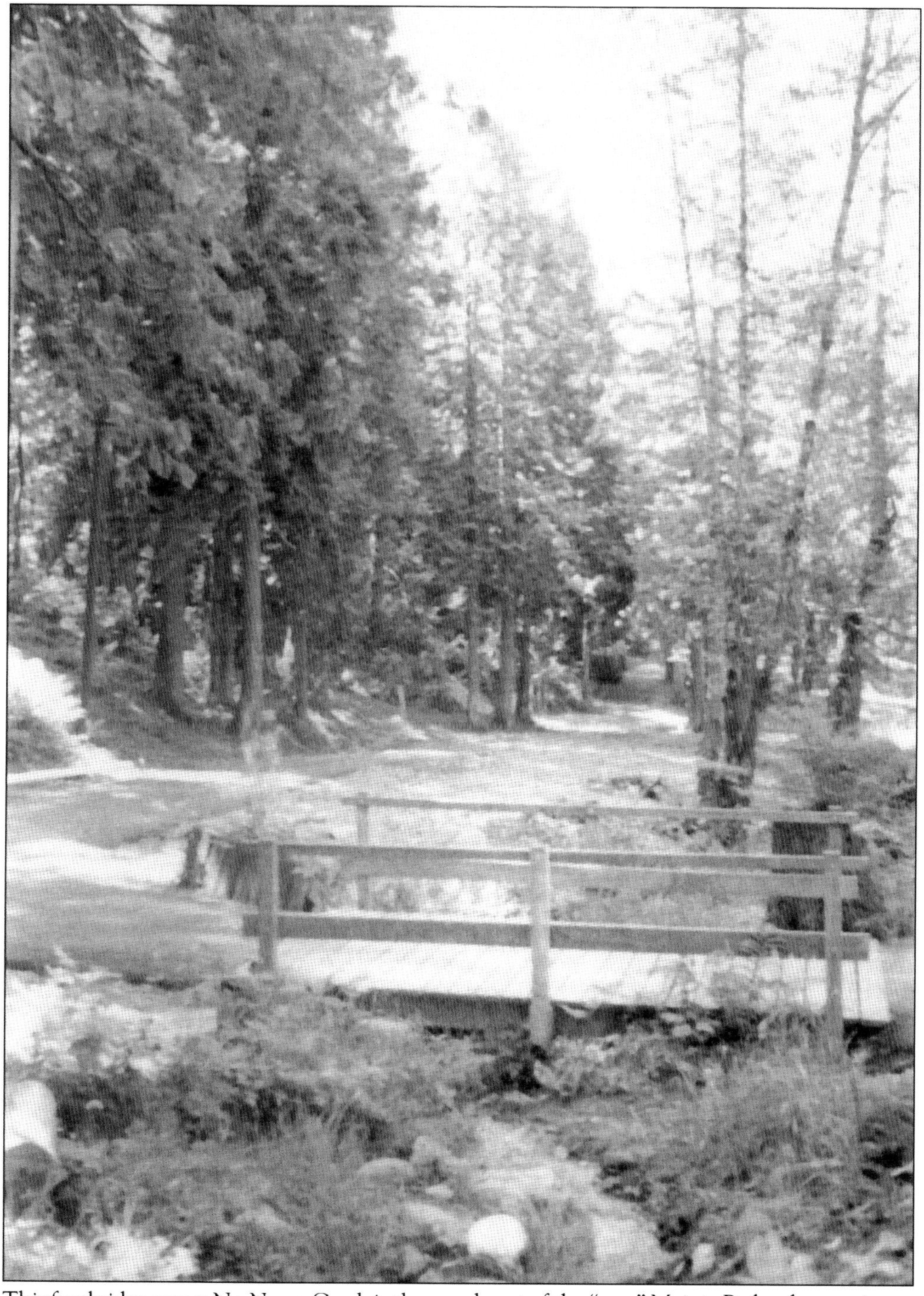

This footbridge across No-Name Creek is the very heart of the "new" Meinig Park, where artisans, musicians, and 50,000 visitors to Sandy mingle at the Mountain Festival on the weekend after Independence Day. In 1845, when Samuel Barlow passed this way, it was covered with tall firs, 12 feet in diameter. In 1972, it was covered in blackberry vines. Now, it is a quiet place to contemplate nature.

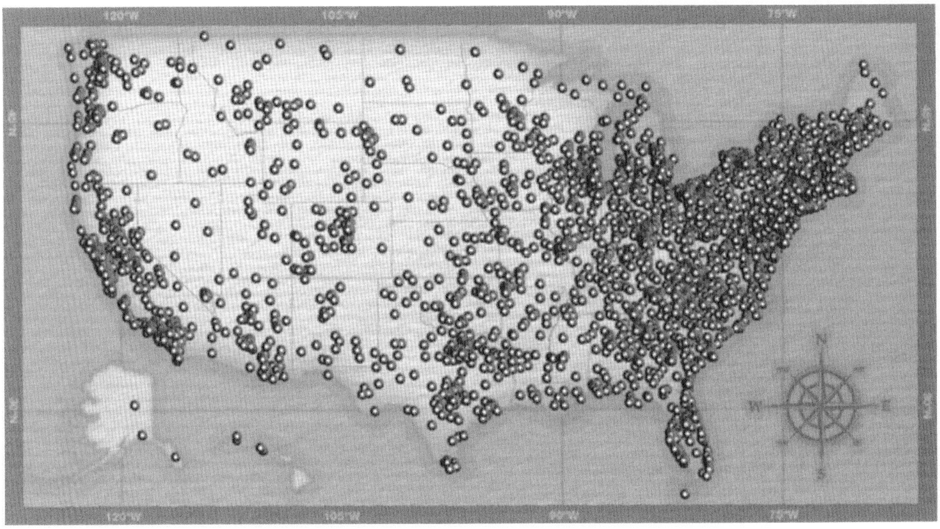